THE KING'S WAR

THE KING'S WAR

MARK LOGUE
AND PETER CONRADI

Quercus

First published in Great Britain in 2018 by Quercus.

Quercus Editions Ltd
Carmelite House
50 Victoria Embankment
London EC4Y 0DZ

An Hachette UK company

A CIP catalogue record for this book is available
from the British Library

HB ISBN 978 1 7842 9571 4
TPB ISBN 978 1 78206 597 5
Ebook ISBN 978 1 78206 598 2

10 9 8 7 6 5 4 3 2 1

Typeset by CC Book Production

Printed and bound in Great Britain by Clays Ltd, Elcograf S.p.A.

To my wife Ruth, who contributed substantially to this book.

To my children Amy, Hannah and Laurie,
even though they still haven't read *The King's Speech*.

To my mother-in-law Beryl, for her support
(especially over the past year).

To all my close friends for their kindness and love.

Contents

Foreword

The King's Speech was a huge critical and commercial success when it was released at the end of 2010, picking up seven BAFTAs and four Oscars, including Best Picture and Best Director for Tom Hooper, Best Actor for Colin Firth for his memorable portrayal of George VI, and Best Screenplay for David Seidler. It must have been watched by at least forty million people at the cinema alone. In the years since, millions more have viewed it on DVD, Netflix, Amazon and on television.

It is not difficult to understand the film's appeal: the story of the future King's battle with his life-long stammer and the help he received from Lionel Logue, his irreverent Australian speech therapist, clearly struck a chord with audiences. Cinema-goers revelled in its Englishness, were touched by Firth's performance as the gentle, vulnerable monarch and applauded Geoffrey Rush's portrayal of Logue with his determination to cut through protocol to help his royal patient. It helped that the story was true: George VI did have a stammer and, yes, he was helped by an Australian commoner who used highly unconventional methods.

For me the film meant something much more: Lionel Logue was

my grandfather, but he died in 1953, twelve years before I was born, so he was always something of a mystery. His story was told to me when I was a child, but I never paid too much attention to what seemed like ancient history – even though, growing up, I became fascinated by the medals, signed royal photographs and mementoes scattered around the house.

In fact, it wasn't until my own father, Antony – the third of Lionel's three sons – died in 2001 that I began to appreciate the role that my grandfather had played in the history of the royal family. It fell to me to organize his personal papers, which had passed first to his eldest son, Valentine, an eminent brain surgeon, and then, on Valentine's death in 2000, to my father, who had locked them away in a tall grey filing cabinet in his study.

Coming face to face with my grandfather for the first time, on 31 August 2010, at a private screening of the film at the Odeon in Panton Street, London, was an extraordinary experience. It was a year earlier, when Seidler's script was already written and the shooting of *The King's Speech* was about to begin at Elstree Studios and on location around London, that the film-makers got in touch with me. Although I, too, live in London, the connection came via an academic website published by Caroline Bowen, a Sydney-based speech and language pathologist, which at the time was the only online source of information on Lionel Logue. The producers were excited to learn I had my grandfather's papers, most of which had never been seen before. As the papers were transcribed, Hooper and Seidler rewrote the script to incorporate the gems of information that I found.

None of this, though, could fully prepare me for seeing Rush as my grandfather, alongside Firth, Helena Bonham Carter as the Queen and Jennifer Ehle as my grandmother Myrtle. It was surreal to see my father depicted as a ten-year-old boy. I still remember the day when I was invited on the set and met Ben Wimsett, who played him. A scene they were filming particularly resonated with me: Rush's character hovered over my father and Valentine while they recited Shakespeare. It reminded me of a scene from my own childhood when I struggled to do the same, while my father, who had a prodigious memory, repeated verbatim the lengthy passages he had learnt as a boy.

The success of the film provided me with a series of even more surreal experiences: during the first few weeks following its release, I made countless newspaper and television appearances in both Britain and America, during which I was asked to talk about 'the real Lionel Logue'. Then came the Oscars themselves, when I was invited to a party at the Chateau Marmont in Los Angeles. As the ceremony ended in triumph for *The King's Speech*, the room filled with every Hollywood star you could mention. The celebrations went on until dawn.

I went to another party later that day hosted by the film's producers, Simon Egan and Gareth Unwin, at a luxury villa in the Hollywood Hills. Glimpsing Simon's fifteen-month-old daughter, I thought she would look cute photographed with the Oscar, so I handed her the statuette and stepped back to take the picture. She lost her grip just as I was clicking the shutter, and the Oscar fell to the ground with a loud bang, bouncing down the stone steps. Everyone at the party fell silent. The horror was evident on everyone's face – not least mine, where it was mixed with embarrassment and shame.

The statuette suffered several dents: it had a bashed head, damaged shoulder and a dented stand, and gold plating had flaked off the chest. The Academy of Motion Picture Arts and Sciences was contacted immediately, and, to my relief, it turned out they have an 'Oscar Hospital' to cope with the all-too-common injuries sustained by the statuettes during victory celebrations. When Simon went to have it repaired, he was half expecting to see a queue of sheepish Oscar winners in there with their own damaged statuettes nursing hangovers.

There is only so much you can show in 118 minutes, however brilliant the director – and Hooper, for whom this was only his second feature, was certainly that. That was why, after having become involved in the making of the film, I also set out to tell the real-life story behind the events it depicted, working with Peter Conradi, a journalist with the *Sunday Times*. We entitled our book *The King's Speech: How One Man Saved the British Monarchy.* Published to coincide with the film, it was a bestseller in both Britain and America and translated into more than twenty languages.

During the more than a quarter of a century they worked together, my grandfather remained loyal to the King, respecting his privacy and the confidential nature of the treatment he gave him. He chose to remain behind the scenes, largely silent, rarely giving interviews, never publishing his work or having his methods scrutinized by peers or teaching them to students. He also always worked alone. Perhaps this was because he felt like an imposter, never having received any formal training or qualifications, and was forced to battle the prejudices of established medical institutions, as well as a degree of anti-Australian sentiment.

Yet he was immensely proud of his achievements, as became clear to me when I examined the papers he left behind. The hundreds of pages I transcribed included correspondence between the King and my grandfather from their first meeting in 1926 – when the future monarch was still Duke of York and, as second son of George V, never expected to be King – until his death in 1952. The letters from the King, the majority on Buckingham Palace headed paper (but with a few sent from Sandringham and from Windsor Castle), were handwritten and signed George R. The draft replies from Lionel were scribbled in barely legible handwriting, always in pencil on Basildon Bond paper. Occasionally, he would note down anecdotes so as not to forget them, using whatever came to hand: an empty envelope, the cover of a book, a scrap of paper, all of them painstakingly filed for posterity.

There are also four large scrapbooks in which Lionel – or perhaps Myrtle – had carefully pasted press cuttings, almost all of them relating to the King's struggle with his speech impediment and the treatment my grandfather gave him. One has '1937' embossed in gold leaf on its front cover. This was a memorable year for Lionel, following the King's accession to the throne after the abdication of his elder brother, Edward VIII, in December 1936 to marry Wallis Simpson, and marked a turning point in his career. Into the scrapbook have been pasted all the paperwork surrounding the coronation that May, including his and Myrtle's invitation to Westminster Abbey, photographs of the pair of them in their court dress, and all manner of tickets and scraps, however trivial.

Inevitably, over time, the frenzy that surrounded the film faded, and my life returned to normal, leaving me to reflect on a crazy two years and the relentless pace and unquenchable appetite of the publicity machine that had monopolized my time and, for a while, had taken me in as one of its own. Those involved with the film moved on to other projects, but for me there was no question of turning my attention elsewhere. There was still more that I wanted to find out about my grandfather.

The speech that the King made in September 1939 on the outbreak of war – which formed the climax of the film – was not the end of his relationship with Lionel Logue. Far from it; it was the beginning of an even more intense phase of their work. With Britain's very survival as an independent nation at stake, the King found himself thrust further into the limelight. This meant greater pressure, too, on my grandfather, who was to play a crucial role in preparing the King for the countless speeches he made during the course of the conflict.

Constraints of time and space meant we were able to consider the war years only briefly in our first book. *The King's War* sets out to study this period in considerably greater depth. The main elements of the story will be familiar to those who read *The King's Speech*: quotes and some descriptive passages that were first published there are necessarily repeated here for completeness. Yet the years that have passed have also given us the opportunity to go back into the archives and tease out more material relating to the two men. We have also made greater use of the diary kept by Myrtle, which provides a very different perspective on her and Lionel's life in wartime London.

We have been able to enrich our narrative with the reminiscences of some of those whose lives were touched by Lionel Logue. At the end of the Introduction in *The King's Speech*, I appealed to readers to write in with their memories of my grandfather. It proved a shrewd move. In the months and years since, countless people have sent me letters and emails: former patients, the children and grandchildren of patients or people who knew him; even the nurse who cared for him in hospital. Others have approached me at events at which I have spoken about the book.

Some told me what it was like to have been my grandfather's patient, describing the techniques he encouraged them to employ to tackle their stammers. Others shared snippets about his life or copies of letters they exchanged with him. I have been presented with an inscription discovered inside a book cover and a letter discovered in a second-hand shop in New Zealand. Others wanted to know what – if anything – I had found in the archives about them or their fathers.

The result is not just a more detailed portrait of the two men's relationship from 1939 onwards than we were able to provide in our first book. We have also set out to put this relationship into a broader context. This is essentially a story of two families at war – the Windsors and the Logues – whose respective experiences of the conflict were in many ways so different, yet in some respects so similar.

I hope you enjoy this book. In the meantime, I am continuing my quest to find out more about my grandfather. For that reason, I am repeating my appeal for anyone with further information that could add to my knowledge of his life to email it to me at lionellogue@gmail.com, or to write to our publisher: Quercus, Carmelite House, 50 Victoria Embankment, London EC4Y 0DZ.

Acknowledgements

I would like to thank my lovely wife Ruth although I would have appreciated a bit more support with the first one. Also our children Amy, Hannah and Laurie, for letting this project take over our home, and my siblings Sarah, Patrick and Nickie for their help and reminiscences. Thanks also to my Aunt Anne and her daughter Victoria Logue.

Thanks also to the London Metropolitan Archives, the British Library, the National Archives, the Imperial War Museum, Southwark Library, Lewisham Library, Dulwich College Library and the University of London. Thanks to the Ministry of Defence, the Royal Army Service Corps, Army Personnel Centre and the Scots Guards for my father's and uncle's military service histories. And finally thanks to the local historians Steve Grindlay, Brian Green, Ian McInnes and Bernard Nurse who helped add so much detail to what life was like in south London during the war.

Mark Logue,
London, July 2018

The King's Funeral

It was a rumble of drums that they heard first, followed by the wail of a piper's lament and the blast of trumpets. The crowds, standing thirty deep along the Mall, stirred as the funeral cortège approached. Caps were doffed and hands pulled from pockets; conversation faded away. The artillery in Hyde Park sounded a salute that made the pavement shake: the guns boomed fifty-six times, once for every year of a life cruelly cut short. It was 15 February 1952 and the people of Britain – and of the Empire – were bidding farewell to their King. The cortège was headed by the Household Cavalry, flanked by the pipers and band of the Scots Guards. Then came the Earl Marshal and a few personal servants, and behind them the dull green gun carriage that was serving as the King's bier, its highly polished brass flashing in the pale sunshine. The coffin was dressed in the red, blue and gold of the Royal Standard. Surmounting it lay the Imperial State Crown, resting on a cushion of royal purple, together with the gold orb, sceptre and insignia of the Order of the Garter. Beside them lay a wreath of white flowers from the woman who had spent the previous three decades at the King's side and was now known as the Queen Mother.

She rode in a carriage immediately behind the gun carriage, accompanied by her daughters, the Queen and Princess Margaret, and her sister-in-law, Mary, the Princess Royal. They were all shrouded in black. Following on foot were the closest male members of the family: the Duke of Edinburgh, the Duke of Gloucester, the Duke of Kent. Joining them was the Duke of Windsor, back from exile in France. The crowd strained forward to get a better view of a man whose decision to give up the throne sixteen years earlier to marry Wallis Simpson, a twice-divorced American, still divided the nation. Simpson herself was not present. It had been made clear to her husband she would not be welcome; this was not the moment for reconciliation.

The funeral procession had set off from Westminster Hall, to which the King's body had been brought from Sandringham. During the four days in which he lay in state, more than 300,000 people filed past his coffin, which lay within a circle of candlelight set like a jewel against the darkness enveloping the hall. Supported on a catafalque, it was draped with the Royal Standard and topped by a brass cross from Westminster Abbey and candles from the Tomb of the Unknown Warrior. The Yeomen of the Guard and officers of the Household Cavalry stood guard in their brilliantly coloured uniforms.

Then, just after daybreak, the carefully choreographed ceremony began. At 8.15, the RAF detachment in the guard of honour, their belts gleaming white against the blue of their greatcoats, marched through one of the west gates to a position on the left of the line, facing the great door of Westminster Hall. They were followed by a detachment of Royal Marines and Coldstream Guards, both dressed in field grey. The Sovereign's Standard was borne by a warrant officer of the Household Cavalry, attended by the Standard Coverer and a trumpeter. The silence hanging over New Palace Yard was broken by the cry of military commands.

As the bells of the Abbey tolled, the gun carriage on which the King would make his final journey was set in position outside the hall. The bearer party of the King's Company, Grenadier Guards, their heads uncovered as a mark of respect, carried out the coffin and placed it in on the bier. Big Ben chimed for the first time. Then, as the sound of funeral brass and drums carried across faintly from Whitehall, the bier moved forward towards the west gate and onwards across London, followed by seven carriages bearing the royal family and representatives of other monarchies.

It was nine days earlier that the people of Britain – and of the Empire – had learnt of the death of George VI. The country was plunged into mourning; Winston Churchill, who had returned as Prime Minister the previous October, set the tone with a characteristically robust broadcast in which he praised the King and described the news of his death as having 'stilled the clatter and traffic of twentieth-century life in many lands, and made countless millions of human beings pause and look around them'. Similar tributes followed, praising above all the decisive role that 'King George the Good', as the newspapers had begun to call him, had played in rallying morale during the Second World War when his nation's existence as an independent state had hung in balance. There was discussion, too, of the King's stammer, a subject that, although obvious to anyone who had ever heard him speak, had been largely taboo during his lifetime – and of the help he had received in overcoming his impediment from a plain-talking Australian speech therapist named Lionel Logue.

The stress of war had certainly taken a heavy toll on the King's always delicate health. During the late 1940s he suffered a series of scares that culminated in September 1951 with the removal of his cancerous left lung. His speech for the opening of parliament that November had – exceptionally – to be read for him by Lord Simonds, the Lord Chancellor, and his Christmas message pre-recorded in a tortuous process that had taken the best part of two days. He had nevertheless seemed well on the path to recovery by the end of the following January when the then Princess Elizabeth set off with the Duke of Edinburgh on a tour that began with East Africa and was intended to take them on to Australia and New Zealand.

On 5 February, back in Sandringham, the King seemed happy and carefree as he set out in the morning for a day of shooting with his neighbour, Lord Fermoy, during which he bagged nine hares and did not return home until dusk. After a relaxed dinner, he went to bed at midnight. The next morning at 7.30, his valet, James MacDonald, came to bring him his usual morning cup of tea. When he did not receive any reply to his knock, MacDonald entered the King's bedroom and found his master's lifeless body. Dr James Ansell, 'Surgeon Apothecary' to the royal household, was called and declared the King dead. The cause of death was not cancer but instead a coronary thrombosis – a fatal blood clot to the heart – that he appeared to have suffered soon after falling asleep.

A well-oiled machine swung into action: at 8.45 Alan Lascelles, the King's principal private secretary, telephoned his deputy, Sir Edward Ford, who was in London at home in his flat in Park Lane. Lascelles – a veteran of the royal establishment who had served George VI's elder brother and father before him – used the agreed code word.

'Hyde Park Gardens,' he told Ford. 'Tell Queen Mary and the Prime Minister.' He did not need to say any more.

A clergyman's son, and the product of Eton and Oxford, Ford had become the King's Assistant Private Secretary in 1946 after a spell as tutor to King Farouk of Egypt and several years at the Bar followed by a 'good war' in the Grenadier Guards. Half an hour after Lascelles's call, he arrived at 10 Downing Street and was shown up to see Winston Churchill. He found the Prime Minister still in bed, Foreign Office papers strewn around him and a chewed cigar in his mouth. On the table next to it was the candle he used to relight it.

'Prime minister, I've got bad news for you,' Ford told him. 'The King died last night. I know nothing else.'

'Bad news, the worst,' exclaimed Churchill, slumping back in shock. He had been preparing a speech on foreign affairs to the House of Commons, but threw the papers to one side, deeply moved. 'Our chief is dead,' he said. 'How unimportant these matters seem.'

Ford then had to travel on to Marlborough House to break the news to Queen Mary, the late King's mother. It was sixteen years since her husband, George V, had died. Now her son was to follow him to the grave. Ford had the impression when he arrived that she knew already what he had come to tell her, yet this did not soften the blow. 'What a shock,' she told him. 'What a shock.'

It was time to tell the world: at 10.45 news agencies released a brief statement announcing the King had 'passed peacefully away in his sleep'. Half an hour later, the announcer John Snagge broke the news to the nation on the BBC.

Yet the woman whose life was to be most affected by the King's death was still in the dark. Princess Elizabeth, as she was then, had spent the previous night with Prince Philip at the Treetops Hotel, a game-viewing lodge in the foothills of Mount Kenya, watching wild-life drinking at the waterhole beneath. The young couple returned at dawn to Sagana Lodge, a farm a hundred miles north of Nairobi that had been given to her as a wedding present by the Kenyan government. It was only several hours later that Martin Charteris, her private secretary, heard the news from a shocked local journalist at the nearby Outspan Hotel. Charteris told Lieutenant Commander Michael Parker, Philip's equerry and close friend. 'Mike, our employer's father is dead,' he said. 'I suggest you do not tell the lady at least until the news is confirmed.' It fell to Parker to inform Philip, who looked, as Parker later put it, 'as if you'd dropped half the world on him'. Pulling himself together, the Duke took his wife for a walk in the garden where, at 2.45 that afternoon he told her she was now Queen. When Charteris arrived at Sagana fifteen minutes later, he found her surprisingly composed. She had an emotional walk around the grounds of the lodge with Philip and then prepared for the long journey home. The royal party flew the few hundred miles to Entebbe, over the border in Uganda, and then on to London. Already flags were flying at half mast across the Empire, crowds were beginning to gather at the royal residences and diplomats were making their way to Buckingham Palace to express condolences on behalf of their nations.

The cortège's route took it along the Mall past Marlborough House, where eighty-four-year-old Queen Mary, too frail to take part, watched from a window, a large bowl of flowers by her side, and then continued on through St James's Street to Piccadilly, past number 145 where the then Duke of York had begun his married life. The building had been hit by a German bomb and reduced to a single storey, draped in black and purple. A Union flag on top flew at half mast. From there the mourners continued through Hyde Park Corner, Marble Arch, Edgware Road and by way of Sussex Gardens to Paddington Station. The royal train was waiting at platform eight, the black funeral coach in the middle, with an expanse of red carpet covering the platform beside it. Accompanied by the shrill piping of a naval party, the bearers, walking in slow motion, carried the coffin on board, and the doors of the funeral coach were sealed. A few seconds later, the Queen and the other female members of the royal party stepped into the coach behind it, with the royal dukes in the one behind that. Then, as the guard of honour presented arms and the bands of the Coldstream and Scots Guards played Chopin's Funeral March, a thin shaft of smoke rose from the funnel of the engine, and the royal train moved slowly out of the station. Its destination was Windsor, where the King was to be laid to rest in St George's Chapel, as his father and grandfather had been before him.

CHAPTER ONE

The First Wartime Speech

The red light faded and silence descended briefly on the room. It was just after 6 p.m. on 3 September 1939. The sense of relief on the King's face was clear for all to see. The broadcast had lasted only a few minutes, but it had been the most important of his life, and he knew it. Despite the huge pressure, he had risen to the challenge. Finally able to relax, he allowed himself a smile.

Lionel Logue extended his hand.

'Congratulations on your first wartime speech, your Majesty,' he said.

'I expect I will have to do a lot more,' replied the King.

As the two men walked out of the door, the Queen was waiting in the passage. 'That was good, Bertie,' she said.

The King went to his study to have his photograph taken. As ever, at Logue's insistence, he had broadcast standing up. During all the years that the King had worked with the Australian speech therapist to overcome the stammer that had blighted his life since childhood, one of the most important lessons he had learnt was the importance of deep breathing, which he found easier when he was on his feet. Yet he was always photographed sitting down; it looked more intimate that way. Today was no exception: the photograph that would appear the next day on the front pages of newspapers across the world was of the King, dressed in his admiral's uniform, complete with ribbons, sitting bolt upright at a table, the microphones positioned straight in front of him.

The Queen began to chat with Logue. She had arrived at Euston from Scotland five days earlier aboard the night train. After a gruelling four-week tour of North America that May and June, she and the King had been longing for the peace and quiet of Balmoral. They had travelled north at the beginning of August, but, as the threat of war grew, the King had been required back in London. The Queen stayed on a few days in Scotland and now she, too, had returned to the capital. During the tense days that followed, she was constantly at her husband's side, her presence invaluable. She left the two princesses, Elizabeth, aged thirteen, and Margaret Rose, nine, behind, with instructions that if war broke out they should be moved to Birkhall, a smaller property on the Balmoral Estate that was thought to be less vulnerable to enemy bombers. The Queen wrote to her eldest sister, Rose, asking her to look after them if anything happened to her and the King. In the meantime, the girls' governess, Marion Crawford, known to all as 'Crawfie', was instructed to 'stick to the usual programme as far as you can'.[1]

It was thirteen years earlier that the then Duke of York had for the first time climbed the two flights of stairs leading to Logue's consulting room at 146 Harley Street, beginning a relationship that was to shape both men's lives. The Duke had initially been reluctant to make the visit. Over the course of the years he had seen too many so-called experts who had turned out to be quacks – nine, by one count – but the outlandish cures they proposed merely added to the sense of anger and frustration he felt whenever he tried to speak and no words came out. His staff had become used to what they called his 'gnashes', sudden outbursts of unrestrained anger that were terrifying in their ferocity. But his wife, who seemed to feel his anger and frustration as much as he did, was insistent that he make one last attempt.

Logue had arrived in London from his native Australia in 1924 aboard the *Hobsons Bay*, a ship of the Commonwealth and Dominion Line, together with his statuesque wife, Myrtle, and their three sons, Laurie (fifteen), Valentine (ten), and Antony (three). The journey took six weeks; they travelled third class. A few weeks short of his forty-fourth birthday, Logue had worked as a speech therapist in various places in Australia besides his native Adelaide. Speech therapy in those days was still in its infancy; like many of his fellow practitioners, Logue did not have a medical or scientific background or indeed formal training of any sort. His background was instead in oratory and amateur dramatics. But he had put the techniques he acquired in public speaking and on the stage to good use in helping Australian soldiers who struggled to speak after falling victim to gas attacks during the First World War. He found the same techniques effective in helping people with stammers – among them a young journalist named Keith Murdoch, father of the future media mogul, Rupert.

Coming to Britain was a considerable gamble: Logue had built up a name for himself in Australia, but London, home to seven and a half million people and the bustling capital of the Empire that ruled a quarter of the world's population, was a different matter. He had £2,000 of savings – the equivalent of £110,000 in today's money – and just one introduction: to John Gordon, an ambitious young Dundee-born journalist who was chief sub-editor of the *Daily Express* and would go on to become one of the most influential British newspapermen of his generation.

Logue began modestly, settling in simple lodgings in Maida Vale and offering his services to local schools. Then he took the plunge, taking a flat in Bolton Gardens in South Kensington and leasing a consulting room in Harley Street. Number 146 was at the cheaper and less prestigious end, of the street, near to the bustle of the Marylebone Road, but it was still Harley Street. The gamble began to pay off. Logue's reputation spread and he started to acquire a number of wealthy patients, whom he charged hefty fees to subsidize the lower rates paid by the poor. This, though, was to be his first contact with royalty.

That he and the Duke met at all was thanks to Lord Stamfordham, a royal equerry who had been told about Logue by John Murray, a member of the publishing dynasty who had been his patient. Stamfordham was impressed by what he found and proposed that Logue call on the Duke at his home in Piccadilly. But Logue was adamant that his prospective royal patient should visit his consulting room, just like everyone else.

'He must come to me here,' Logue insisted. 'That imposes an effort on him which is essential for success. If I see him at home we lose the value of that.'

And so, two days later, the Duke came to him. On 19 October 1926, Logue opened the door of his consulting room to a slim, quiet man, fifteen years his junior. Logue was struck by his tired eyes. It soon became apparent how heavily the Duke's stammer weighed on him. In his quest to find the source of his patients' problems, Logue would quiz them on their past. As he did so, the Duke described his childhood and the lack of understanding shown towards his problem by his father, George V, and by his tutors. The advent of adulthood had not cured his problem: instead it brought public speaking duties that drew his stammer to the attention of a far wider audience.

The day of their first consultation, the Duke was still reeling from the humiliation that he had suffered eighteen months earlier when he had been obliged to make a speech at the Empire Exhibition in Wembley. His stammer had given him an understandable horror of public speaking, and this was an especially high-profile speech that was to be broadcast across the Empire. Through force of will, the Duke managed to make it through to the end, but his performance had been marred by several embarrassing pauses during which his jaws were still moving but no words came out. Now he and the Duchess were about to embark on a six-month tour of Australia and New Zealand that would require countless public speeches. He was dreading it.

The two men spent an hour and half together. 'I can cure you,' Logue told him. 'But it will need a tremendous effort by you. Without that effort, it can't be done.' The record card he filled out after their meeting began 'Mental: Quite Normal, has an acute nervous tension which has been brought on by the defect', and went on to describe the Duke's physique, as 'well built, with good shoulders but waist line very flabby', his top lung breathing as 'good' and commented on his 'nervous tension with consequent episodes of bad speech, depression' and his 'extraordinary habit of clipping small words'. This initial consultation cost £4 4s – the equivalent of about £250 today. Over the next 14 months, the Duke had a further 82 appointments, taking his total bill to £197 3s (or £11,000 today). And so began an extraordinary relationship in which the Australian would play the role as much of counsellor to the future King as his speech therapist.

During the early years they worked together at his practice in Harley Street, Logue had used a variety of methods to help the Duke. As with all his patients, he placed most emphasis on learning to breathe properly. The chest was not to expand with inhalation, but instead the lungs should push the diaphragm down and allow it to rise on expiration; this had ideally to be performed in a relaxed, standing pose, with legs apart and hands on hips, following a process of conscious relaxation that started with the feet and moved upwards. Logue invariably taught such techniques with the window of his consulting room wide open, even at the height of winter. This was supplemented with various exercises: practising vowel sounds preceded by an 'H' such as Hay, Hee, Hi and Ho or else reciting fiendish tongue twisters such as 'the Regagie Roller Ram'. When faced with a word that seemed likely to trip them up, patients were urged by Logue to use a different word instead, or else to leave off the initial consonant, since no stammerer ever struggles over a vowel. As Frank Weeks, a former patient put it: 'If one spoke of the King and the Queen and the 'k' was the problem one simply said "the 'ing and the queen". If one could get a small "k" in there so much the better, but the sentence would be understood and was far better than having a K-K-K-King.'[2] Such techniques were informed by Logue's instinctive knowledge of human nature that led him to understand the causes of stammering were often psychological as much as physiological.

Despite all his years with Logue, the King was never 'cured' as such; it is arguable whether anyone can ever really be cured of a stammer. But he nevertheless made considerable progress. Over time, his defect became barely noticeable in private conversation, among friends, family and members of the royal household. 'With others,' according to one of his wartime equerries,* 'he stammered occasionally, but the stammer was not a "stutter" with visible movements of the head or the lips. It took the form of a silence during which he tried to emit, pronounce the offending word or a synonym.'[3]

---

* Peter Townsend, who later became Princess Margaret's lover.

The King's accession to the throne in December 1936, following the abdication of his elder brother Edward VIII – or David as he was known in the family – to marry Wallis Simpson, heralded a new phase in Logue's relationship with the King. His broadcasts and other public speeches assumed an importance they had never had when he was Duke of York; the outbreak of war elevated them further. With it would come a widening of Logue's role: whenever the King had an important speech or broadcast, Logue would go through the text to remove difficult words and help him rehearse his performance. As the years passed, Logue became increasingly close to the King and Queen until he had almost become a member of the royal family. Like her husband, the Queen opened up in the presence of this cheery, good-humoured Australian who was refreshingly free of the stuffiness of the others with whom they were surrounded at court, and she confided in him to an extent she did not with other people. This evening, the first of the war, was no exception: she shared with Logue the strange feeling of relief that she and King felt now that the die had been cast and a conflict that had long seemed inevitable had finally been declared.

'Bertie hardly slept at all last night, he was so worried, but now that we have taken the decisive step he is much more cheerful,' she told him.

That morning, a Sunday, Sir Nevile Henderson, the British ambassador to Berlin, had given Hitler until 11 a.m. to withdraw the troops he had sent into Poland two days earlier. If he failed to do so, Britain would declare war. The ultimatum was met with silence. At 11.15 Neville Chamberlain addressed the nation from the cabinet room at 10 Downing Street.

'This morning, the British Ambassador in Berlin handed the German government a final note, stating that unless we heard from them by 11 o'clock that they were prepared at once to withdraw their troops from Poland, a state of war would exist between us,' Chamberlain said. 'I have to tell you now that no such undertaking has been received, and that consequently this country is at war with Germany . . .'

> The situation in which no word given by Germany's ruler could be trusted and no people or country could feel itself safe, has become intolerable. And now we have resolved to finish it, I know that you will all play your part . . .
>
> May God bless you all. And may He defend the right, for it is evil things that we shall be fighting against – brute force, bad faith, injustice, oppression and persecution; and against them I am certain that right will prevail.

No sooner had Chamberlain finished speaking than the air raid siren blared. Robert Wood, the BBC sound engineer in charge of the broadcast, watched with amazement as the Prime Minister led his entire cabinet down to his special air raid shelter underneath the building. Rather than follow them, Wood went instead to the front door of Number 10, lit a cigarette and looked at the people outside rushing about in confusion to try and find a shelter. It quickly became clear that it was a false alarm: there were no enemy aircraft, merely a little British spotter plane. Whoever was responsible had apparently been overreacting to the enormity of the news they had just heard. The all-clear sounded before Wood could finish his second cigarette, and the cabinet 'trooped rather sheepishly back and began the business of waging all-out war'.[4]

Chamberlain then went to the House of Commons, which was meeting on a Sunday for the first time in its history. Just after midday, he began to address MPs. Since becoming Prime Minister in May 1937, he had devoted all his energies to avoiding war by appeasing Hitler. Now this policy lay in tatters. 'This is a sad day for all of us, and to none is it sadder than to me,' he told the House, which cheered as he rose to his feet.

> Everything that I have worked for, everything that I have hoped for, everything that I have believed in during my public life, has crashed into ruins. There is only one thing left for me to do; that is, to devote what strength and powers I have to forwarding the victory of the cause for which we have to sacrifice so much. I cannot tell what part I may be allowed to play myself; I trust I may live to see the day when Hitlerism has been destroyed and a liberated Europe has been re-established.

The King listened closely to his Prime Minister's words. He had been a wholehearted supporter of appeasement, inviting Chamberlain to stand with him on the balcony of Buckingham Palace, their respective wives at their sides, in September 1938 after the Prime Minister returned from his meeting with Hitler in Munich with the false promise of 'peace in our time'. The 'pro-Chamberlain appeasement point of view prevailed at court . . . from the highest to the lowest,' complained Alexander Hardinge, the King's private secretary, who was unhappy with the monarch's stance.[5] By associating himself so closely with a specific government policy that was to be subject to a vote in parliament, the King's behaviour verged on the unconstitutional. Yet the rapturous applause with which he and Chamberlain were greeted by the crowds gathered below showed this was a view also shared by many – perhaps the majority – of his subjects who were desperate to avoid another world war, especially one expected to involve the large-scale bombing of Britain. 'They all complain about Chamberlain nowadays but at the time he had a great deal of support,' noted the Queen many years later.[6]

The bankruptcy of Chamberlain's policy had been exposed by Hitler's subsequent actions, which culminated that Friday when Germany launched simultaneous attacks by land, sea and air on Poland, introducing the world to a new kind of hell: Blitzkrieg. At a stroke, any prospect of negotiating a peaceful settlement had been swept away. The following evening, as London was hit by a massive thunderstorm that sent cascades of water crashing down onto the city, the King was told that his Prime Minister was now ready to act and to issue Hitler an ultimatum. As he went to bed that night, he knew the Nazi leader would refuse to comply.

The Queen woke at 5.30 on the Sunday determined to experience a last bath at leisure and her final cup of tea in a country still at peace. At 10.30 she joined the King in his sitting room to listen to Chamberlain's broadcast. Tears were running down her face as the Prime Minister spoke. When the siren sounded the false alarm after his broadcast, she and the King looked at each other. Their hearts beating fast, they went down into the basement, which had been converted into an impromptu air raid shelter, gas masks in hand, and waited for the first bombs to fall. When the all-clear was sounded they came back upstairs and gathered for prayers in the 1844 Room, so named because it had been decorated in that year for the state visit of Tsar Nicolas I of Russia.

The Logues had been listening to Chamberlain speak at their home, Beechgrove House, on Sydenham Hill in south-east London. Like many people in Britain, their reaction to the declaration of war was a feeling of release. 'A marvellous relief after all our tension,' Lionel recorded in his diary. 'The universal desire is to kill the Austrian house painter.' As he wrote later to Rupert Gruenert, Myrtle's brother in Perth: 'To have a war was the only way out. We are well prepared (not like last November at Munich) and already have demonstrated our planes are superior to the Germans."

It was a measure of how well Lionel's career had been going that he and Myrtle had moved in 1932 from their flat in Bolton Gardens to this imposing mid-Victorian villa on the edge of Dulwich Woods. The house, which dated from the early 1860s, was enormous: it had twenty-five rooms, five bathrooms and five acres of grounds, including a tennis court – and some illustrious former owners. It was built by William Patterson, an East India merchant, who first named it 'Singapore' but then decided Beechgrove would be more appropriate. The house changed hands several times after Patterson's death in 1898. Subsequent owners included Samuel Herbert Benson, regarded as one of the pioneers of modern advertising thanks to his campaign for Bovril, and Sir William Watson Cheyne, who went on to become president of the Royal College of Surgeons. Shortly after the Logues moved in, the Alleyn's College of God's Gift, the charity that owned the freehold of Beechgrove and much of the other land in Dulwich, granted him permission to put up a small brass plate outside with his name on it to advertise his services as a curer of speech defects.

The house had provided the Logues with more than enough room in which to bring up their three sons, but its size meant it required money and staff to maintain – both of which they knew would now be in short supply. That Friday Myrtle had broken the news to her housemaid that, with war coming, she could no longer afford to keep her. Myrtle was relieved that she took it so well. 'She is so optimistic and says, "there ain't going to be a war, madam. Old Moore's Almanack says so",' Myrtle wrote in the diary that she was to keep for a large part of the war. The housemaid was still cheerful when Myrtle saw her off the next day, telling her that she wouldn't have their only son 'excavated' to the country, preferring that he remain in London and take his chances.

By contrast, their cook, Therese, a Bavarian who had lived in London for a decade, was worried about how she would fare as an enemy alien once Britain and Germany were at war. Coming downstairs, Myrtle found her in floods of tears.

'Oh, Madam, I am caught – it is too late to get away,' Therese wailed.

Myrtle suggested they go upstairs to listen to the wireless, which they did, only to hear, to their alarm, a notice of general mobilization.

'I look at her tear-stained swollen face and think I must do something, so suggest that as war has not yet been declared she should ring up her Embassy and enquire,' Myrtle wrote in her diary. 'She does and is informed that there is a last train leaving at 10 a.m. on the next day. I send her upstairs to pack.'

Therese was still looking miserable and tear-stained when she set off the next day. Myrtle, meanwhile, was left to contemplate with horror how she was going to look after the house with her sole remaining domestic help – a young Czech refugee who had little experience of domestic service and drove Myrtle to distraction with her pidgin English.

About midday, shortly after Chamberlain had finished speaking, the Logues' telephone rang. It was Sir Eric Miéville, who after a highly distinguished career of public service in China and India had been appointed assistant private secretary to George VI shortly before he came to the throne. The King was to broadcast to the nation that evening at six o'clock and needed Logue to help him to prepare. Logue was driven to the Palace by their eldest, Laurie, who was now aged thirty and living with his wife of three years, Josephine – or Jo, as she was always known in the family – in nearby Crystal Palace. It could have been any late-summer day in London had it not been for the sun shining on the barrage balloons, turning them silvery blue. Laurie dropped his father off at 5.20 and turned the car round. He wanted to be back at Beechgrove in time to listen to the broadcast. Logue left his hat, umbrella and gas mask in the Privy Purse Hall and climbed the stairs.

The King received Logue in his private study, rather than the room they normally used, which was being readied for the post-broadcast photograph. He had already changed into his admiral's uniform. From that moment on until the end of the war, he never appeared in public except in military garb, to indicate he was permanently on active service. He handed Logue a copy of the text of the broadcast: it was a simple one, intended to prepare his subjects for the struggle that lay ahead and unite them in their determination to achieve victory. Logue read through it, just as he had read through countless past speeches, looking carefully for words that the King might stumble over and, where possible, substituting something easier. Thus 'government' was replaced with 'ourselves', while 'call' took the place of 'summon'. He also marked points at which to take a pause.

As the King rehearsed, Logue was impressed with how well he read. He felt proud of how far he and his patient had come since their first meeting all those years ago in Harley Street. He was also struck by how sad the King sounded. Logue tried in vain to lighten the mood, reminding him how the two of them had sat in the same room, together with the Queen, on Coronation night in May 1937 preparing for the broadcast he had been due to make to the Empire, which, at the time, had seemed equally daunting. Logue made the King laugh as they talked about how much had happened during the intervening two and a half years.

At that moment, the door at the other end of the room opened, and the Queen came in to give her husband last-minute encouragement. They did not have long to talk. With just three minutes to go, it was time to move into the Broadcasting Room. Normally, the only other people in the room for the broadcast would be Logue and Wood, the BBC sound engineer who had worked with the King since his accession to the throne, and was, according to Logue, 'a great tower of strength . . . [he] does know his job'. This time, Frederick Ogilvie, the economist who had taken over from John Reith as Director General of the BBC the previous year, had asked Logue if he could also be present. Logue said he would have to consult the King; he did not want anything that would make him even more nervous. As they crossed the corridor, the King beckoned to Ogilvie to join them. The room had been redecorated since Coronation night and was bright and cheerful, but the mood was sombre. The King knew how much was riding on this speech, which would be heard by millions of people across the Empire.

After fifty seconds, the red light came on. Logue looked at the King and smiled as he watched him step up to the microphone. The King allowed himself the tiniest glimmer of a smile in return. The clock outside in the Quadrangle struck six.

'In this grave hour,' the King began, speaking with great feeling, 'perhaps the most fateful in our history, I send to every household of my peoples, both at home and overseas, this message, spoken with the same depth of feeling for each one of you as if I were able to cross your threshold and speak to you myself.

For the second time in the lives of most of us we are at war. Over and over again we have tried to find a peaceful way out of the differences between ourselves and those who are now our enemies. But it has been in vain. We have been forced into a conflict. For we are called, with our allies, to meet the challenge of a principle which, if it were to prevail, would be fatal to any civilised order in the world.

It is the principle which permits a state, in the selfish pursuit of power, to disregard its treaties and its solemn pledges; which sanctions the use of force, or threat of force, against the sovereignty and independence of other states. Such a principle, stripped of all disguise, is surely the mere primitive doctrine that might is right; and if this principle were established throughout the world, the freedom of our own country and of the whole British Commonwealth of Nations would be in danger. But far more than this – the peoples of the world would be kept in the bondage of fear, and all hopes of settled peace and of the security of justice and liberty among nations would be ended.

This is the ultimate issue which confronts us. For the sake of all that we ourselves hold dear, and of the world's order and peace, it is unthinkable that we should refuse to meet the challenge.

It is to this high purpose that I now call my people at home and my peoples across the seas, who will make our cause their own. I ask them to stand calm, firm, and united in this time of trial. The task will be hard. There may be dark days ahead, and war can no longer be confined to the battlefield. But we can only do the right as we see the right, and reverently commit our cause to God. If one and all we keep resolutely faithful to it, ready for whatever service or sacrifice it may demand, then, with God's help, we shall prevail. May He bless and keep us all.

CHAPTER TWO

Sitzkrieg

The evening was beginning to draw in as Logue left Buckingham Palace and drove back south-eastwards towards Sydenham Hill. Soon London would be plunged into complete darkness. The blackout had begun two days earlier. Mea Allan, a journalist from the *Daily Herald*, stood on the footway of Hungerford Bridge and looked out across the Thames as the lights went out. 'The whole great town was lit up like a fairy land, in a dazzle that reached into the sky,' she wrote.

> . . . and then one by one, as a switch was pulled, each area went dark, the dazzle becoming a patchwork of lights being snuffed out here and there until a last one remained, and it too went out. What was left us was more than just wartime blackout, it was a fearful portent of what war was to be. We had not thought that we would have to fight in darkness, or that light would be our enemy.[7]

The blackout was an important part of military preparedness. Those responsible for Britain's defence were convinced that in the event of war German bombers would hit London and the country's other main industrial and population centres. They therefore set out to remove any points of reference that could guide the enemy to their targets. A form of blackout had been introduced in 1915 during the First World War; when a Zeppelin was known to be en route, lights were dimmed rather than put out completely. In the intervening two decades, the threat from the air had grown considerably. The Germans had held their own first blackout exercise in Berlin in 1935, and two years later, Britain followed suit: the Home Office launched an appeal to recruit 300,000 'citizen volunteers' to be trained as air raid precautions (ARP) wardens. Blackout rehearsals began early in 1938, with RAF bombers flying overhead to check for leakages of light.

Traffic emerged as the main problem: even cars driven on only sidelights rather than headlights were clearly visible from above, creating a stream of light that revealed the pattern of the roads. These could then be correlated by enemy bombers with their pre-war maps, allowing them to identify their targets. And so cars' headlights were masked to reveal only a crack of light, windows were covered by blackout curtains and blinds and railway stations lit by candles. Britain was to endure this enforced darkness until 23 April 1945, eight days after the liberation of Belsen, by which time the Allied armies were moving on Berlin.

Like other Londoners, the Logues had been working to get their home ready for the air raids that were widely expected to begin almost immediately after the outbreak of war. On 1 September, the day the lights went out, their youngest son, Antony, an athletic eighteen-year-old with wavy brown hair known in the family as Tony or simply 'Kid', had been dispatched to the local library and came back with a sheet of blackout paper. The mammoth task of blacking out the house was made easier by the fact that many of its windows had shutters. Myrtle had been planning to rip them out ever since they moved into Beechgrove, but, thankfully, seven years later, she had still not got round to doing so. The shutters would also help to protect them against flying glass. The house was so large, though, that even with the blinds, there was still not enough paper to cover all the windows, so Antony left the one in the bathroom uncovered.

This did not seem much of a problem, but at 10 p.m. as Myrtle was brushing her teeth before going to bed, there was a knock on the front door. She opened it to two ARP wardens, who, along with their colleagues, had been touring London to take to task those whose windows were not properly blacked out. Politely but firmly, they told her to put out the light. Myrtle recorded in her diary that she found it very 'trying' sleeping in a heavily shuttered room. 'One has the feeling of a chrysalis in the semi-gloom; all the windows covered with black out paper,' she wrote in her diary.

Walking the streets of London during the blackout could be even more disorientating, as was clear from other contemporary accounts. 'For the first minute going out of doors one is completely bewildered, then it is a matter of groping forward with nerves as well as hands outstretched,' wrote one diarist, Phyllis Warner.[8] Unused to the darkness, people would bang into strangers or tumble over piles of sandbags. The effects of the blackout were not just psychological: by the end of the first month of war it had been blamed for 1,130 road deaths. Coroners urged pedestrians to carry a newspaper or a white handkerchief to make themselves more visible. The casualty departments of hospitals began to fill up with people who had been run over by cars whose headlights had been reduced to little more than a pinprick, broken their legs while stepping off trains onto nonexistent platforms or sprained their ankles stumbling over unseen kerbs.

A number of the injured ended up at St George's Hospital, where the Logues' middle son, Valentine, by then aged twenty-six, was working as a junior doctor after having qualified in 1936. The hospital, situated in Lanesborough House, a grand neoclassical building on Hyde Park Corner, became a unit of the Emergency Hospital Service, providing 200 beds for war casualties and 65 beds for the civilian sick – many of the latter victims of the blackout. During the first night of the war, Valentine was up all night tending to patients who had come to grief on the streets of the capital. The casualties kept on coming in the weeks that followed as the nights got longer.

The blackout was part of a series of measures to protect London and other cities from what it was assumed would be a massive air assault: air raid sirens were installed and barrage balloons, each as big as three cricket pitches and tethered by giant cables, sent up to force bombers to fly to a higher altitude where they could be shot down more easily by anti-aircraft guns. Hospital patients were evacuated from the capital in anticipation of a flood of air raid casualties. Trees, pavements, letter boxes and lamp-posts were marked with bands of white paint. During the Munich crisis, local authorities had begun to dig trenches in parks to provide shelters, which the government afterwards decided to turn into a permanent feature, with a precast concrete lining. Those with gardens of their own dug holes in which they half-buried Anderson shelters, simple structures made up of galvanized corrugated steel panels with room for up to six people, which took their name from Sir John Anderson, the Lord Privy Seal. Those whose homes had cellars or basements were given steel props to provide more protection. Sandbags were stacked around the more vulnerable public buildings. Authorities built public shelters and selected the basements and other suitable parts of shops and office blocks for use in air raids, often to the displeasure of their owners.

One of the greatest fears was of chemical warfare. Poison gas had been used to horrific effect in the trenches during the First World

War, and there was concern that the Germans might use it against civilians in this conflict. By September 1939, some thirty-eight million black rubber gas masks had been handed out, accompanied by a propaganda campaign. 'Hitler will send no warning – so always carry your gas mask,' read one advertisement. Those caught out and about without one risked a fine.

Such preparations had been stepped up as Chamberlain's hopes of avoiding conflict with Hitler began to look increasingly forlorn. A decisive step towards war was passed on 23 August 1939 when Vyacheslav Molotov, the Soviet Foreign Minister, and Joachim von Ribbentrop, his German counterpart, signed a non-aggression pact. Far from heralding peace, the pact gave Hitler a free hand to invade Poland and then unleash his forces on his western neighbours. Two days later, Britain signed a treaty with the Polish government pledging to come to its assistance if it were attacked. Chamberlain had not yet given up hope of negotiating with Hitler. The King, who had immediately taken the night train down from Balmoral, offered to write a personal letter to the Nazi leader, but the Prime Minister turned him down – just as a suggestion that the King might send a friendly message to the Emperor of Japan, from one head of state to another, to try and detach him from the other Axis powers, was rejected for fear of almost certain rebuttal.

On 28 August Logue had received a call from Hardinge.

'Hold yourself in readiness to come to the Palace,' the King's private secretary told him.

Logue did not need to ask why. 'I said I was ready at any time day or night – but much as I would like to see, and speak with His Majesty, I sincerely hoped I would not be sent for,' he wrote in his diary. 'Have given orders at Harley [St] and at home – everyone knows exactly when to get me, day or night.'

Yet even at that late stage, war did not seem completely inevitable.

There was still a hope that Poland's defence pact with Britain might dissuade Hitler from invading. Calling at Buckingham Palace on 26 August, the day after it was signed, Sir Miles Lampson, the British ambassador to Egypt, found the King in 'admirable form', his main concern that the political crisis had disrupted some excellent grouse shooting – '1,600 brace in six days' – at Balmoral. 'It was utterly damnable that that villain Hitler had upset everything,' Lampson reported. 'H.M. thought that there would almost certainly now be peace and that this time Hitler's bluff had been called.'[9]

Preparations for war had nevertheless begun to acquire a momentum of their own. At 11.07 a.m. on 31 August, the terse order 'Evacuate Forthwith' was issued, marking the mass evacuation of London and other towns and cities. In the first four days of September, nearly three million mothers and children thought to be in danger from enemy bombers were transported to places of safety in the countryside. Many of the children, labelled like pieces of luggage, had been separated from their parents and accompanied instead by an army of 100,000 teachers. 'Keep calm, keep a cheerful British smile on your face . . . Good luck, and a safe return to dear old London,' was the parting message of Herbert Morrison, at that time Minister of Supply, to an early wave of evacuees who set off on 1 September. In the event, only half of those eligible actually left the city; many parents could not bear to be separated from their children. Civil servants, by contrast, had no choice in the matter. In the weeks and months that followed, thousands of them were also evacuated from the capital, as were a number of employees of private companies. Pets fared less well: a pamphlet issued by the government aimed at animal owners published on 26 August urged them to send their pets to the countryside but, if this was not possible, 'it might be kindest to have them destroyed' for fear that during an emergency there might be 'large numbers of animals wounded, gassed or driven frantic with fear'. By the end of the first week of war, 750,000 had been put down.

Then, in the early hours of 1 September, Hitler launched his assault on Poland, undeterred by the defence pact it had signed with Britain. At around 4.45 a.m. the *Luftwaffe* began bombing raids on airfields, ships and troops, while the *Schleswig-Holstein*, on a visit to the free port of Danzig (Gdansk), opened fire at the Polish garrison. A few hours later, the King presided over a meeting of the Privy Council at which he signed an Order in Council mobilizing Britain's armed forces. When he visited Chamberlain in Downing Street that afternoon, he was wildly cheered and said to have been 'deeply touched' by the spontaneous demonstration of loyalty.[10] That evening Henderson, the British ambassador, delivered an ultimatum to the German Foreign Ministry saying his government would 'without hesitation fulfill their obligation to Poland' if Germany did not withdraw its forces and cease its aggression. The official German news agency responded by accusing Britain of being 'an aggressor who desires a European war.'

The next day Logue received a summons to go to the Palace. The weather was hot; it reminded him more of a summer's day in Sydney or Ceylon than England. He arrived just before 4 p.m. and was shown in to see Hardinge. The son of a former Viceroy of India, Hardinge had been appointed assistant private secretary to George V in 1920 at the age of twenty-six and had served him until his death sixteen years later. When Edward VIII acceded to the throne, Hardinge was promoted to become his principal private secretary and, as such, had to negotiate his abdication, during which, like many at court, he had little sympathy either for the departing King or for Wallis Simpson. He was much happier working for his successor, their earlier difference over appeasement, although not forgotten, rendered irrelevant by the march towards war.

Logue was surprised to see Hardinge, usually formally dressed as befitted a long-standing member of the royal household, in his shirt sleeves. Invariably calm, he was uncharacteristically tense, his mood exacerbated by the heat. 'The only time I have ever known him lose his temper was when he opened out on the Nazi regime, and the Russia–German pact,' Logue noted in his diary. 'He told me lots of funny things were happening in Germany, but they could not quite find out just what they were. As he said, this waiting is too terrible for words.'

As they parted Hardinge told Logue: 'Only one thing will satisfy us and that is the removal of Hitler,' which Logue 'thought was a good tip'.

The King was in similarly grim mood. There was nothing left of the optimism Lampson had encountered a few days earlier. Instead the monarch seemed as frustrated as everyone else in Britain at trying to work out what was going on.

'Hello, Logue, can you tell me, are we at war?' the King enquired.

'I don't know, your Majesty,' replied Logue.

'You don't know, the Prime Minister doesn't know, and I don't know,' the King shot back, a note of irritation in his voice that could presage one of his 'gnashes'. 'It is so damn unreal. If only we knew which way it was going to be.'

But by the time Logue left the Palace he was convinced that war was 'just around the corner'. The following evening, he stood at hand as the King made his broadcast.

Logue collapsed into bed shortly after arriving home on the first night of war. Despite the grave nature of the occasion, he was pleased with the way the King's broadcast had gone. His slumbers proved brief: at 3 a.m. came another air raid warning that sent him and Myrtle rushing down to Beechgrove's stuffy basement. 'The only feeling is one of irritation,' she wrote in her diary. 'It is strange how things work out – no panic, no fear, only plain mad at being disturbed.' Like the warning the previous day, this too was a false alarm.

The Germans had already struck at sea, however. A few hours earlier, the SS *Athenia*, a transatlantic passenger liner on charter to Cunard, with 1,103 passengers and 315 crew on board, was hit by a torpedo off the coast of Northern Ireland as it made its way from Glasgow to Montreal. The ship was targetted about 250 miles northwest of Inishtrahull, as its passengers, a mixture of Jewish refugees, Americans, Canadians and Britons, were sitting down to dinner. The missile was fired by a German U-boat, whose captain mistook the *Athenia* for an armed merchant cruiser and attacked without warning. The ship sank with the loss of ninety-eight passengers and nineteen crew – twenty-eight of them Americans. Fifty of the victims died when their lifeboat was crushed by the propeller of a Norwegian tanker that came to their assistance.

This unprovoked attack on a civilian vessel, in contravention of all the rules of naval warfare, and just hours after the declaration of war, caused outrage on both sides of the Atlantic – all the more so because the Germans refused to admit responsibility. In Canada, the death of Margaret Hayworth, a ten-year-old from Hamilton, Ontario, who had been on board the stricken ship, helped rally that nation behind its government's decision a week later to follow Britain in declaring war on Germany. The scale of the disaster, and large loss of American lives, fuelled hopes that the United States would now follow suit: comparisons were drawn with the 1915 sinking of the *Lusitania*, which helped stiffen American resolve against the Kaiser's Germany. 'Hitler is unlucky,' noted Myrtle. 'American neutrality will soon go.'

Such hopes were misplaced, however. Just as it took two years after the attack on the *Lusitania* before the United States entered the First World War, despite the loss of 1,128 American lives, so the sinking of the *Athenia* was not enough to change the isolationist mood of a country reluctant to be dragged into another European conflict so soon after the last. It did, however, help to change American public opinion sufficiently to lead to the amendment of the neutrality laws to allow Washington to sell munitions and supplies to Britain and France – a first step towards taking on the Nazis directly.

For the people of Britain, the war nevertheless still seemed far away. The weather in London that September continued fine, with warm days and calm nights. At times it was stifling inside the Logues' shuttered house. Myrtle cooked for the first time in a long while and was pleased to note that her hand 'had not lost its cunning'. Beechgrove's huge garden was well stocked with vegetables, but their gardener was due to leave to start as an air raid warden that week, which would mean it would be her job to harvest them all. She and Lionel also got down to work chopping up eight oak trees that had been felled, taking as much of the wood into their storehouse as they could. Myrtle was proud of how skilled she had become at cutting the smaller pieces of timber into short lengths. 'The rangers patrolling the railway at the foot of our garden are much amused at the sight of me wielding a saw,' she noted.

Air raid warnings were becoming a regular feature of life in London, even though they had yet to be followed by the arrival of a single enemy plane, let alone the much-feared mass aerial bombardment. On 6 September, a Wednesday, the Logues were woken by the sirens at 6.45 a.m. and went down to the basement. While they waited, they had breakfast. Bored, they finally made their way back upstairs. It was, noted Myrtle, 'so beautiful a day for men to kill one another'. After the all-clear sounded at nine o'clock they went into London to have their hair cut; Laurie drove. Myrtle had not been to the centre of the capital for six weeks and was struck by its transformation: the lights at crossings had been blacked out so that all that was visible were little Xs of light and the kerbs were painted black and white to help people find their way.

The warning had been yet another false alarm – caused by German reconnaissance planes that had been turned back – but it had still made everyone late for work. Yet Myrtle was struck by how cheerful people seemed as they hurried through the city, gas masks slung over their shoulders. She was also entranced by the sight of the barrage balloons. 'Hundreds of these silver things fill the sky, and were it not for the menace they will protect us from, it would be a joy to watch,' she wrote.

The next day came news that the French had tried to help their Polish allies by taking the war onto German soil with what was to prove a short and ill-fated invasion of the Saar region. Myrtle, meanwhile, was busy on the home front, cutting wood and picking more fruit and vegetables to preserve for the winter. She made blackberry jam for the first time in fifteen years and was pleased with how well it turned out. She dug so many potatoes that she was losing a pound in weight per day. 'At the end of the war I hope to be a sylph,' she noted. Valentine was a good shot and brought them back rabbits he had killed in Epping Forest.

Myrtle marked her fifty-fourth birthday that Sunday by cooking a good dinner – complete with cake – for her whole family, together with several friends. Yet everyone seemed to be struggling to come to terms with the reality of war. 'Life seems to be suspended – one seems to have no aims or desire to do anything but routine jobs,' she wrote in her diary.

'We still carry on in this dream-like existence, and this feeling seems to be universal. Our whole life has changed. Life socially is at a standstill, also, owing to the blackout, one dare not venture out after dark. The street accidents are terrifying. Val is operating every night until the early hours.'

On the day that war was declared, cinemas, together with sports arenas and theatres, had been ordered closed, ostensibly because of potential mass casualties in the event of an air strike, but also as part of a broader policy by the government aimed to show it took the conflict seriously. The closures were denounced by the playwright George Bernard Shaw in an open letter to *The Times* as a 'masterstroke of unimaginative stupidity' that could only be disastrous for morale. 'What agent of Chancellor Hitler is it who has suggested we should all cower in darkness and terror "for the duration"?' he demanded.[11] People went to the pub instead, and the number of street brawls rose accordingly. Conscious of the negative effect on civilian morale, the government soon changed tack and allowed the cinemas to reopen. Myrtle and Antony went to their local picture house that Friday afternoon. Several theatres both in the West End and in the suburbs were also soon back in business. Concerts, too, began to be staged again, although it was not until March 1940 that the Albert Hall reopened. The public dance halls were full as never before. Spectator sports were harder hit: although football fixtures soon resumed on a limited basis, Arsenal's ground was turned over to civil defence, the pitch at Twickenham was dug up and replaced by vegetables and the Oval cricket ground converted to a prisoner of war camp, though never used.

Britain's move to a war footing gathered pace. On 16 September, petrol rationing was introduced. Post offices and local taxation offices had begun to issue ration books just over a week earlier; drivers had to produce their car's registration book and in return received the number of coupons to which they were entitled, based on its engine size. Hundreds of buses were withdrawn from service. Taxis were allowed only three gallons of petrol a day and gave up cruising the streets in search of passengers. London began to turn into a country village, its residents walking on the roads rather than keeping to the pavement. Sections of Greenwich Park, Primrose Hill and London's other green spaces were turned over to allotments as posters exhorted people to 'dig for victory'. Tailors' windows were devoted to uniforms, and policemen wore tin hats instead of their traditional helmets. The Chancellor of the Exchequer Sir John Simon's budget on 27 September raised income tax from five shillings to seven shillings and sixpence in the pound and sharply increased the duties on beer, wine, spirits and tobacco.

Yet normal life continued: on the evening of budget day, Lionel and Myrtle went round to play bridge with their friends, Dr Gerald Tattersall Moody, a scientist and a barrister, and his wife Hester, who lived at the Cedars, an imposing house a few minutes' walk away from Beechgrove, on the other side of the Sydenham Road. It was a lovely moonlight night, all the more striking because of the blackout – even though, as Myrtle noted, the sky in London was always faintly luminous, in contrast to the 'pitch blackness of an Australian sky' that she remembered from life back home.

They were woken at 2 a.m. by the telephone. It was Laurie. Jo had just gone into labour and he said he was about to go with her by ambulance to Queen Charlotte maternity hospital. Suddenly all thought of war was replaced by concern for Jo. Four hours later, she gave birth to a baby girl, Alexandra – who became known as Sandra. 'Great rejoicing,' wrote Myrtle. 'We haven't had a girl in the family since I was born. It feels strange to be a grandmother – the whole family calls me "Gran". Laurie is staying with us. It gives me a warm feeling to have him near if only for a short time.'

Laurie himself was working for Lyons, the food company. Having risen to become second-in-command of the ice cream department, he was in charge of supplying cinemas, all the dog racing tracks and Wimbledon during the tennis tournament. Since he was in food distribution, he had not been among the first wave of men to be called up when conscription was introduced for all males aged between eighteen and forty-one.* Antony, meanwhile, had been accepted to study medicine, following in the footsteps of Valentine. A few weeks before he was due to start his course at King's College, London, he learnt the faculty was being shifted to Leeds for the duration of the war. A fun-loving young man who had inherited his father's passion for poetry, Antony had cheered up life at Beechgrove, and his parents were sad when they saw him off at King's Cross on 5 October. 'His being away takes a lot of laughter out of my life,' wrote Myrtle in her diary. With her three sons now gone and Lionel often at work, she was grateful for the company of her two young dogs, Digger, a fox terrier, and Tov, a cairn, even though it was becoming a struggle to find enough beef in the shops to feed them.

A few weeks later, the hospital gave Valentine a couple of days off work, and he and his mother drove up to Leeds to see how Antony was settling in. It was pouring with rain, and the journey northwards in Valentine's sports car was an arduous one, especially after the windscreen wipers broke halfway into the journey. Antony's landlady seemed kind-hearted, though, and cooked them an 'excellent dinner' when they arrived. Myrtle was pleased to see how well her youngest was settling into his digs. 'He looks so well, big and manly, evidently the cold North country suits him,' she wrote in her diary. She was less impressed by their trip the next day to nearby Harrogate, the spa town. 'Once affluent Harrogate has been taken

---

* Plans for limited conscription applying to single men aged between twenty and twenty-two were given parliamentary approval in the Military Training Act in May 1939. This required men to undertake six months' military training, and some 240,000 registered for service. On the day Britain declared war on Germany, parliament immediately extended conscription to all males aged eighteen to forty-one, with exceptions for some in key industries.

over by the government and all the residents of the lovely hotels turned out at a few hours' notice, many had been resident in the one hotel for 20 or 30 years,' she wrote. 'Great curative spa ruined for a senseless bureaucracy. The hotels remain empty, not being used for the purpose which was intended. There should be many questions asked about the panic administration of this country.'

By then, Britain and Germany had been at war for almost two months, but the much-feared air raids had still not begun, and all remained quiet on the Western Front. Many of the children who had been evacuated to the countryside had begun to make their way home. By mid-October as many as 50,000 mothers and children had returned; a month later the figure had more than doubled, putting a strain on the education system in London and other large cities. Many school buildings had been taken over by civil defence and few had adequate shelters. The government struggled to maintain morale. The popular perception of a 'phoney war' or 'Sitzkrieg' was at its height.

'Just gardening and cooking, it's strange how one can go on in the same rut day after day without boredom,' Myrtle wrote that November in her diary, which she filled with descriptions of flowers tended and vegetables harvested. She also started doing work for the Australian Women's Voluntary Service Committee, which was set up to help the growing number of the country's troops arriving in Britain.

Her and Lionel's frequent trips to the theatre and cinema continued, as did bridge and dinner parties with friends, often accompanied by a bottle of champagne. Lionel's connections and renown also meant the chance to meet new people – among them William Hillman, an American foreign correspondent who had been based for a time in Berlin, whom they invited round for dinner. 'He was so interesting,' wrote Myrtle. 'He has known Hitler and his gang since 1929 and talked so interestingly about them. Val came out also and was thrilled.' They ate a brace of pheasant that had been given to Lionel by a grateful patient.

Despite the deceptive calm at home, the war at sea was now beginning in earnest, with devastating results: in the early hours of 14 October the German submarine U-47 succeeded in penetrating the defences at Scapa Flow in Orkney, off the extreme northern tip of Scotland, which, because of its great distance from German airfields, was to serve as the main British naval base during the war. The U-boat's commander, Günther Prien, fired his first torpedo at the *Royal Oak*, an elderly battleship with 1,234 men on board. After scoring a hit, Prien turned to make his escape, but, realizing there was no immediate threat from British surface vessels, returned to make another attack. The second torpedo blew a 30-foot (9-metre) hole in the British ship, which flooded and sank within just thirteen minutes. Some 833 men were killed, many of them as they slept in their hammocks. Few of those who escaped survived the freezing water. Others were rescued but succumbed to their wounds. More than a hundred of the ship's complement were 'boy sailors', teen-agers who had been assigned to the British fleet before they became ordinary seamen at the age of eighteen.

One of five Revenge-class battleships built for the Royal Navy during the First World War, the *Royal Oak* was slow, outdated and no longer suited for front-line duty. But its sinking was a major blow to morale and showed the ability of the German navy to bring the war to British waters in a base that had been thought impregnable to submarine attack. Prien became a celebrity in Germany and was the first member of the *Kriegsmarine* to receive the Knight's Cross of the Iron Cross with Oak Leaves. 'Horrible news of Scapa flow with 810 dead,' Myrtle wrote in her diary. 'It seems too horrible to be true.'

*

The King had been in Scapa Flow a few days earlier on a trip that also took him to Invergordon. The visit will have brought back memories of his own naval career more than a quarter of a century earlier: days before Britain declared war on Germany on 3 August 1914, the battleship HMS *Collingwood*, on which the then Duke had been commissioned, had been sent to Orkney. His service record had not been an especially glorious one, however: after just three weeks he began to experience violent pains in his stomach and suffer difficulty with his breathing; he was diagnosed with appendicitis and sent to Aberdeen for surgery. He subsequently returned to his ship and took part in the Battle of Jutland in May 1916. But he endured repeated stomach problems that were eventually diagnosed as an ulcer, and by July the following year, ill once more, he was transferred ashore to a hospital near Edinburgh. Reluctantly he accepted that, after eight years of either training or serving in the navy, his naval career was over. 'Personally, I feel that I am not fit for service at sea, even after I recover from this little attack,' he wrote to his father.[12]

On this occasion, the King travelled up to Scotland aboard a special bulletproof train that set off from Euston Station in conditions of utmost secrecy. Police guarded all the approaches as he boarded at platform six; another engine with empty carriages drew alongside to shield him from view. Neither the driver nor the fireman knew their final destination as they steamed out of the station. Once on board, the King and Queen were able to relax in some comfort. The train had every conceivable comfort including air conditioning, coach-to-coach telephones, electric fires and a mechanical cushioning system to reduce vibrations. The royal couple had a coach each, fitted with a lounge, dining car, sleeping cabins and bathrooms, as well as accommodation for their respective valet and maid.[13] It was in this manner that the King was to travel some 52,000 miles during the war, often accompanied by the Queen, meeting and encouraging his subjects.

With the outbreak of the conflict, the Palace moved swiftly onto a war footing: many members of the royal household departed for military service, while large numbers of those who remained were transferred to Windsor Castle. Guards and sentries appeared in khaki and steel helmets, while members of the household dressed in khaki and blue uniforms. The finest pictures and other artworks were stored underground in Windsor – as were the Crown Jewels – and display cases emptied of miniatures, gems and porcelains. Skylights were painted black, windows covered and the great cut-glass chandeliers in the state rooms at Windsor lowered to just three feet above the ground to reduce the impact if they fell. The carriage horses in the Buckingham Palace Mews were put to work on farms.

The King's two younger brothers joined the war effort: Prince Henry, the Duke of Gloucester, aged thirty-nine on the outbreak of war, joined the British Expeditionary Force and was appointed Chief Liaison Officer. Prince George, the Duke of Kent, a stylish and fast-living thirty-six-year-old who had been due to become Governor General of Australia that November, went instead to the Admiralty. Several members of the royal household also took up war duties.

For the King himself, the outbreak of war brought new duties and responsibilities. He was not just head of state but also Commander-in-Chief of the armed forces of Great Britain and of the Empire. Although with no formal powers as such, he had the monarch's right to be consulted, to encourage and to warn his government. To help him fulfil this role he was given numerous briefings by the Prime Minister and other members of the cabinet containing large amount of sensitive military information. He was also one of the few people allowed access to Ultra, the intelligence derived from the cracking of the Nazis' Enigma code. In Buckingham Palace he kept a chart showing aircraft production and losses. 'The King took a very great interest in things – people talked to him and he could make his points,' recalled Lieutenant General Sir Ian Jacob, military assistant to the war cabinet.[14] The king nevertheless found his role frustrating. 'I wish I had a definite job like you,' he wrote to his distant cousin, Louis Mountbatten, captain of HMS *Kelly* and commander of the 5th Destroyer Flotilla in October 1939. 'Mine is such an awful mixture, trying to keep people cheered up in all ways, and having to find fault as well as praising them.'[15]

War or no war, the State Opening of Parliament was due to take place on 28 November. There had been speculation that, for reasons of security, the King would not appear, with the government's programme read out instead by Viscount Caldecote, the Lord Chancellor. In the end, it was decided the King should take part after all. To help him prepare, Logue went to the Palace that morning. He arrived at 10.30 and was shown upstairs to a large room. There was no one in it, but through the half-open door of the King's study, he could hear the monarch going through the speech.

At that point, the Queen, who had been in the room listening to her husband rehearse, caught a glimpse of him.

'Oh, here is Mr Logue,' she said.

Logue bowed over the Queen's hand and congratulated her on a speech, the first of the war, that she had made to the women of the Empire on 11 November, Armistice Day. The Queen had been reluctant to make the broadcast at first but had faced multiple calls to do so and eventually agreed. She proved herself an effective speaker. Listeners wrote to the BBC full of admiration. Reith, the former Director General, reportedly called it 'one of the best broadcasts that have ever gone out to the world'.[16] Now Logue added his words of praise.

'She blushed like a school girl and told me that she was so nervous at the start that she hardly knew what she was saying,' he recalled.

'I told her that I had almost written to congratulate her, but that I was shy about it.'

'I wish you had,' she replied.

'I will next time,' replied Logue.

The Queen put her hand on heart. 'I hope there never will be a next time.'

'You can never tell,' chipped in the King.

'Anyway, if I do have it again, I will get you to hear through it first,' the Queen said to Logue, laughing, and added: 'Now I must leave you two and go and get dressed.'

The two men went through the speech. 'A good effort, despite the fact that the redundancy of words is dreadful,' was Logue's verdict afterwards. He timed their run-through – eleven minutes exactly – and wondered how long it would take the King to deliver it. Logue was not going to be in parliament to hear the result of his work, but one of the equerries promised to call him at 2.15 to let him know how it had gone.

The State Opening of Parliament is the occasion for a great show of British pageantry. The previous year, in accordance with tradition, the King and Queen had set off from Buckingham Palace aboard a golden coach, their path to parliament lined with cheering, flag-waving crowds. This year, by contrast, the royal couple arrived at the Palace of Westminster by car and with the minimum of retinue; the King wore the uniform of an Admiral of the Fleet, with the Imperial Crown carried by a senior naval officer; the Queen was in velvet and furs embellished with pearls against the cold. The peers in attendance wore morning dress or military uniform rather than their robes. The speech itself, which in peacetime would have set out the government's proposed legislative programme in some detail, was short and to the point: 'The prosecution of the war demands the energies of all my subjects,' the King began. The text gave nothing else away besides telling MPs that they would be asked to make 'further financial provision for the conduct of the war'. It had taken the King thirteen minutes to deliver the speech, two minutes longer than during their run-through, and he had hesitated four times.

A few days later, on 4 December, the King travelled to France to inspect the British Expeditionary Force. A gale was blowing in the Channel, but no sooner had the warship nosed out of the harbour than he walked to the bridge, where he remained for the entire one-and-a-half-hour crossing. 'The King earned the admiration of the Royal Navy by his magnificent conduct on one of the worst Channel crossings for weeks,' wrote Bernard Gray, the *Daily Mirror's* reporter with the force.[17] 'The deck below was frequently awash as the man-of-war buried her nose in the swirling waves. The King . . . stood serene and calm, revelling in the battle against the elements.'

During his stay of just under a week he met Lord Gort, the Commander-in-Chief of the Expeditionary Force, as well as the French President, Albert Lebrun, the Prime Minister, Edouard Daladier, and General Maurice Gamelin, Gort's French counterpart. The British press noted that the King would be stepping ashore almost exactly twenty-five years after his father had paid a first visit to the front during the First World War. It was, according to Gray, to be 'the most democratic royal visit ever made'. 'He will tramp through the mud just like [the troops] do. He will see their trenches, their forts, their guns. And, equally important, how they live.'[18] The King's visit gave a much-needed morale boost both to the British troops and to the French. The weather was already bitterly cold. Three months after the start of the war there had been little action on the Western Front. There was tension between British High Command in France and the government in London, and Anglo-French cooperation was under strain.

The King returned to London to the welcome news of the sinking of the *Admiral Graf Spee*, the German 'pocket battleship', in the Battle of the River Plate in Argentina. The ship, which had taken part in his Coronation Review in 1937, had been sent to the South Atlantic in the weeks before the outbreak of war to be in position in the merchant sea lanes. By December it had sunk nine vessels but was confronted by the British cruisers, the *Ajax*, *Achilles* and *Exeter*, on 13 December. The German ship inflicted heavy damage on the three but was damaged and forced to put into port at Montevideo. Hans Langsdorff, its commander, was convinced by false reports that superior British forces were approaching and scuttled his ship. The news of the vessel's loss was a major morale booster for the British cause. 'The *Graf Spee* is our sole topic,' Myrtle wrote in her diary.

The next day, 14 December, was the King's birthday. Along with his birthday greetings, Logue sent him a couple of books he thought he would like, in accordance with a practice he had begun more than a decade earlier (and would continue until the King's death). Logue did not record the books' titles in his diary but told the King he thought he would find them both 'very light and very entertaining'. That afternoon he was invited to the Palace to discuss the King's upcoming Christmas message. While he was waiting to be summoned, Lord (Stanley) Baldwin came in, walking with a stick. They got into a discussion about the sinking of the *Graf Spee*, in the course of which Logue noticed how deaf the former Prime Minister had now become. When Baldwin was sent for and limped out the room, Logue was struck by the realization of the extent to which he and Ramsay MacDonald, whom he had succeeded at Number 10 in 1935, were 'the two men responsible for all the troubles we are going through'.

Logue was received by Alan Lascelles, the King's assistant private secretary. The grandson of the 4th Earl of Harewood and a product of Marlborough College and Trinity College, Oxford, Lascelles had been associated with royalty since 1920 when he was appointed assistant private secretary to Edward, Prince of Wales – the same year Hardinge had started work for George V. Although initially an admirer of the future King Edward VIII, Lascelles – known to his intimates as Tommy – swiftly became disillusioned with his poor work ethic and even poorer morals. He resigned in 1929, declaring 'I have wasted the best years of my life,' and went to Canada as private secretary to the Governor General, only to be persuaded by George V to return in 1935 shortly before his death. Such was Lascelles's sense of duty that he remained in his post for Edward VIII's brief reign, but he was far more comfortable serving his successor, whose sense of duty matched his own.

Lascelles told Logue the King would make his broadcast from Sandringham, where he and the Queen had decided to spend the Christmas holidays. Their daughters would come down from Scotland to join them. It had been three months since they had seen the princesses and their reunion was to be a joyful one. The family – or 'us four' as the King called them – had always been a close one, its warmth a contrast to the stultifying formality that had blighted his own childhood. 'There was something unique about the King's home life,' said Princess Alice, who as the wife of the Duke of Gloucester was to observe several generations of the royal family. 'The four of them made a small, absolutely united circle. They shared the same jokes and they shared each other's troubles.'[19]

The prospect of having to address the nation on Christmas afternoon nevertheless cast a shadow over the festivities. 'This is always an ordeal for me & I don't begin to enjoy Christmas until after it is over,' the King wrote in his diary.[20] Wood, the BBC sound engineer, learnt this for himself one Christmas Day when a younger member of the Royal Family was trying unsuccessfully to interest the King in some event when he suddenly exclaimed: 'I can't concentrate on anything because I've got that damned broadcast coming up this afternoon.'[21]

What was to become a beloved national tradition that has endured to this day had been initiated by his father, George V, in 1932. Seated at a desk under the stairs in Sandringham, the monarch read out words that had been written for him by Rudyard Kipling, the great imperial poet and author of *The Jungle Book*. He spoke again in 1935, less than a month before his death, reflecting not just on his Silver Jubilee but also on two other major royal events of the year, one joyous, the other sad: the Duke of Gloucester's marriage to Alice and the death of his sister, Princess Victoria. The broadcasts, which were mildly, but not overly, religious in tone, were intended to cast the monarch in the role of head of a great family that embraced not just the United Kingdom but also the countries of the Empire.

George VI had been reluctant to follow suit, not least because of his stammer, which turned every public speech into a painful ordeal. At Christmas 1936, with his elder brother's abdication just two weeks old, there had been no expectation that he should speak. A year later, the situation was different, and there had been a clamour from the Empire for him to make a broadcast. Thousands of letters began to arrive at Buckingham Palace urging him to speak. After considerable hesitation, he bowed to the pressure. The broadcast had turned out well, but the King had made clear, in a phrase picked up by the newspapers, that this was to be a one-off rather than a continuation of the practice established by his father. 'I cannot aspire to take his place – nor do I think that you would wish me to carry on, unvaried, a tradition so personal to him,' he said. True to his word, he did not make a speech in 1938.

The following year, with Britain – and the Empire – at war, there could be no question of the King not addressing his subjects. It was decided he would deliver a personal message at the end of the BBC's *Round the Empire* programme on Christmas afternoon. The purpose of the speech was to counter the mood of anticlimax, apathy and complacency engendered by the phoney war. The King was also keen to point out that the conflict was about defending Christian civilization; he spoke of what he had seen at first hand since September: of the Royal Navy, 'upon which, throughout the last four months, had burst the storm of ruthless and unceasing war'; of the Royal Air Force, 'who were daily adding laurels to those that their fathers had won'; and of the British Expeditionary Force in France: 'Their task is hard. They are waiting, and waiting is a trial of nerve and discipline.'

'A new year is at hand,' the King concluded. 'We cannot tell what it will bring. If it brings peace, how thankful we shall all be. If it brings continued struggle we shall remain undaunted. In the meantime, I feel that we may all find a message of encouragement in the lines which, in my closing words, I would like to say to you.'

Then he quoted from a hitherto unknown poem that had been drawn to his attention by the Queen. It had been written in 1908 by Minnie Louise Haskins, an academic at the London School of Economics, and privately published in a collection four years later.

The poem began:

And I said to the man who stood at the gate of the year: 'Give
    me a light that I may tread safely into the unknown.'
And he replied:
'Go out into the darkness and put your hand into the Hand of
    God. That shall be to you better than light and safer than
    a known way.'

After the broadcast ended, Wood quipped that in a few years' time he expected the King to be making his Christmas broadcast on television. The King looked at Logue with a grin and said: 'I expect you will be under the table then, Logue.'

Thanks to the broadcast, Haskins's poem became enormously popular under the title 'The Gate of the Year'. It was reproduced on cards and widely published. The Queen was especially moved by it, and in the late 1960s, when a new side chapel was added to St George's Chapel at Windsor Castle as a permanent resting place for her late husband, the words were inscribed on a panel to the right of the iron gates. When she died in 2002, the poem was read out at her state funeral.

No one had let Haskins herself know in advance that her words were going to be quoted, and she did not listen to the broadcast. 'I heard the quotation read in a summary of the speech,' she told the *Daily Telegraph* the following day. 'I thought the words sounded familiar and suddenly it dawned on me that they were out of my little book.'

Haskins had Logue to thank for ensuring her work reached such a large audience. When he was rehearsing the text of the broadcast with the King five days earlier, he had been told that the Archbishop of Canterbury wanted to paraphrase her verses and turn them into prose. Logue had objected and talked round the King's advisors into agreeing to block the suggestion. He was disappointed, though, with the King's delivery. 'It began badly, voice high-pitched, and it was at once evident that he was suffering under some emotional stress,' he noted afterwards. 'After the first minute, he settled into his stride, and spoke well, in a good voice, but only took 9½ minutes instead of 10 or 11. Too quick.'

CHAPTER THREE

The Big Freeze

The first full year of the war began with a big chill: the newspapers proclaimed it the coldest since the Battle of Waterloo. The Thames was frozen for eight miles between Teddington and Sunbury, and ice covered stretches of the Mersey, Humber, Severn, the Lakes and all the Scottish lochs. Hundreds of barges were unable to move on the Grand Union Canal. Temperatures in central London were below zero for a week and there was skating on the Serpentine on six inches of ice. Trains were trapped in snow drifts, water pipes froze, boilers exploded and birds were said to have fallen from the sky into the Channel. The average temperature in January was minus 1.4° C.

Despite the war and the worsening weather, the Logues had enjoyed a remarkably normal Christmas break – even though, as had become a habit, Lionel spent the day itself with the King. Guests began arriving at Beechgrove on the twenty-third, which was a Saturday. Together with the Logues, there would be ten of them for Christmas. The visitors would be staying in the house because the fog made travelling almost impossible, even within London. Myrtle viewed the challenge ahead with some trepidation: it would be the first time since they had left Australia that she had to look after so many people without any staff to help. In the run-up to Christmas she had also been struck down by a bout of bronchitis – although at least this afforded her time to finish knitting a pullover for Valentine.

On Christmas Day itself, they had a 'jolly cold luncheon'. 'Champagne cocktails at 6.30 p.m.; the presents given, goodness knows when we shall be able to afford champagne again,' noted Myrtle. As the guests washed up after dinner, they listened to Gracie Fields on the radio singing to the troops. 'Didn't have our usual dance as nobody felt inclined for it.'

By 27 December the guests had all departed, and life settled down into the usual lull between Christmas and New Year, though it was enlivened by the arrival home of Valentine, who had been given a ten-day break from the hospital after having worked all through Christmas. It began to snow; Beechgrove, to Myrtle's eyes, 'looked divine', even though Valentine and Antony, who was back from Leeds for the holidays, were disappointed that not enough of it had settled to make it worth getting out their toboggan. On New Year's Eve, they all set off for a party hosted in Wimbledon by their Australian friends, Gilbert and Mabel Goodman, which meant a ten-mile drive through blacked-out London. 'The fog came up and we had the most terrifying experience getting there in Valentine's little open sports car,' Myrtle wrote in her diary. 'Dozens of people telephoned cancelling, we had another party in town to go to, left early and went to the Lyceum club and saw the New Year in, then started for home, which took 1½ hours instead of 30 minutes. Pedestrians led us with torches, their hands on the top of the car. I really must not try an experience like this again.'

And then it was all over. That Sunday, Antony left early to go back to Leeds to look for new digs; Valentine stayed until after lunch. 'It is lonely without them,' wrote Myrtle after they had both gone. 'Back again to the old routine. Frost again, and snow nearby, the whole of Europe suffering likewise.'

In the days that followed, Myrtle chronicled the worsening arctic conditions engulfing London:

9 January: 'Freezing today, so I'm not allowed out, so have decided to repair bed linen, have not had to do this myself many years.'

10 January: 'Fall of snow, which had hardened on top of frost and making roads very dangerous, so decide to clear out the drawers of discarded toys belonging to the boys . . . This cold is certainly keeping the Huns quiet.'

18 January: 'This icebound land is becoming boring, our place is a sheet of snow, with only the marks of the birds across the smooth surface.'

Keeping a large house such as Beechgrove liveable in such temperatures was a near impossible task. At the beginning of the winter, to save money, Lionel and Myrtle had decided to heat only the few rooms they were using and to turn off all the radiators in the top part of the house. On 19 January, as the temperature plunged, three of the radiators burst. Myrtle spent two hours fighting an ever increasing cascade of water using a spanner as a lever until she managed to shut off the stop cock. 'Oh boy, do we have fun,' she wrote. The next day, according to Met Office records, after an early low of close to minus 9° C, the temperature crept up only as high as minus 2.4° C.

Antony, up in Leeds, was faring even worse, as Myrtle recorded: 'All the pipes froze in his digs, and he had not had a bath for nine days. Then soot fell down the chimney which put the lid on things. He moved to new digs today, do hope he'll have a little more comfort.'

Despite the extreme cold, the roads remained passable. The next day, a Sunday, Valentine came round to Beechgrove in his new car. Myrtle was delighted to see it was a saloon – unlike the open tourer he had previously driven. She put down the change to Gilbert Goodman, who, hearing about how much she hated the sports car, had said to Valentine: 'Why didn't you cut your mother's throat outright instead of freezing her to death in your open car.' Laurie also called by to fit the car radio – which gave Myrtle the chance to nurse her granddaughter Sandra – a 'wee, fat thing' now almost four months old.

The temperatures were dropping again, though: the following Wednesday, Lionel and Myrtle came home after a film and dinner to hear the sound of rushing water when they were still twenty yards from home. 'Lionel did a bulldog rush, bellowing "main burst", and sure enough it was, in three places . . . [It] flooded the garage and cascaded out of the drive,' Myrtle wrote. 'Telephoned the plumber who crawled out of bed to come, nothing to be done at that hour but turn the water off at the main and draw the furnaces. What fun we have!'

The next day, there were 'plumbers all over the house, no hot baths, no central heating, cold is intense, but thawing. Managed to get the holes cut out and replaced.'

There was worse to come: for forty-eight hours starting on 26 January, Britain was in the grip of a devastating snow storm that created drifts as much as two feet deep in the north. In the south, it fell largely as super-cooled rain that froze as soon as it touched the ground. Roads and pavements turned into skating rinks, making sloped surfaces impossible to climb. Telegraph poles and wires snapped under the weight of the ice.

By the following day, a Saturday, the snow was six inches deep in London. 'Traffic held up all over the country, no coal deliveries, just enough to see us through until Monday,' wrote Myrtle.

There was little respite from the frozen conditions:

Tuesday, 30 January: 'Slight thaw and then hard freeze, no vehicles can get up steep hill. It's a lovely sight, but we are sick of it.'

Wednesday, 31 January: 'Fog, so cancelled the James's dinner party. The way we break treaties is worthy of Hitler. Snow drifts to knees.'

Thursday, 1 February: 'Have been down garden at danger to life and limb. Digger dug up a rat and made his first kill. Lionel said it was a good scrap, he's come in very cock-a-hoop.'

Friday, 2 February: 'Snowbound, cancelled Mrs Plummer's lunch. People were creeping along pavements holding to railings. I ventured out and nearly landed on my hands and knees.'

Saturday, 3 February: 'The snow is thawing and freezing to such an extent that it is impossible to walk on pavements. Another burst drain and a waste pipe inside which necessitates everyone using the cloakroom lav using an open umbrella, because the ceiling is streaming. The sum total to date is three burst radiators, main burst twice in three places, burst waste. Lionel shovelled the ice off a frozen gutter and precipitated a hundredweight of ice through a large window, so until a man can repair it, it is covered with brown paper.'

Sunday, 4 February: 'We decided to go out today, [even] if we had to crawl, and nearly had to. There was a thaw and a freeze, we clung to railings and slithered down the 400 foot to the railway, Lionel finishing in a sprint, calling to the porters to hold the train – which they obligingly did – for one padding along in the rear . . . I never want to see snow again.'

The next day, the weather was warmer and the snow melted, leaving the roads inches deep in water. Myrtle went out to pack up papers and books for Australian troops. The ground had thawed sufficiently for her to work in the garden. She took the opportunity to clear up the garden and start a bonfire, but because of the blackout she had to extinguish it by dusk.

The frost was getting worse; by Saturday it was three inches deep and Myrtle, pressing on with her gardening, struggled to get her fork into the hardened ground. 'This winter has been the worst I ever remember,' she wrote the next day. 'Life is strange. Hardships on top of war conditions.'

Monday brought yet more snow and impassable roads. 'Never again will I admire a snowy landscape, trains held up, traffic and standstill, no coke nor coal,' wrote Myrtle.

Amid the freeze, there was news from afar of a dramatic post-script to the sinking the previous December of the *Admiral Graf Spee* in the South Atlantic. The *Altmark*, a newly built German tanker and supply vessel, had been assigned to support her, and when the *Graf Spee* went down, the *Altmark* took on board seamen who had been rescued from her – among them 300 captured British merchant navy officers and seamen. The *Altmark* then attempted to take its human cargo back to Germany, steaming around the north of Scotland and through the territorial waters of neutral Norway. On 14 February, as it was heading south, it was discovered by three British Lockheed Hudson Mk II aircraft from RAF Thornaby in North Yorkshire and pursued by several British destroyers led by HMS *Cossack*. The following evening, when the *Altmark* was in the fjord of Josing, in western Norway, the *Cossack* caught up with her. According to a breathless account in the *Sunday Express*, thirty British seamen 'threw up grappling irons from the *Cossack*, climbed them, and, armed with cutlasses, swept on to the Nazi crew'.[22] Leaping twelve feet in the dark across the water, a British officer grasped the ship's rail, hauled himself abroad and then, revolver in hand, stormed his way onto the bridge and reversed the engines so the German vessel ran aground on the rocks. The German sailors fled across the ice to land from where they turned and opened fire on the ship. The other British seamen, meanwhile, set about rescuing their comrades, who were locked in shell rooms, storerooms and an empty oil tank, battened down beneath hatches strengthened by cables and chains. The British prisoners emerged with lurid tales of the brutality of their captors. 'It was a filthy place with no fresh air. Conditions were terrible, and the Germans made them as miserable as they possibly could with their cruel, heartless treatment,' one man told the paper. Another said he had not seen daylight for three weeks.

This story of British derring-do on the high seas prompted rejoicing back home. 'I am delighted with this exploit,' wrote the King. 'I have been thinking of the Altmark for the last 2 days, & thanks God we have rescued these men from a "living hell".'[23] Like other Britons, the Logues heard the news on 17 February. Bored with the weather, they had put on snow shoes and ventured out to the cinema and, on their return, had seen the newspapers hoardings were carrying reports of the attack, which they stood in the street and read. Myrtle proclaimed herself to be 'overjoyed', writing in her diary: 'Our spirits seem lighter, what a story, it must be a century since our sailors boarded a ship in real earnest and took what they wanted . . . Rejoicing.'

A few days later, to help boost their depleted coke and coal supplies, Myrtle and Davey, their gardener, sawed down one of the trees in the garden at Beechgrove, but 'the wretched thing jumped off the stump and wedged itself upright in the soil, entwined in the branches of another tree. I left Davey sawing it about four foot up, hoping it would drop clear of the top branches.' The next day, a bailiff arrived unexpectedly and informed Myrtle that the penalty for chopping down a tree without permission was £50 – a considerable amount, equivalent to £3,000 today. 'I felt guilty,' she wrote, 'but reasoned that the only thing they could do would be to send one to jail. However we'll wait and see.'

Adding to the misery of the cold was food rationing, which the government finally introduced on 8 January after several months of discussion. Each adult was permitted just four ounces of butter a week, twelve ounces of sugar and four ounces of bacon or ham (uncooked) and three ounces (cooked). Extra sugar rations were allowed for making jam and marmalade. On 11 March meat was also 'put on the ration', with just over one pound per person per week. That July, so, too, were tea, margarine, cooking fats and cheese; jam, marmalade, treacle and syrup followed in March 1941.

The Logues coped surprisingly well; not only did they turn over much of Beechgrove's garden to growing vegetables, but Valentine obliged by continuing to contribute the occasional rabbit shot during his trips to Epping Forest. 'We are living well within our ration,' wrote Myrtle. 'Four ounces of butter each per week. It's marvellous how we can do without.' Food prices were rising, though, and maintaining such a large house was proving increasingly tough. For that reason, they went ahead that March in letting out the basement to another couple and moving upstairs themselves. 'We are now much more compact,' wrote Myrtle, while bemoaning the fact that making the required changes to the house necessitated an army of electricians and other workmen that made them feel for a few days 'that we are living in the middle of Piccadilly Circus'. The tenants settled in well, although Myrtle was livid the next month when she discovered that their only child, George, had dismantled the rockery and pitched it, stone by stone, into the pond. 'He is so truthful, one is so amazed that rage evaporates before "yes, madam, I done it weeks ago", she wrote in her diary. 'So after a homily on giving way to destructive feelings, holding up Hitler as an awful example, I leave him.'

With the ordeal of his first wartime Christmas message out of the way, the King had been able to relax with his family at Sandringham for a few more days. He and the Queen now had to decide what to do with the princesses; they were reluctant to send them hundreds of miles back to Scotland and decided they would go instead to Windsor and stay at Royal Lodge, a house in Windsor Great Park, three miles south of the Castle, that he had been granted by his father as a country retreat in 1931. 'Birkhall is too far off, & at their age, their education is too important to be neglected,' he wrote in his diary.[24]

No sooner were the holidays over than the King became embroiled in the growing crisis surrounding Leslie Hore-Belisha, the colourful Secretary of State for War, whose relations with the military, and Lord Gort in particular, had become increasingly fraught. The two men's mutual animosity plunged new depths over the so-called Pillbox Affair that erupted when Hore-Belisha complained after a visit to the British Expeditionary Force in November 1939 that Gort was not doing enough to build defences to protect his troops. The King learnt first hand about the ill feeling of the top brass towards his minister when he went to France the following month. He also appears to have helped to fuel the animosity – inspired, in part, by his continued resentment of the support that Hore-Belisha had given his elder brother during and after the abdication crisis, even going to Paris to meet the Duke in September 1937. The King duly passed on his concerns to Chamberlain, who then went to France a few days later. Ultimately, thanks to the King's intervention, the generals managed to get their way: on 5 January, Hore-Belisha was forced to resign and left the cabinet, refusing an offer from Chamberlain to stay on in the less prestigious job of President of the Board of Trade. His sacking provoked a media storm, described variously by the newspapers as a result either of society intrigue, 'hostility of the brass hats' or opposition to the ousted minister's attempts to 'democratise' the army.

In a letter to the King three days later Chamberlain said he had told Hore-Belisha, who was Jewish, there 'existed a strong prejudice against him for which I could not hold him altogether blameless', adding: 'In these circumstances I felt the change had better come when things were quiet than be forced later when perhaps some crisis might have arisen.'[25] Ambitious and often tactless, Hore-Belisha had made a lot of enemies, but there was also more than a whiff of anti-Semitism about the affair; Henry Pownall, the chief of staff to the British Expeditionary Force, wrote of the relationship between Gort and Hore-Belisha: 'The ultimate fact is that they could never get on – you couldn't expect two such utterly different people to do so – a great gentleman and an obscure, shallow-brained, charlatan, political Jewboy.' Hore-Belisha himself claimed later that senior army officers resented his appointment because he was 'a Jew and an ordinary person not of their caste'.[26]

Sir Henry 'Chips' Channon, the diarist, believed the King had played a crucial role in turning Chamberlain against his minister – and thought Hore-Belisha knew it. 'London is agog with Belisha tales ... as it has now leaked out that the King himself insisted on Leslie's resignation,' he wrote in his diary on 8 January. 'Ever since the Abdication, the Court Minions have been intriguing his downfall ... all this will do the Monarchy harm, as they should not intrigue or dabble in politics.'[27] For that reason, the King was understandably expecting an awkward encounter when Hore-Belisha came to Buckingham Palace the next day to surrender his seals of office. In the event, the ousted minister behaved graciously, prompting the relieved King to write in his diary: 'I saw Hore-Belisha on my arrival at B.P. Luckily he was pleasant, and there was no need for me to open up the question of his resignation.' In his resignation speech the following week, however, Hore-Belisha made 'two clever digs', which, according to Channon, 'could be taken by the uninitiated to be slurs on the PM, but which now seem certainly to have been sad, sly allusions to the Sovereign'.[28]

The affair cast further gloom over the public mood. By March 1940, Britain had been at war for six months. Contrary to all expectations, the country, on the home front at least, was enjoying a period of relative calm. The air raids that had been expected by everyone – the government included – had not taken place. While there was military action at sea and in the air, the conflict in Western Europe had hitherto been one of words and propaganda from Germany, which was waging a war of nerves against the neutral countries to pressure them into providing it with food, oil and other raw materials. A general feeling of frustration found expression in growing popular discontent with the government. Though still loyal to Chamberlain, the King shared some of this frustration: 'I am very worried over the general situation, as everything we do or try to do appears to be wrong,' he wrote in his diary.[29]

The King, meanwhile, continued his efforts to rally morale at home, taking to the royal train to travel around the country. During his visit to a munitions factory 'somewhere in the Midlands', one of the female workers who was sorting out live bullets from duds turned to him and said: 'If I had my way, each of these would have Hitler's name on it.' Standing next to her, the King tried his hand at sorting, only to give up and declare with a laugh: 'I'm no good at it.'[30] On another occasion, dressed in his admiral's uniform, he spent several hours inspecting the naval forces; while there he acted, for a while, as ticket collector for troops from the British Expeditionary Force who were boarding trains for a spell of leave – much to the amazement of one sergeant who, on recognizing him, 'gave a gasp of surprise, straightened to attention and saluted'.[31]

One crucial issue in these months was the attitude of Washington, a subject in which the King had a personal stake. The birth of what in the decades since has become known as the 'special relationship' can be traced back to the few days he and Queen spent in the United

States in June 1939 during their tour of North America, in what was the first visit by a reigning British monarch to the former rebellious colony. For the King, the highpoint had been their twenty-four hours at Hyde Park, Franklin D. Roosevelt's country house on the bank of the Hudson River in Dutchess County, New York, where he and the President discussed the worsening international situation over beer and hotdogs. The King left, convinced that Britain could count on Washington's support in the event of war, telling an American reporter in an unguarded moment later in the trip: 'It's in the bag.'[32]

Events showed how wrong the King had been. Despite strong sympathy for the British and French cause, a poll in September 1939 showed at least ninety-five per cent of Americans strongly opposed to becoming 'involved in Europe's wars'. Roosevelt, though keen to do what he could for Britain, had his hands tied by his attempt to win re-election in November 1940, given that he was already under fire for pursuing policies that critics claimed had brought America too close to military intervention.

The King was nevertheless keen to build on the rapport he had established with the President. In the first instance this meant working on Joseph Kennedy, the US ambassador to London, who had been a strong supporter of appeasement. During a lengthy meeting with the King a few days after the outbreak of war, Kennedy expressed his incredulity that Britain should be involved in a conflict that could potentially ruin her for the sake of the Poles. The King was alarmed at what he had heard and was concerned the ambassador's views were colouring the reports he sent back to Washington. In a frank letter to Kennedy the following day, the King described America, France and the British Empire as the 'three really free peoples in the World' and noted that two of the three were now fighting against 'all that we three countries hate & detest' in the form of Hitler and his Nazi regime. He concluded: 'We stand on the threshold of we know not what. Misery & suffering of War we know. But what of the future? The British Empire's mind is made up. I leave it at that.'[33]

Yet Kennedy continued to send his gloomy reports back to Washington. In January 1940 he informed Lord Halifax, the Foreign Secretary, that Sumner Welles, the Under-Secretary of State, would shortly be coming on a visit to Italy, Germany, France and Britain to 'place the President in a position to judge whether there was or was not the possibility of finding the way of settlement'. By 'settlement' he meant a negotiated peace with Germany. The King's meeting with Welles left him depressed. 'The fact is the US is not coming to help us, & nothing yet will make them,' he wrote, though he added: 'But they are pro-British in the main.'[34]

There was grim news, too, from northern Europe where Finland was heading towards defeat in its Winter War against the Soviet Union. The origins of the conflict lay in the Molotov–Ribbentrop Pact. Although ostensibly a non-aggression pact between Germany and the Soviet Union, the treaty had a secret protocol that divided the countries of Eastern Europe into spheres of interest. Finland, along with parts of Poland and the Baltic States fell into the Soviet sphere. Stalin had begun with Poland, sending his forces into the east of the country on 17 September – sixteen days after Hitler had invaded from the west. The Soviet leader then forced Estonia, Latvia and Lithuania to accept treaties that allowed the Russians to establish military bases and station troops on their soil. The following month, he made a number of territorial demands on Finland, including the shifting of its border with the Soviet Union on the Karelian Isthmus westwards, in return for other territory elsewhere. The Finns refused, however, and on 30 November, after a fake border incident staged by the NKVD, the forerunner of the KGB, Soviet forces invaded with twenty-one divisions, totalling 450,000 men, and bombed Helsinki. It was an unequal contest: the Soviets had more than three times as many soldiers as the Finns, thirty times as many aircraft, and a hundred times as many tanks, but the Red Army's officer class had been crippled by Stalin's purge of 1936–38 and the Finns fought hard. Battle raged in freezing temperatures that hit a record low of minus 43° C at one spot in Karelia on 16 January. Often travelling on cross-country skis and dressed in snow camouflage, the Finnish soldiers used guerrilla tactics to great effect against their conventionally equipped Soviet foes.

The David versus Goliath struggle caught the imagination of many in Britain – among them Myrtle. 'Russia is unleashing something. One wonders what this convulsion of civilisation is opening up,' she wrote on the day of the Soviet attack. On 4 December, she added: 'How valiant the Finns are to stand up to Russia, do hope this small nation withstands annihilation.' And then four days later: 'Sure the Finns rejoiced over yesterday. They're doing a lot of damage to the Bolshies. Do hope they can hold out.' On 13 January came news of a great Finnish victory that saw the destruction of the Russian 44th division. 'I always thought I was soft-hearted,' wrote Myrtle, 'but I openly rejoiced at this news.'

Thanks to their overwhelming numbers, however, the Russians began to prevail, prompting growing demands in Britain and France to intervene militarily to help the Finns. But the Swedes and Norwegians were unwilling to give either Germans or the Soviets a pretext to attack them and refused to grant the Allies transit rights, leaving the Finns with little alternative but to sue for peace. On 12 March a formal peace treaty was signed, obliging Helsinki to cede even more territory than it had stood to lose under the terms of the original Soviet proposal.

Adding to the King's problems was his increasingly prickly relationship with the former Edward VIII, now Duke of Windsor. Bertie, as the King was called by his family, had grown up in awe of his elder brother, known as David. Given the amount of time they spent together – and the distant attitude of their parents – it was natural that the two boys should become close. Yet it was an unequal relationship: as the oldest child, David looked after Bertie and their younger siblings, Mary, Henry, George and John, but also told them what to do. 'I could always manage Bertie,' he wrote in his autobiography. His attitude increasingly jarred – as Henry Hansell, their tutor, noticed to his concern. 'It is extraordinary how the presence of one acts as a sort of "red rag" to the other,' he reported.[35]

This was more than usual sibling rivalry. David was not just older than Bertie, he was good-looking, charming and fun. Both boys were also aware from an early age that he was destined one day to become King. Bertie had been less blessed by fate. No great intellectual, he had come sixty-eighth out of sixty-eight in his final examinations at the Royal Naval College. Growing up, he began to suffer from poor digestion and had to wear splints on his legs to cure him of knock knees. He was also left-handed but, in accordance with the practice of the time, was made to use his right hand. Adding to Bertie's problems – and to some extent a result of them – was the emergence of his stammer, which was worsened by the attitude of his father, whose response when his son was struggling for words was a simple: 'get it out'. The letter 'K' – as in King – was to prove a particular challenge, something of a problem for someone born into the royal family.

As an adult, although undoubtedly a hard worker with a strong sense of duty, the future George VI was far from glittering company. Nancy Mitford called him 'a very dull man', while the art historian Kenneth Clark's first impression of the King and Queen was damning: 'She is not much better than the kind of person one meets at country houses, and the King somewhat worse.'[36] Edward

VIII was also a hard act to follow. 'It will be years for Albert the Good to build up a legend comparable to that of his brother,' Harold Nicolson, the writer and MP, predicted to his wife and fellow writer, Vita Sackville-West, on the day of the abdication in December 1936.[37]

Edward VIII's decision to renounce the throne inevitably transformed the relations between the two men. It was not that his younger brother had wanted to become King. Far from it. As Queen Mary later revealed to Nicolson: 'He was devoted to his brother and the whole Abdication crisis made him miserable. He sobbed on my shoulder for a whole hour – there, upon that sofa', when he knew he had to take his brother's place.[38] His wife was equally appalled at the prospect of her husband ascending to the throne, not just because of the strain she feared it would put on him, but also because of the impact on her. When the then Elizabeth Bowes-Lyon finally agreed to marry the Duke of York in 1923, almost three years after they first met, she had done so in the expectation of a quiet life. Part of her husband's reluctance to become King was due to his horror of public speaking and the realization that, as monarch, it would become a vital part of his role. Logue was aware of this – and had experienced first hand the King's nervousness in the run-up to his coronation and to the radio broadcast he had to give to the Empire the same evening.

The King's dismay at the way his elder brother had forced him into the limelight went a long way to explaining their future animosity. The Queen also disapproved deeply of Wallis Simpson, who was often disparagingly referred to in the royal family as 'Mrs S' or simply 'that woman'. Such feelings were accentuated by concern at the damage that the abdication had done to the monarchy.

Nor did the former King make matters any easier for himself with his sense of grievance at his family's failure to satisfy his increasingly outrageous financial demands and his anger at what he saw as the humiliating treatment meted out to his beloved wife. Although she had been elevated to Duchess, the highest rank in the British nobility, the King deemed that she could not be styled 'Her Royal Highness' or received at court. Other aspects of the Duke's behaviour had not endeared him to his younger brother, not least the visit he paid to Nazi Germany in October 1937, where he met Hitler. The sight of the former British monarch doing a Nazi salute, albeit a half-hearted one, was chilling. It also appeared to plant the dangerous idea in the minds of the Nazi leadership that the Duke could be a potential ally – a consideration that was to colour both sides' respective attitudes to him during the conflict.

The outbreak of war, which found the Duke and Duchess at their home in Antibes, could have provided an opportunity for reconciliation and a chance to heal wounds; instead, it seemed to harden attitudes on both sides. It also presented the King – and the British government – with a ticklish problem. The Duke, who still held the titles of Field Marshal, Admiral of the Fleet and Marshal of the Royal Air Force, was keen to serve his country. But in what capacity? A few days later, he and the Duchess travelled to Britain in an attempt to resolve the issue, the first time he had set foot on British soil since December 1936 when he sailed into exile. The King offered the couple a plane; they insisted on a destroyer instead. The royal family awaited the return of the Duke – and even more so, of the Duchess – with some trepidation. 'What are we going to do about Mrs S?' the Queen asked Queen Mary.[39] 'Personally, I do not wish to receive her, tho' it must depend on circumstances; what do you feel about it, Mama?' Queen Mary's response is not known, but she is likely to have been equally hostile to the idea. For his part, the Duke was also apprehensive. 'I don't know how this will work out,' he confided to his wife as their ship entered Portsmouth

Harbour. 'War should bring families together, even a Royal Family. But I don't know.'[40]

The reality of the Duke's situation was brought home to him when they docked: no member of his family had come to meet him; they had not even sent a courtier or car to help with the luggage. On 14 September the two brothers met for the first time since the abdication. The encounter went all right, 'but it was very unbrotherly', the King told the Duke of Kent, who had always been close to their eldest brother. 'He was in a very good mood, his usual swaggering one, laying down the law about everything.'[41] The description the King gave the Prime Minister of their meeting was even more telling. 'He seems very well, & not a bit worried as to the effects he left on people's minds as to his behaviour in 1936,' he wrote to Chamberlain. 'He has forgotten all about it.' Wallis was not invited to come to the Palace, and, just in case, the Queen had made sure she was away while the Duke and Duchess were in Britain.

The King offered his elder brother a choice of two jobs: either to go to the British military mission in France or to help organize civil defence in Wales. The latter appointment appealed more to the Duke, but the King then had second thoughts and told him there was no choice: he had to go to France. A request by the Duke to set off with Wallis on a month-long tour of troops stationed in Britain was vetoed. The official reason given was that their presence would risk drawing enemy attention to strategic locations. In reality, the King was worried about the enthusiasm with which his brother might be greeted just three years after the abdication. As he remarked ruefully to Hore-Belisha: 'All my ancestors succeeded to the throne after their predecessors had died. Mine is not only alive but very much so!'[42]

Posting the Duke to France nevertheless brought with it problems: chiefly, to what extent could he be entrusted with secret information? His own loyalty was not seriously in doubt, but many

– rightly or wrongly – were not convinced that the same could be said of Wallis. The King was also reluctant to have his elder brother visit British troops in France, for the same reason he had been opposed to his proposed tour of the United Kingdom – though for months no one had the courage to tell him directly. The Duke was livid: it was 'merely fresh evidence of my brother's continued efforts to humiliate me by every means in his and his courtiers' power', he told Churchill.[43] Reports of the Duke's growing disillusionment were seized on by German spies and relayed back to Berlin. This was a problem that would not go away.

CHAPTER FOUR

The 'stab in the back'

Neville Chamberlain was in buoyant mood when he stood to address a Conservative Party gathering at Central Hall, Westminster on 4 April 1940, 'When we embarked on this war in September I felt we were bound to win, but that we might have to undergo some heavy trials and perhaps severe losses,' the Prime Minister told his audience.

That may be so still. But after seven months of war, I feel ten times as confident of victory as I did at the beginning . . .

Long before the war Germany was making preparations for it. The result was that when war did break out German preparations were far ahead of our own, and it was natural then to expect that the enemy would take advantage of his initial superiority to make an endeavour to overwhelm us and France before we had time to make good our deficiencies.

Is it not extraordinary that no such attempt was made? Whatever may be the reason – whether it was that Hitler thought he might get away with what he had got without fighting for it, or whether it was that, after all, the preparations were not sufficiently complete – however, one thing is certain: he missed the bus.

General Sir Edmund Ironside, the chief of the Imperial General Staff, struck a similarly defiant tone in a front-page interview with the *Daily Express* the next day, headlined "'Come on Hitler!" dares Ironside'. 'Time is against Germany. She cannot forever keep her armies in the battle area, poised for action, and then make no move. Her morale is certain to suffer,' the general declared. 'Frankly we would welcome an attack. We are sure of ourselves. We have no fears.'[44]

Ironside did not have to wait long to have his wish fulfilled: a new phase in the war was about to begin, with devastating consequence for Europe and for Britain. Five days later, in the early morning, German forces invaded Denmark and Norway, in Operation *Weserübung*. The assault on Denmark began just before 4 a.m by land, sea and air. Two hours later, with their country's forces completely outnumbered and faced with a German threat to bomb Copenhagen, King Christian X and the entire Danish government capitulated. The operation was over within six hours, in what was the shortest Nazi military campaign of the war. Norway's size and geography made it a much harder nut to crack, and Allied forces came to its aid. By the end of the month, however, the southern parts of Norway were in German hands and by 4 May the Allies were left with nothing more than a precarious foothold in Narvik, which, it was clear, could not be sustained for much longer.

The Nazis' successes in Scandinavia brought to a head long-running frustrations with Chamberlain, who, it was becoming increasingly clear, was no wartime leader. On 7 May, the House of Commons began a heated two-day debate on Norway in which speaker after speaker turned on him. David Lloyd George, 'the man who had won the war' of 1914–18, appealed to the hapless Prime Minister to 'give an example of sacrifice, because there is nothing that can contribute more to victory than that he should sacrifice the seals of office'. Some of the harshest criticism came from within Chamberlain's own party: Leo Amery, a former Conservative cabinet minister, famously quoted to him the words that Oliver Cromwell had used to the Long Parliament almost three centuries earlier: 'You have sat too long here for any good you have been doing. Depart, I say, and let us have done with you. In the name of God, go.'

Chamberlain initially appeared determined to tough it out. When he went to see the King that evening he said, with a smile, that he was not coming to resign. The King was keen to hold on to him, and even offered to speak to Clement Attlee, the Labour leader, to try to persuade his party to join a National Government. 'I told the P.M. that I did not like the way in which, with all the worries and responsibilities he had to bear in the conduct of the war, he was always subject to a stab in the back from both the H of C and the Press,' the King wrote.[45] Chamberlain was not averse to the idea, but suggested the King wait until the Labour Party conference due to be held that coming weekend, which would give a better sense of feelings within the party.

Despite the political forces ranged against him, Chamberlain won the vote the next day by 281 to 200, but many Conservative MPs abstained or voted against him. Even so, Chamberlain still held out hopes of remaining at Number 10, provided he could do so at the head of a coalition – which meant persuading Labour to serve under him. He was to be disappointed: the party made clear that while it was prepared to join a Conservative-led administration, it would have nothing to do with one headed by Chamberlain. Matters came to head on 10 May when Hitler's troops poured into Holland, Belgium, Luxembourg and France, beginning a dramatic new phase of the war. That afternoon, Chamberlain went to the Palace.

The King accepted Chamberlain's resignation, telling him how 'grossly unfairly' he thought he had been treated and how 'terribly sorry' he was that the crisis had erupted. When it came to a choice of successor, the King made clear his preference for Lord Halifax. One of the era's most senior Conservative politicians, Halifax had endeared himself to the King as one of the main architects of appeasement since replacing Anthony Eden as Foreign Secretary in March 1938. He was also a personal friend: his family had long served the crown, and the King and Queen would often dine with the Halifaxes at their home in Eaton Square. The King even gave him a key to the gardens of Buckingham Palace, which we would walk through on his way to work.

But Chamberlain made clear it would be impossible to have a peer at the head of the government and urged him to send instead for Winston Churchill, who, after a decade in the political wilderness, had been brought back into government on the outbreak of war as First Lord of the Admiralty. It was a controversial choice: Churchill, who had changed parties twice in his career – moving from the Conservatives to the Liberals in 1904 and then back again twenty years later – continued to arouse widespread suspicion because of his bloody-mindedness. Thanks to his role at the Admiralty, he bore a major part of the responsibility for the Norwegian debacle – even though, to his own surprise as much as that of others, he managed to escape the blame, which was taken by Chamberlain. The King appears to have shared the widespread view of Churchill as a political adventurer, and during a press campaign the previous summer to have him readmitted to the cabinet, he had left Chamberlain in no doubt as to his opposition to the idea. Nor had he forgotten Churchill's championship of Edward VIII during the abdication crisis.

The King had little alternative, however, but to follow Chamberlain's advice – and summon Churchill to the palace.

'I suppose you don't know why I have sent for you,' he told his guest after looking at him searchingly and quizzically for a few moments.

'Sir, I simply couldn't imagine why,' Churchill quipped back, playing along with the joke.

'I want you to form a Government.'[46]

The King went away from the meeting convinced that Churchill was 'so full of fire & determination to carry out the duties of prime minister'. Yet he still had his doubts: 'I cannot yet think of Winston as PM,' he wrote in his diary the next day, 11 May. 'I met Halifax in the garden and told him I was sorry not to have him as PM.'[47]

Despite such initial misgivings, the King's relationship with Churchill was to become a powerful and enduring one. By that September the traditional formal weekly audience granted by the monarch to his Prime Minister had been replaced by an informal Tuesday lunch at which the two men would discuss the progress of the war, serving themselves from a side table; the Queen often joined them for conversations that ranged more widely than merely the conduct of the war. The following January, Churchill wrote to the King to say he had been 'greatly cheered by our weekly luncheons in poor old bomb-battered Buckingham Palace, & to feel that in Yr. Majesty and the Queen there flames the spirit that will never be daunted'.[48] The Queen declared many years later that she felt very much a part of a team with the King, who 'got on terribly well, like a house on fire', with Churchill.

Nevertheless the new Prime Minister's behaviour with the King was very differently from his predecessor's: while Chamberlain was always generous with his time, Churchill often arrived late, staying for only a few minutes and sharing little information. As Lady Hyde, one of the Queen's ladies-in-waiting, told John Colville, Churchill's private secretary:

Although the King and Queen appreciate Winston's qualities and see that he is the man for the occasion, they are a little miffed by the off-hand way in which he treats them. They much preferred Chamberlain's habit of going to the Palace regularly, once a week, and explaining the situation in a careful and unhurried way. Winston says he will come at 6.00 p.m, puts this off by telephone to 6.30 and is inclined to turn up for ten hectic minutes at 7.00.[49]

In hindsight, the King's complaints seem unreasonable given the large number of competing claims on Churchill's time when Britain's very existence as an independent country hung in the balance. Yet, despite this difficult start, the King gradually transferred the enormous loyalty he had previously felt towards Chamberlain to his successor. By the New Year, he wrote in his diary: 'I could not have a better Prime Minister.' For his part, Churchill 'valued as a signal honour the gracious intimacy' with which he was treated. Although, in some ways, a rival to the King as father of a nation, he was also aware of the importance of monarchy in binding together not just the United Kingdom but also the Empire and so went out of his way to praise the King. 'Winston, however cavalierly he may treat his sovereign, is at heart a most vehement royalist,' noted Colville.[50]

Churchill quickly got down to work, inviting Attlee and the Liberal leader, Sir Archibald Sinclair, to join his government; Chamberlain remained in the war cabinet, leading the House of Commons as Lord President of the Council; Halifax stayed on as Foreign Secretary. Churchill's first speech to the Commons as Prime Minister on 13 May set the tone of his premiership – which was a complete contrast to Chamberlain's: 'I would say to the House, as I said to those who have joined this government: "I have nothing to offer but blood, toil, tears and sweat". Britain's policy, he declared, was 'to wage war by sea, land and air, with all our might and with all the strength that God can give us: to wage war against a monstrous tyranny, never surpassed in the dark, lamentable catalogue of human crime'. Such dramatic resolve quickly turned Churchill into a source of comfort and inspiration, his refusal to contemplate anything short of outright victory giving his nation the lead it needed. Quentin Reynolds, an American journalist, described how drinkers in a Fleet Street pub fell silent when his voice came on the radio. 'All eyes were glued on the loudspeaker, almost as if the listeners believed that by concentrating they could see Churchill's face,' he wrote.[51]

The German forces, meanwhile, were making short work of the Dutch, who had insufficient weapons and equipment, much of it dating from the First World War. Dutch hopes that the British and French would come to their aid were rapidly fading. At 5 a.m. on the day of Churchill's speech, the King had been woken by a police sergeant who told him he had a telephone call from Queen Wilhelmina. At first he thought it was a hoax, but took the call anyway. To his surprise, it was indeed the Dutch monarch.

'She begged me to send aircraft for the defence of Holland,' the King wrote in his diary. 'I passed this message on to everyone concerned, & went back to bed. It is not often one is rung up at that hour, and especially by a Queen. But in these days anything may happen, & far worse things too.' Even if Britain could have sent the planes, time was running out to save the country. Later that day, Wilhelmina telephoned the King again, this time from Harwich. A special train was waiting to take her to London. She and the King had never met before, but George VI went to Liverpool Street Station to receive his fellow monarch. 'She was naturally very upset, & had brought no clothes with her,' he wrote. Given the Queen's ample frame, finding her suitable replacements proved a challenge.

Wilhelmina's initial intention had been to go back and join Dutch forces in Zeeland, in the south-west of the country, which were still resisting, but the military situation had deteriorated so sharply that everyone thought a return was impossible. The next day, the Nazis bombarded Rotterdam from the air; when they threatened to do the same to Utrecht, the Dutch surrendered. Wilhelmina remained in Buckingham Palace, where she attempted to rally resistance at a distance. Britons were horrified by the speed of the German victory. 'Holland lays down her arms. The Dutch who were such great fighters have capitulated after five days of war. It's terrifying,' wrote Myrtle in her diary

The same day, the German army advanced through the Ardennes and crossed the River Meuse – a feat the French had thought impossible. Paul Reynaud, the French prime minister, telephoned Churchill to tell him his country was defeated. The next day, Churchill flew to Paris to assess the situation for himself.

'*Où est la masse de manoeuvre?*' (Where is the strategic reserve?) he asked Gamelin, the French Commander-in-Chief.

'*Aucune*' (None), replied Gamelin.

German forces, meanwhile, broke through the Maginot Line, the supposedly impregnable fortifications along France's eastern border. The British Expeditionary Force was in danger of being cut off from the sea by the advancing German forces. By 20 May, the first German units reached Abbeville on the English Channel, overran the 25th Infantry Brigade of the 50th (Northumbrian) Infantry Division and captured the town.

It was against the backdrop of this rapidly deteriorating military situation that the King was scheduled to make a broadcast to mark Empire Day on 24 May, his first such speech since the previous Christmas. Three days earlier at 11 a.m. Logue had received a call from Hardinge asking him to go and see the King that afternoon at 4 p.m. to help him prepare. Logue arrived fifteen minutes early and was welcomed by Hardinge, who was fretting over the bad news from Abbeville.

Logue nevertheless found the King in a strangely cheerful mood when he was called up to see him. Standing on the balcony, and dressed in his military uniform, he was whistling to a young corgi sitting under a plane tree in the garden of Buckingham Palace, which could not work out where the sound was coming from. The hair on the side of the King's temples was a little greyer than Logue remembered it. The strain of war was taking its toll. As Logue approached, the King turned and gave him his usual grin.

They went into the King's study. With all the pictures and other valuables put away in storage for the war, it was bare, the only decoration a vase of flowers. Logue was impressed by the text of the speech he was to deliver, but they nevertheless went through it together to see if they could make improvements. While they were doing so, there was a light tap at the door. It was the Queen, dressed in powder grey, with a large diamond butterfly brooch on her left shoulder. As the King noted the changes they had agreed, he talked to Logue about the wonderful effort he thought the RAF was making – and 'how proud one should be of the boys from Australia, Canada and New Zealand'.

Soon afterwards, Logue went to leave. 'It was a wonderful memory as I said goodbye and bowed over the King's and Queen's hands, the two of them framed in the large window with the sunshine behind them, the King in field marshal uniform and the Queen in grey,' he wrote in his diary.

On Empire Day itself, Logue went to the Palace after dinner. Ogilvie, the BBC Director General, was there, as was Wood, the sound engineer, who had become close to the King in the three years he had been working with him. As well as dealing with the technical arrangements, he would, like Logue, also often chip in with suggestions to modify the text of the speeches to make them easier by removing words that the King might stumble over.* Wood and Logue generally worked well with each other, but they had their disagreements, in particular over Logue's insistence that the King should make his broadcasts standing up at a high desk because, with his belief in the importance of deep breathing, he thought this made it easier for the King to speak more clearly. Wood disagreed and thought it made him more uncomfortable. Over time Wood prevailed and was able to persuade the King to sit down at a desk like any other broadcaster. 'It was very difficult for me,' he recalled. 'I had to be very tactful because I was not a famous Harley Street specialist; I was only a specialist in microphones, and it took time to overcome this and win his trust. But we did it.'[52] On this occasion, Wood, as ever, had done a good job and made sure the room had been properly prepared for the broadcast. He had also run a cable down into the dugout in case the King was forced by an air raid to speak from there. 'It didn't matter what happened,' wrote Logue. 'The broadcast would go on.'

Logue accompanied the King into the broadcasting room which,

---

* As Wood describes in his memoirs, the King often took some convincing. The words 'oppression' and 'suppression' were a particular challenge, but when Wood tried to remove them from a speech on one occasion, the King insisted he could say them perfectly well – which may have been true if he had plenty of time, but not if they came up in the middle of a sentence. Wood did not try to argue but changed the conversation to another matter and then out of the blue challenged the King to say them. 'Caught unawares, he would try, trip up on those infernal Ss and then give up with good humour,' Wood noted. (Robert Wood, *A World in Your Ear*, London: Macmillan, 1979, p.103)

to their relief, was pleasantly cool: the windows had been left open
to prevent a repetition of the previous day's disaster when the
unfortunate Queen Wilhelmina had made a lunchtime broadcast
to the Dutch colonies in the Caribbean and the room was so hot
and stuffy it felt as if it were on fire. Logue proposed only minor
changes to the text: rather than beginning 'It is a year ago today', he
suggested to the King that it would be better to start: 'On Empire
Day a year ago.' They had a last run-through and, with just eight
minutes to go, the King walked off into his room to focus on the
more difficult passages.

There was a sense of anticipation across Britain. Cinemas ended
their programmes early and, as nine o'clock approached, crowds
of people began to gather outside radio shops and a hush fell over
clubs and hotel lounges. Millions more were sitting in front of their
radios at home. Empire Day had assumed additional importance
during wartime because of the massive contribution being made
by the nations of the Empire. The King's broadcast was to be aired
at the end of a programme entitled *Brothers in Arms*. Featuring
men and women born and brought up overseas, it was intended
to 'demonstrate in no uncertain fashion the unity and strength of
which Empire Day is the symbol'. At twelve and a half minutes, the
speech would be the longest he had made – and a major test of all
the time he had spent working with Logue.

A minute before he was due to begin, the King walked across
the passage into the broadcasting room and stared out of the open
window towards the failing light. It was a beautiful spring evening
and perfectly peaceful. 'It was hard to believe that within a hundred
miles of us, men were killing each other,' thought Logue.

The red studio light flashed four times and went dark – the
signal to begin. The King took two steps to the table, and Logue
squeezed his arm for luck. The gesture underlined the closeness of

78

the relationship between the two men; no one was meant to touch a King unbidden in that way.

'On Empire Day last year I spoke to you, the peoples of the Empire, from Winnipeg, in the heart of Canada,' the King began, adopting the first of Logue's changes. 'We were at peace. On that Empire Day I spoke of the ideals of freedom, justice, and peace upon which our Commonwealth of Free Peoples is founded. The clouds were gathering, but I held fast to the hope that those ideals might yet achieve a fuller and richer development without suffering the grievous onslaught of war. But it was not to be. The evil which we strove unceasingly and with all honesty of purpose to avert fell upon us.'

The King continued, smiling to himself like a schoolboy – or so it seemed to Logue – whenever he managed a hitherto impossible word without difficulty. The 'decisive struggle' was now upon the people of Britain, the King continued, building up the tension. 'Let no one be mistaken: it is no mere territorial conquest that our enemies are seeking; it is the overthrow, complete and final, of this Empire and of everything for which it stands and, after that, the conquest of the world. And if their will prevails they will bring to its accomplishment all the hatred and cruelty which they have already displayed.'

The King paused after he had finished speaking. At Logue's suggestion, they were trying a new way of working. Previously the red light – or the 'red eye of the little yellow god' as Logue used to call it – stayed on throughout the broadcast. But it was always a distraction, and so this time they were trying without it, although this had the disadvantage of making it difficult for them to know for sure when they were actually off the air. The two men continued to look at each other for a few moments in silence before either dared to speak.

A few minutes later, Ogilvie came in. 'Congratulations, your Majesty, a wonderful effort,' he said. He was followed by the Queen, who kissed her husband and also told him how well he had spoken. They all stayed there talking for another five minutes.

'And then,' as Logue put it, 'the King of England says "I want my dinner" – and they all said good night and went down the stairs into another world.'

The King was proud of his effort. He was also relieved that, despite the rapidly changing military situation, he had not been obliged to make any major last-minute changes to the text. 'I was fearful that something might happen to make me have to alter it,' he wrote in his diary that evening.[53] 'I was very pleased with the way I delivered it, & it was easily my best effort. How I hate broadcasting.'

The newspapers the next morning were effusive in their praise of the King's performance. The *Daily Telegraph* called it 'a vigorous and inspiring broadcast', adding: 'Reports last night indicated that every word was heard with perfect clarity throughout the United States and in distant parts of the Empire.' The next day, the *Sunday Express* went further. 'The King has finally cured his speech defect,' it proclaimed, in a triumph of wishful thinking over reality that may have been inspired by Logue's old friend, John Gordon, who had moved from the *Daily Express* to become editor of its Sunday sister title in 1928. 'The hesitation which marred many of his earlier speeches has gone. Experts who listened to the King's war broadcast on Friday night declared yesterday that his delivery was so smooth that there was no reason why the old trouble should ever recur.' One such expert, whom the newspaper did not name, declared that 'even the most difficult consonants and words which formerly would have caused hesitation were delivered without the trace of a stumble'.[54]

Logue's telephone, meanwhile, had been ringing constantly. 'Everyone is thrilled over the King's speech,' he wrote in his diary.

'Eric Miéville [the King's assistant private secretary] rang me from Buckingham Palace and told me that the reception all over the world had been tremendous. Whilst we were speaking the King rang for him, so I sent my congratulations through again.'

Others were more sceptical: according to the government's Home Intelligence Reports on morale and public opinion, the speech had 'a steadying but not a deep effect. It was generally liked but most frequent comments were on the improvement in H.M.'s delivery and on the slightly impersonal note of the broadcast.'[55] The Conservative MP, Cuthbert Headlam, wrote in his diary after listening to the broadcast: 'Poor little man – one is very sorry for him.'[56]

Lionel and Myrtle celebrated the King's success by going the next day to see a matinee of *My Little Chickadee*, a comedy-western set in the 1880s, starring Mae West and W.C. Fields. Afterwards, Valentine took his parents to their favourite Hungarian restaurant. It was their first visit since the beginning of the war, and the band played all Myrtle's favourite tunes.

CHAPTER FIVE

Dunkirk

In his headquarters deep below Dover Castle, set in a maze of musty chalk tunnels that had been carved out of the cliffs at the time of the Napoleonic Wars, Admiral Bertram Ramsay convened a meeting of officials from the Admiralty and the Ministry of Shipping. Ramsay had been brought out of retirement on the outbreak of war and appointed officer-in-charge of Dover. He was now to lead one of the greatest and most audacious maritime rescues ever attempted. The meeting was held in the operations centre, a large chamber in the complex that had housed an electric power plant during the First World War. Known as the Dynamo Room, it lent its name to the operation.

A few days earlier, on 19 May 1940, amid growing concern over the fate of the 400,000 British troops in northern France facing the advancing German troops, Ramsay had been summoned to the War Office. He was ordered to plan for a 'partial evacuation' of the British Expeditionary Force – partial, because at that stage no one in the government seemed able or willing to recognize the severity of the situation in which the force's members now found themselves. Over the days that followed, Ramsay lobbied the Admiralty, War Office,

Ministry of Shipping and the commanders of the other coastal ports for help in assembling the vast number of ships and boats he reckoned he needed for the evacuation. Conscious of the lack of piers at which large vessels could dock, Ramsay also sent out an appeal for hundreds of fishing boats, pleasure steamers and other small craft capable of plucking troops straight off the beaches.

Such an evacuation was initially anathema to Churchill, who, despite what he had seen of the parlous state of the French army, continued to hope it would launch a counter-attack against the Germans. By contrast, Gort, the commander of the British Expeditionary Force, had little confidence in the abilities of his allies and warned the war cabinet that his men might be forced to make a fighting retreat towards Dunkirk, which was the only usable harbour left. As a precaution, at cabinet on 20 May, Churchill gave orders for the Admiralty to 'assemble a large number of small vessels in readiness to proceed to ports and inlets on the French coast'.

In the days that followed, the Allied forces were embroiled in ferocious street fighting. Stukas dive-bombed while British and French warships, sailing perilously close to the coast, shelled German motorized columns as they advanced along the coastal road. Explosions rocked the air as demolition crews blew up bridges and other facilities. Palls of black smoke rose into the air. Starting on 23 May, the evacuation of Boulogne began; over the course of the next two days, some 4,300 men were rescued, though 300 were left behind. There was no attempt to save the forces in Calais, however. Amid French protests that the men of the British Expeditionary Force were doing nothing but preparing their own escape to England, the 3,000 British troops, together with 800 French, who were caught in the town were ordered to stay and fight. Out of ammunition and water, they were overrun. Then, on 24 May, came an unexpected reprieve: as two German army groups were closing in on Dunkirk for the kill,

Hitler ordered his armoured spearheads to halt for three days. With the bulk of the French army still undefeated, he wanted to preserve his forces for his drive on Paris. The Germans also did not appear to realize quite how many British forces they had trapped on the coast.

Matters were further complicated by the collapse of the Belgian army following the Dutch defeat. The same day that the King broadcast to the Empire, his Belgian counterpart, Leopold III (having assumed command of his country's army) had a last meeting with his ministers before they left for France, where they intended to continue to operate as a government in exile. They urged Leopold to leave with them. The Belgian King refused, insisting he must 'share the same fate as my troops' and on 25 May, convinced further resistance was hopeless, he instead sued for terms of capitulation. From his headquarters in Bruges, he wrote a letter to George VI explaining his action. The King was dismayed, chiefly because of the potentially disastrous implications for the British forces trapped in France. 'This came as a great shock to me as the evacuation of the B.E.F. will be almost impossible, with the Germans on three sides of us,' he wrote.[57]

The next day, a Sunday, the decision was taken to launch Operation Dynamo. That morning's newspapers, operating under wartime censorship, talked up the Allies' military successes, but it was clear the British Expeditionary Force's prospects were bleak. At the King's request, the day had been declared a day of People's Prayer and was marked by special church services across the country, including one at Westminster Abbey, which he and the Queen attended together with Queen Wilhelmina and Churchill. The King went on to visit RAF stations to decorate pilots involved in bombing Germany, but his mind was on the hundreds of thousands of their fellow servicemen still trapped in France. 'The thought of losing Gort & his band, all the flower and youth of our country, the Army's backbone in officers and men is truly tragic,' he wrote in his diary.[58] That evening, at three minutes before seven, the Admiralty signaled Ramsay: 'OPERATION DYNAMO IS TO COMMENCE.' Ramsay had already jumped the gun and dispatched the first flotilla four hours earlier. The first men arrived exhausted at Dover in the early hours of the next morning, the only equipment with them their rifles.

When he learnt that the British were escaping, Hitler realized the folly in halting his attack and ordered the destruction of the Dunkirk pocket. German artillery and bombers pounded the town, turning it into a living hell for the desperate men waiting on the beaches and in the dunes to be picked up. Yet day and night the rescue ships kept on coming, even though they, too, came under relentless fire as they neared the coast.

The continuing heroics in the Channel coincided with a ferocious political battle within the war cabinet. On one side was Churchill, determined that Britain should fight on against the Nazis, if necessary alone, and, standing against him, Halifax who thought the military situation now so desperate the government should pursue a negotiated peace with Hitler – brokered by Mussolini, who had yet to enter the war on the German side. Over the course of three days from 26 May, the war cabinet met nine times; the bitterness of the discussion exposed the strength of feeling on both sides. When Halifax demanded to know what was so wrong with 'trying out the possibilities of mediation', Churchill retorted that 'nations that went down fighting rose again, but those who surrendered tamely were finished'. Halifax was initially backed by Chamberlain and a sizeable section of the Conservative Party, but Churchill finally outmanoeuvred them on 28 May by appealing over their heads to the full twenty-five-member outer cabinet, which supported him.

The same day the Belgians surrendered. News of their

capitulation was broadcast at 8.30 the next morning by Reynaud, the French Prime Minister, who said Leopold had surrendered against the wishes of his government and of the army and made clear his fear that this meant the British Expeditionary Force was lost. Leopold was branded by the newspapers as the 'traitor King'. 'From the purely cynical point of view, breaking the news to the British public in this way is not a bad thing,' noted Harold Nicolson, who was now working at the Ministry of Information.[59] 'It will at least enable them to feel that the disaster was due to Belgian cowardice as indeed to some extent it was.' Myrtle put it simply in her diary: 'Darkest day. My cousin who understands French, heard Reynaud's communiqué and telephoned us, we are horrified. Indeed luck seems to have deserted us. It is a ghastly blow. Leopold must be unhinged.'

Yet, miraculously, the British Expeditionary Force was not lost. The Admiralty thought they would have a window of just two days before the Germans overran Dunkirk, and expected to be able to rescue 45,000 men at best. The Allied forces held on, however, and, despite the relentless German bombardment, the rescue continued throughout the week. When the King saw Anthony Eden, who had returned to the government and was now Secretary of State for War, on 29 May he told him 30,000 men had been evacuated in the previous forty-eight hours.[60] Each evening thereafter the King chronicled in his diary the number rescued: by the next day, the total had reached 80,000 and by the day after, 133,000 men from the BEF and 11,000 Frenchmen. By the ninth day, a total of 338,226 soldiers – 198,229 British and 139,997 French – had been plucked from the beachhead. Although the flotilla of yachts, motorboats and skiffs was to become the stuff of popular legend, the majority of the men were rescued by British destroyers, cross-channel ferries and Irish Sea packets.

On 4 June Churchill made one of the most memorable speeches of the war – or, indeed, of all time – in which he warned that Britain faced imminent invasion. 'Even though large tracts of Europe and many old and famous States have fallen or may fall into the grip of the Gestapo and all the odious apparatus of Nazi rule, we shall not flag or fail,' he told the House of Commons. 'We shall go on to the end . . . we shall fight on the beaches, we shall fight on the landing grounds, we shall fight in the fields and in the streets, we shall fight in the hills, we shall never surrender.' In her diary the next day, Myrtle noted more simply: 'All our men off. God be praised. Have met some of the nurses, they have a story to tell which will live for ever.'

Amid the rejoicing, the Logues had more immediate worries: that week, while all eyes in Britain were turned on Dunkirk, they learnt that Laurie, who had received his call-up papers in March, had been accepted for the Royal Corps of Signals. When Myrtle heard the news, she and Jo had 'a little weep'.

Despite the war, Lionel and Myrtle tried to continue with normal life at Beechgrove. Myrtle spent much of her time gardening and planting vegetables, even though the summer heat in the green-houses was terrific – hitting 44° C. On 8 June they went to their friends, the Moodys, to drink champagne to celebrate the 'Dunkirk miracle', but the mood turned gloomy the next day, a Sunday, when Laurie and Jo came round with baby Sandra to arrange storage of their furniture in anticipation of Laurie's departure for war and Jo's return to her home town of Nottingham. Myrtle was 'sad to see their little home disintegrated'. A few days later, Laurie sent up his first load of furniture. 'So sad; he looked drawn and very thin,' noted Myrtle. Then she went off to the Moodys' for more champagne. 'The old boy's drinking his cellar dry with our help.'

The next weekend, Laurie and Jo came to Beechwood again for

dinner; Valentine was there too. Myrtle served them a brace of guinea fowl, new potatoes and green peas; 'not bad for wartime'. She was struck by how well her daughter-in-law was holding up. 'Jo is so brave, poor darling,' she noted. Valentine, meanwhile, who had been under the weather, returned to work at hospital very much better in health.

A few days after Dunkirk came another evacuation of a very different nature, this time from Norway. When the German forces invaded, the sixty-seven-year-old King Haakon and his son, Crown Prince Olav, fled Oslo, together with their government and much of the country's gold reserves. They travelled seventy-five miles to the north, seeking refuge in the woods as German war planes tried to attack them. Vikdun Quisling, the Norwegian fascist installed by the Nazis as puppet Prime Minister, appealed to the monarch to return to the capital and recognize his government, but Haakon refused, choosing exile instead. On 7 June the King, together with other members of the Norwegian royal family and the government, were spirited away from Tromsø aboard HMS *Devonshire* to Britain. George VI and Haakon were close: Haakon had been married to George's aunt, Maud, the daughter of Edward VII, who had continued to spend considerable time in England after her husband became King in 1905, much of it at Appleton House on the Sandringham Estate. When Maud died in a London nursing home in 1938, George followed her coffin with Haakon on the first stage of its journey back to Norway.

Haakon was put up at Buckingham Palace, joining Wilhelmina of Holland, who was still staying there. Wilhelmina's daughter, Juliana, her husband, Bernhard, and their two daughters had also been accommodated at the Palace for a few weeks before going on to exile in Canada. Looking around at what he called 'this influx of foreign cousins', the King, tongue in cheek, wondered, to Wood, the BBC sound engineer, 'where *he* was going to sleep that night'.[61]

The flight of the Norwegian royals, combined with fears that Britain, too, could soon be invaded, prompted serious thought about how to ensure the safety of the Windsors. There had initially been talk of Princesses Elizabeth and Margaret being sent to Canada, following the example of the children of many upper-class British families, but the Queen was having none of it: 'The children could not go without me, I could not possibly leave the King, and the King would never go,' she declared.'[62] Instead, the two princesses were moved, first to the Royal Lodge in Windsor Great Park and then to Windsor Castle itself, although, for their safety, official pronouncements said merely that they were 'living in a house in the country'. The King and Queen also slept at the Castle, initially in a dugout constructed under the Brunswick Tower and then, from early September 1940, on the ground floor of the Victoria Tower (also known as the Queen's Tower), which was specially reinforced against bombs. They spent weekends there as well, but during the week would travel up and down to Buckingham Palace in an armour-plated car, their gas masks and steel helmets always to hand.

Although the Palace was a prime target for German attack, the security precautions were somewhat amateurish: a royal air raid shelter was created out of the housemaids' basement sitting room, which was reinforced with wooden partitions and equipped with baskets of sand and hand pumps. 'The first thing that strikes you is that the shelter is not excessively elaborate,' observed a journalist who visited later that year[63] – even though the many readers, who, unlike the Logues, did not have a basement and were instead forced to rely on more primitive arrangements in their back gardens or public shelters, may have begged to differ.

The linoleum on the floor is covered with rugs which neither fit nor match in colour, and the big old-fashioned housemaid's sink still remains with nothing to screen it. A well-scrubbed deal table pushed against one wall was formerly piled high with sheets and towels. Now it has a small mirror standing on it, with ivory brushes and a comb – in fact, it has been promoted to be the Queen's dressing-table.

The walls of the room are papered with rather a faded flowery design, and the biggest bits of furniture are two large sofas and two armchairs, which have been brought down from one of the state apartments. They are covered in rich red brocaded satin, and the sofas are so long and so wide that they make comfortable beds. Folded rugs lie across them with large pillows, and beside one of them is a small, round, gilt table. On it stands a tray with quite a small teapot and two cups of thin white and gold china, marked with the royal crown, so that just as they did when taking refuge in a public shelter last week, the King and Queen may have a 'nice cup of tea' – though in this case they can make it themselves with a small electric kettle. On another table, beside the opposite couch, are set out patience cards, bottles of mineral water and glasses, a notebook and pencils, two electric torches, and a bottle of smelling salts. There is a house – or rather a palace – telephone. Although the windows are heavily shuttered and sandbagged outside, one of them has a flight of rough wooden steps, leading to an emergency exit. Beside it stands a stirrup pump, buckets of sand and water, a couple of entrenching tools, and two hurricane lamps.

There is a full-sized radio set similar to the one the King uses in his own sitting-room, and the doors and windows have been treated so as to make the whole room gas-proof. Nearby are separate shelters for the ladies-in-waiting, equerries, and for every single person in the palace, each of whom goes to his or her appointed place when the sirens sound.

It was not until 1941 that a full-scale concrete air raid shelter was built adjoining the palace, with proper gas-proof rooms, and kitchen and bathroom facilities. Security on the ground was barely more professional. On one occasion, Haakon asked the King what precautions had been taken against a possible attack on the Palace by German parachutists. As an answer, the King pressed an alarm signal to summon a member of the Coats Mission, a special unit set up to provide round-the-clock protection for the royal family and evacuate them if necessary. No one came. An equerry was promptly dispatched to find out what had gone wrong. It turned out the duty police sergeant had assured the officer of the guard that 'no attack was impending' and its members had stood down. When the situation had been explained, a party of guardsmen came rushing into the garden and, to the astonishment of Haakon – and the amusement of the King and Queen – 'proceeded to thrash the undergrowth in the manner of beaters at a shoot rather than of men engaged in the pursuit of a dangerous enemy'.[64]

The King took great interest in the Coats Mission, which he described on one occasion as 'my private army'. But incidents such as this one made him realize he should also take measures to protect himself. Thus he had firing ranges laid down in the gardens of Buckingham Palace and Windsor Castle, where he and his equerries practised with rifles, pistols and tommy guns. If the Germans invaded and occupied Britain, the King told one guest, he would offer his services to the leader of a British resistance movement. The Queen also learnt how to fire a revolver. 'I shall not go down like the others,' she vowed to Harold Nicolson.[65]

What became known as the 'Dunkirk spirit' perfectly described the determination of the people of Britain to pull together at such times of national emergency and adversity. Yet, however great the heroism and however remarkable some of the escapes, there was no disguising the fact that Dunkirk had been no victory. On the contrary: as Churchill told his junior ministers in private, it had been 'the greatest British military defeat for many centuries'.

The bad news kept on coming: on 5 June, the day after Churchill's speech to the Commons, the second act of the Battle of France began as the Germans struck southwards from the River Somme. The French fought well in many areas, but they were no match for the Germans. Then five days later, Mussolini, Hitler's ally, finally declared war on Britain – 'a stab in the back but not unexpected', as Myrtle put it in her diary.

The Germans meanwhile had launched a major offensive on Paris on 9 June, and four days later the French capital was declared an open city, as the country's government fled to Bordeaux. Early the next morning, a little more than a month after the beginning of the campaign, the first German troops entered the city. In her diary, Myrtle echoed the disappointment felt by many Britons at the speed with which their ally had given up. 'Bosch had entered Paris at 6 AM,' she wrote the next day. 'We are all stunned, we so hoped the French could hold them.'

During a speech to the Commons on 18 June, Churchill announced that the Battle of France was now over and the Battle of Britain about to begin. 'Upon this battle depends the survival of Christian civilisation,' he told MPs. 'Let us therefore brace ourselves to our duty, and so bear ourselves that, if the British Empire and its Commonwealth last for a thousand years, men will still say, "This was their finest hour".'[66]

France's final act of surrender came three days later with the signing of an armistice with Germany in the Compiègne forest. This established a German occupation zone in northern and western France, leaving the remainder of the country 'free' to be governed by the French. The location was chosen by Hitler because this was where Germany had surrendered at the end of the First World War. Hitler insisted the document of capitulation be signed in Marshal Ferdinand Foch's personal railway coach, the same one that had been used in 1918. He later had the coach destroyed.

'This is the blackest day we have ever known,' wrote Myrtle. 'I heard the news that France had stopped fighting in a bus from a disgusted bus conductor who proclaimed to the entire world what he would do to the entire French nation and Chamberlain. Surely now, there is nobody left who can rat on us. We are all really alone, and if our government gives up there will be a revolution, and I am in it.'

It was a sentiment shared by the King. 'Personally I feel happier now that we have no allies to be polite to & to pamper,' he wrote to his mother.[67] Dorothy L Sayers, best known for her detective stories, struck the popular mood in her poem, 'The English War', which was published in the 7 September issue of the *Times Literary Supplement*.

> 'Praise God, now, for an English war –
> The grey tide and the sullen coast,
> The menace of the urgent hour,
> The single island, like a tower,
> Ringed with an angry host.'

Such rhetoric apart, there was no disguising the desperate situation in which Britain, now without any Continental allies, found itself. It seemed only a matter of time before the Germans invaded. Fears abounded of enemy parachutists, perhaps abetted by fifth columnists. For that reason, May 1940 saw a sharp rise in the number of people, largely from the far right of the political spectrum, interned as potential security risks, under what was known as Defence Regulation 18B. The regulation, which came into force two days before the outbreak of war, had initially been used sparingly, with the arrest of only a dozen or so people believed to be hardcore Nazis. But the ease with which Quisling seized power in Norway again focused fears on the danger of enemy infiltration, prompting a change of heart. One of the first to be arrested, early on the morning of 23 May, was Sir Oswald Mosley, leader of the British Union of Fascists, who had made no secret of his admiration for Hitler. By the end of the year more than a thousand people were in custody.

The government also set out to strengthen Britain's defences against invasion. In a radio broadcast on 14 May, Eden called on men between the ages of seventeen and sixty-five to enrol in a new force to be known as the Local Defence Volunteers (LDV). By July, nearly 1.5 million men and boys had signed up, and its name was changed to the more inspiring Home Guard. Golf courses, sports fields or other open spaces that could be used for enemy landings were 'sabotaged' by being scattered with junk. Road signs and the names of villages and of railways stations were taken down to confuse the enemy. Metal railings from houses, churches and other buildings were collected to be turned into weapons. The mayor of Camberwell in south-east London appealed for the gift or loan of firearms and binoculars for use by his local force. 'We are seriously in need of rifles, guns, revolvers, either automatic or revolving,' he declared. A week later, in a rare moment of truth, it was reported that the mayor felt very disappointed with the response, complaining: 'All I have received is one pair of binoculars.'[68] For the first months, many members of the Home Guard had to drill with wooden rifles

MARK LOGUE & PETER CONRADI

or hone their street-fighting skills with non-existent machine guns. The Marylebone company of the Home Guard had to make do with forty-eight pikes borrowed from the Drury Lane theatre.

Lionel, who had celebrated his sixtieth birthday that February, joined his local branch of the Home Guard, which was based at the Dulwich & Sydenham Golf Club. He, Val and Antony were members of the club, which lay on the other side of the railway cutting that ran along the back garden of Beechgrove. The volunteers based themselves in the clubhouse at the top of nearby Grange Lane, which, with its elevated views across London, was an ideal vantage point. They were an erudite if eclectic bunch, which, besides Logue, included at least four doctors, a wine importer and several local builders and property developers. There was also the local undertaker and another man who was still waited upon at his home by an elderly uniformed maid. Within a few weeks of the unit's creation, the volunteers were given rifles for which they were issued thirty rounds of ammunition each night from a store kept in a cigar box in the clubhouse. Andrew Rankine, a founder member who later joined the regular army, was in tears of laughter when he first saw *Dad's Army*, the BBC television comedy about the Home Guard that debuted in the late 1960s, telling his nephew Ian: 'That's just how it was.'

Notes compiled by Guy Bousfield, one of the doctors in the unit, and obtained by Brian Green, a local historian[69] contain a mixture of the serious and the absurd. On one occasion, a few nights after mysterious gunshots were heard in Dulwich Woods, a curious figure was seen moving towards the clubhouse, raising fears of a possible fifth columnist. The figure, when challenged, did not respond. Upon closer inspection it was revealed to be the golf club's horse, which was normally used for pulling the lawn mower. As in *Dad's Army*, there was also the inevitable friction between the volunteers and members of the regular army's anti-aircraft battery, who were based only a few hundred yards away.

One entry recorded by Bousfield said: 'Very bad blackout observed in R.A. [Royal Artillery] hut opposite ridge at top of 4th fairway from 10.35 p.m.–10.55 p.m. Proceeded on numerous occasions to corner of hedge on 5th fairway by path without at any time challenge from R.A. sentry. Battery could easily be entered at any time from this direction. Phoned police at West Dulwich to request Yellow Warnings be telephoned.' The volunteers also jealously guarded their privileges. One of them asked if the searchlight personnel operating the Locator Post had permission to use the inside lavatory in the clubhouse. The answer was an emphatic 'no'. Clearly written in the log in pencil were the words: 'outside Lav'.

That August members of the unit were among a 3,000-strong force from across south-east London and Kent inspected by the King in West Wickham. As its members marched across the sports ground, he watched them perform different exercises that included learning how to use a Bren gun, manning road blocks and physical training for the over forty-fives. 'Of the 3,000 men who took part in the parade only a few were without uniform, and the majority were fully armed,' reported The Times,[70] which called the day's events 'a living witness of Greater London's quiet determination to resist the invader'.

Myrtle was also doing her bit for the war effort, working with other women from London's Australian community to welcome troops from their native land who had begun to arrive in large numbers in June. Between then and the end of 1940, some 8,000 members of the Second Imperial Australian Force, all of them volunteers, were stationed in Britain. The basement ballroom of Australia House, the High Commission, was turned into a club and canteen with room for two to three hundred to sit, drink tea and eat sandwiches. When a reporter from the *Sydney Morning Herald* attended the centre's official opening that August she wrote of a 'khaki tidal wave' surging into the building, many of whom were passing through en route to Scotland. 'Two minutes after the first half dozen came in through the doors in Melbourne Place – where red, white and blue placards direct passers-by to "Australia's Social Centre" – Mrs Lionel Logue, wife of the King's voice specialist – was working at top speed looking up trains to Edinburgh and Glasgow,' she wrote.[71]

Hitler's advance across Europe meant new roles for the King's brothers: by giving the Duke of Gloucester the rather ill-defined post of Chief Liaison Officer to the British Expeditionary Force at the beginning of the war, the authorities had intended to create the impression he was playing a militarily significant role while keeping him out of harm's way. This was not how it was seen by Gloucester, who hoped the outbreak of hostilities would finally give him the chance to do some proper soldiering. Often cast as the least intelligent of George V's sons, he had joined the army after Eton, attending Sandhurst in 1919, and aspired to take command of his regiment, the 10th Royal Hussars. The Duke was a competent enough officer, but membership of the royal family brought its constraints: he was not able to serve abroad and often had to break off to perform princely duties, in which he had little interest. The abdication of his eldest brother, which led to his naming as Regent Designate until Princess Elizabeth's eighteenth birthday, put paid to any military career. He retired on his major's pension and devoted himself to farming an estate he had bought at Barnwell Manor in Northamptonshire.

The war and his new role in France seemed to offer Gloucester a second chance. He threw himself into his new duties with enthusiasm, visiting bases, inspecting troops and sending back a series of reports to the King. Always accident prone, he was involved in several car accidents and caught up in a number of dangerous incidents, the most serious of them on 15 May 1940 when he was slightly injured after his staff car came under German attack. 'Motoring about is not nice as many villages are being bombed,' he wrote to his wife. 'We got caught in the middle of a town on Thursday and just had time to quit the car and lie down in a narrow alleyway, when the earth reverberated. We were not hurt but slightly bruised by falling tiles.'[72]

With the retreat of the British Expeditionary Force towards the sea, Gloucester was ordered home, reaching London five days later. As he explained wryly to his mother, his presence had been an embarrassment to the military, 'because wherever I went, or had been, I was bombed'.[73] For his own protection, his military duties thereafter were confined to various morale-boosting visits to troops in Britain and abroad.

Finding a suitable role for the King's elder brother proved a more serious challenge: since late September 1939, the Duke of Windsor had been attached to the British military mission at Vincennes, in the eastern suburbs of Paris. In May, after the Germans invaded the Low Countries, he drove with the Duchess to Biarritz and set her up there before returning to Paris. The future of the British mission was uncertain, however, and the Duke went back to rejoin the Duchess in Biarritz, from where they travelled on to Château de la Croë, their palatial home on the Côte d'Azur, where they continued to live the high life. This was brought to a sudden halt by Mussolini's declaration of war. With the German troops less than two hundred miles away and nothing to prevent their further advance, the Windsors joined a British diplomatic convoy heading to neutral Spain, crossing the border and reaching Barcelona on the evening of 20 June. They later travelled on to Madrid.

The arrival in Spain of the royal couple proved to be of great interest to the Nazis. The Duke's sympathies towards the German regime were well known. General Franco was aligned with Berlin, and the British government was worried the Duke might fall into German hands – with potentially disastrous consequences. When he arrived at the Ritz Hotel he was handed a telegram from Churchill urging him to proceed to Lisbon, where a flying boat would take him and the Duchess back to Britain. The Duke declined unless his wife were given full royal honours. They were not prepared to find themselves 'regarded by the British public as in a different status to other members of my family', he said.[74]

The Duke's attitude convinced the King and Churchill that it would be better if he did not come back to Britain after all. Yet they were equally sure that he had to be kept far from the Germans. Churchill came up with an ingenious solution: the Duke could become Governor of the Bahamas. Churchill asked his friend, Lord Beaverbrook, if he thought the Duke would accept the appointment. 'He'll find it a great relief,' replied Beaverbrook. 'Not half as much as his brother will,' quipped Churchill.[75]

In fact, the King was initially not convinced, fearing that Wallis would be 'an obstacle'. The Queen, who loathed the Duchess with a passion, protested that a woman with three living husbands would 'not be acceptable to the people of the Islands and might set a precedent for a general lowering of standards'.[76] Queen Mary was astonished: she thought her son had merely asked Churchill to help find his brother a house in the Bahamas and that the Prime Minister had misunderstood and made him Governor instead. The appointment, she declared, would be a 'great mistake to my mind on account of *her*'.[77] Hardinge was more realistic about Wallis. 'I think that she will do harm wherever she is – but there is less scope for it in a place like the Bahamas than elsewhere – and the native population probably will not understand what it is all about.'[78]

Churchill's argument of the benefits of putting thousands of miles between the Duke and Duchess and the Germans eventually won the day. 'The activities of the Duke of Windsor on the Continent in recent months have been causing His Majesty and myself grave uneasiness as his inclinations are well known to be pro-Nazi and he may become a centre of intrigue,' Churchill wrote in a first draft of a message to the Prime Ministers of the Dominions announcing the Duke's appointment, which he subsequently amended.[79] Such fears were reinforced by the extent to which the Duke and Duchess, once in Madrid, quickly became a magnet for Nazi sympathizers and agents. Reports sent back to London of the couple's willingness to cooperate with the Germans may have been exaggerated, but the Duke was openly critical of his younger brother, while Wallis made no secret of her anger at the unfairness with which she had been treated by the British establishment. Commenting on the Duchess's 'anti-British activity' and influence on her husband, Hardinge claimed that 'as long as we never forget the power that she can exert on him in her efforts to avenge herself on this country, we shall be all right'.[80]

A few weeks later, the Duke and Duchess moved to Lisbon, where they lived initially in the home of Ricardo de Espírito Santo, a Portuguese banker with both British and German contacts. The Nazis, meanwhile, were working on audacious plan, codenamed Operation Willi, to kidnap the pair while they were on a shooting expedition near the Spanish border. The extent to which the Duke would have been a willing captive remained unclear, though he did succeed several times in delaying his departure for the Bahamas. Ultimately, though, he had no choice, especially after Churchill threatened him with a court martial if he did not comply. At 3 p.m. on 1 August, the Duke and Duchess finally set sail from Lisbon aboard the SS *Excalibur* bound for their new life in the Bahamas.

Concerns by the British authorities that the Duke could have been exploited by the Germans have become all the more plausible in the light of documents that have emerged in recent years about his sympathies. Yet it could be argued the Duke may actually have helped the Allied war effort – albeit unwittingly – by keeping the Germans guessing about his intentions. The thought, however fantastical, that the Duke might be prepared to play a Quisling-type role could have persuaded Hitler against launching what in such an event could have been an unnecessary invasion of Britain, buying the country more precious time during which it stepped up its manufacture of Supermarine Spitfires and Hawker Hurricane fighter planes, some 500 of which a month were pouring off British production lines during the summer of 1940.

Given the success of the German Blitzkrieg in continental Europe, Hitler appears to have expected Britain to sue for peace. But Churchill was not interested in a deal. He was determined to fight on, prompting Hitler to explore military options that he hoped would bring the war against Britain to a quick and successful end. The Nazi leader ordered his armed forces to prepare for an invasion – codenamed Operation Sealion.

For the invasion to have any chance of success, the Germans needed first to secure control of the skies over southern England and remove the threat posed by the RAF. The Nazis believed a sustained air assault on Britain would achieve the decisive victory needed to make Sealion a possibility. What became known as the Battle of Britain began in July 1940 with German attacks on coastal targets and British shipping in the Channel. On 1 August, Hitler gave

Reichsmarschall Hermann Göring, the *Luftwaffe*'s Commander-in-Chief, a directive to launch the air assault. The next day the King received a secret letter from Gustav V, the eighty-two-year-old King of neutral Sweden, offering to make contact between Britain and Germany to explore the possibility of peace. The King's reaction was unequivocal: 'How can we talk peace with Germany now after they have overrun & demoralized the peoples of so many countries in Europe?' he wrote in his diary. 'Until Germany is prepared to live peaceably with her neighbours in Europe, she will always be a menace. We have got to get rid of her aggressive spirit, her engines of war & the people who have been taught to use them.'[81] The British government agreed. On 12 August, the King wrote back to Gustav rejecting the offer. 'The intention of my peoples to prosecute the war until their purposes have been achieved have been strengthened,' he wrote. 'They will not falter in their duty and they firmly believe that with the help of God they will not lack the means to discharge their task.'

Germany, meanwhile, was stepping up its offensive. On 13 August it launched *Unternehmen Adlerangriff* (Operation Eagle Attack), which saw its planes fly further inland, targeting airfields and communication centres. Fighter Command came under enormous pressure, but put up stiff resistance. In a rousing speech to the House of Commons on 20 August, Churchill praised not just the 'brilliant actions' of the fighter pilots who took on the incoming enemy forces but also the skills of the bomber squadrons who flew deep into Germany to 'inflict shattering blows upon the whole of the technical and war-making structure of the Nazi power'. 'Never in the field of human conflict was so much owed by so many to so few,' he declared.

The critical phase came during the last week of August and first week of September when the Germans intensified their efforts to destroy Fighter Command. Airfields were significantly damaged but most remained operational. On 31 August, the British forces suffered their worst day of the entire Battle of Britain: thirty-nine aircraft were shot down, fourteen pilots were killed and a number of airfields across the south-east suffered serious damage. But the *Luftwaffe* was overestimating the damage it was inflicting on the enemy and wrongly came to the conclusion that the RAF was on its last legs. Fighter Command was bruised but not broken. Then came a shift in German tactics.

CHAPTER SIX

The Blitz

It was just after 4 p.m. on the afternoon of Saturday, 7 September 1940, and Virginia Cowles, an American journalist, was sitting down for tea with her friends on the lawn at Mereworth Castle, a splendid Palladian-style villa just west of Maidstone. The weather was unseasonably hot; at its peak the temperature had reached 30° C. The late summer idyll was interrupted by the drone of airplanes coming from the south-east. 'At first we couldn't see anything, but soon the noise had grown into a deep, full roar, like the far-away thunder of a giant waterfall,' Cowles recalled.[82] 'We lay in the grass, our eyes strained towards the sky: we made out a batch of tiny white specks, like clouds of insects, moving north-west in the direction of the capital.'

From their garden in nearby Sissinghurst, Harold Nicolson and Vita Sackville-West watched wave after wave of German planes coming over. 'There is some fighting above our heads and we hear one or two aeroplanes zoom downwards,' wrote Nicolson. 'They flash like silver gnats above us in the air.'[83] A few moments later, Colin Perry was bicycling over Chipstead Hill, in Surrey, when the sound of planes made him look up. 'It was the most amazing, impressive, riveting sight,' he recalled. 'Directly above me were literally hundreds of planes, Germans! The sky was full of them. Bombers hemmed in with fighters, like bees around their queen, like destroyers round the battleship, so came Jerry.'[84]

The 348 Heinkel, Dornier and Junkers bombers and the 617 Messerschmitt fighters had taken off from the Pas de Calais. At 4.14 p.m. they crossed the English coast, bound for London. Forming a block 20 miles wide, they filled 800 square miles of sky.[85] At 4.43 p.m. the capital's air raid sirens began to wail to announce their arrival. The Germans' main target was the docks along the Thames in London's East End, but many of the bombs fell on nearby residential areas that were home largely to the poor. Stepney, where nearly 200,000 people lived, was hit particularly hard. So, too, were Whitechapel, Poplar, Shoreditch and West Ham, as well as Bermondsey on the south side of the river.

When the all-clear sounded at 6.10 p.m., the East Enders assumed their ordeal was over, but their relief was premature. Two hours later, another 318 bombers, accompanied by fighter planes, carried out a second raid. They dropped a further 300 tons of high-explosive bombs and thousands of smaller incendiary devices, guided to their target by the fires burning in the docks. As night fell, the docks were blazing furiously and hundreds of the small houses nearby were in ruins. That morning there had been 1.5 million tons of softwood in the Surrey Commercial Dock; within hours most of it had gone up in flames. The assault did not end until 4.30 the next morning. With the East End bearing the main brunt of the bombing, those living elsewhere in the city initially felt like mere spectators of the destruction taking place just a few miles away; some even rode the Underground eastwards to take a look. The writer E.M. Forster, who had a flat in the west near Chiswick, wrote of 'London burning, a grandiose spectacle'.[86] Any such complacency was shattered just after 11 p.m., however, when a cluster of five 50kg (110lb) high-explosive bombs landed near Victoria, which was bustling with people on their way home after leaving the pubs or nearby theatres. The two raids together killed a total of 436 Londoners and injured more than 1,600. The Blitz had begun.

The next night, the bombers were back, killing 400; on 9 September they came by both day and night, and another 370 died. And so it continued: for fifty-six of fifty-seven consecutive nights, except for one when the cloudy skies provided a reprieve, London was hit by an average of 200 bombers a night.[87] Important military and industrial centres such as Birmingham, Bristol, Liverpool and Manchester were also targeted. By May 1941, when the German campaign ended, more than 43,000 civilians had been killed, half of them in the capital, and more than a million homes damaged or destroyed in the London area alone.

By the time the bombs began to fall, London was already far better prepared than it had been on the outbreak of war. By July, half of its homes had a private shelter, most of them Andersons, which had proved themselves surprisingly effective during early sporadic raids. The programme for building public shelters was largely complete, although conditions were often appalling. The authorities initially refused to countenance the use of Underground stations, largely for fear of disruption to the transport network, but already on the second night of the Blitz a large crowd managed to force their way into Liverpool Street Station. The same was to happen at other stations in the weeks and months that followed. The appeal of seeking refuge deep below ground was obvious, but the stations could turn into death traps if they suffered a direct hit, as was the case at Bank Station in January 1941, when 111 people were killed.

Despite such isolated incidents, the relentless German bombing did not provoke the mass collapse in public order, especially in working-class districts, that the authorities had feared. 'Pessimists had predicted panic and bitterness in the East End, but I saw nothing of the kind,' wrote Harold Scott, who accompanied Churchill on the morning after the first night of attacks on a visit to Silvertown, a riverside area in the East End that had been especially badly hit. 'Smiles, cheers and grim determination showed already that "London could take it".'[88] While this may have been something of an exaggeration, the overwhelming mood was of defiance and resolution.

The onslaught provided the King and Queen with a new role: as the Blitz raged, they, too, toured bomb sites, not just in London but in other cities too. While the King's political judgement was sometimes poor, he was in his element when it came to cultivating the public side of monarchy. The emphasis was on informality: while royal visits in peacetime had been carefully orchestrated affairs in which the King and Queen were shepherded by aristocratic lords lieutenant or mayors and town clerks, now they moved freely among ordinary people, questioning, listening and consoling. 'I was very greatly impressed by the both of them,' wrote Lord Woolton, the Minister for Food, after accompanying the royal couple on some of their tours around the bombed-out streets.[89] 'They were so easy to talk to and to take around, and fell so readily into conversation with the people whom they were seeing, without any affectation or side.' The result was the creation of a bond between crown and people that would have been difficult to achieve in peacetime.

The Queen's contribution was every bit as important as her husband's and reflected serious thought as to how to adapt her role to wartime. Image was all important: while the King invariably appeared in naval uniform, the Queen avoided military garb, even though she had become commander-in-chief of several women's regiments. After consultation with Norman Hartnell, her couturier, it was decided she would wear light colours rather than dark to make her stand out, sticking to her usual pastel pinks, blues and lilacs but in 'dustier' shades than during peacetime. 'She wanted to convey the most comforting, encouraging and sympathetic note possible,' Hartnell recalled.[90] With her hats, gloves and high heels, the Queen consciously dressed up rather than down; even her gas mask, initially carried in a regulation-issue khaki case, was soon transferred to a chic velvet holder made for her by Hartnell. She considered it self-evident that she should be well dressed among the misery. When one nervous courtier summoned up the courage to ask if it was right that she wore her best dresses to visit bomb sites, the Queen replied: 'If the poor people had come to see me *they* would have put on their best clothes.'[91] The Queen's glamour, combined with the warmth she exuded and her willingness always to give the photographers the pictures they needed, helped her to be regarded as the embodiment of what Woolton called 'practical sympathy'.

The royal couple's bond with the nation was further strengthened by a series of German strikes on Buckingham Palace, the first of which was on 8 September, when a delayed action bomb fell on the north side of the building. The next morning the King worked as usual in his office above where it lay, oblivious of the high explosives beneath him. It was only that night, when he and the Queen were far away, sleeping in Windsor, that the bomb went off. There were no casualties, and no damage was done to the main structure of the Palace, but all the windows – including those of the royal apartments – were shattered and some of the ceilings came down.

Over the course of the next few days, the royal couple visited the East End to see the devastation for themselves – and to be seen. They received a warm reception from local people picking their way through the rubble. The scenes of misery made a great impression on them. 'We have seen some of the awful havoc which has been done in East London, & have talked to the people who are quite marvellous in the face of adversity,' the King wrote to his mother.[92] '[They are] so cheerful about it all, & some have had very narrow escapes.'

On the morning of 13 September it was the King and Queen themselves who had a narrow escape. Just after they had arrived at Buckingham Palace for the day from Windsor, a German bomber appeared out of low cloud, flew straight along the Mall and took aim at the building. The royal couple were in the little upstairs sitting room; the Queen was in the process of taking an eyelash out of her husband's eye when Hardinge came into the room carrying a batch of papers. 'All of a sudden we heard an aircraft making a zooming noise above us, saw 2 bombs falling past the opposite side of the Palace, & then heard 2 resounding crashes as the bombs fell in the quadrangle about 30 yds. away,' the King recorded in his diary. 'We looked at each other & then we were out in the passage as fast as we could get here. The whole thing happened in a matter of seconds. We all wondered why we weren't dead.'[93]

The chapel took one of the hits: three men in the workshop below were injured, and although a first aid party sprang into action, one later died of his injuries. The King was badly shaken. 'It was a ghastly experience & I don't want it to be repeated,' he wrote. 'It certainly teaches one to "take cover" on all future occasions, but one must be careful not to become "dugout minded".' A week later he was still suffering from the after effects. 'I quite disliked sitting in my room on Monday & Tuesday. I found myself unable to read, always in a hurry, & glancing out of the window.'[94]

On the afternoon of the attack, after lunch in their shelter, the King and Queen again set off for the East End. The devastation they encountered was terrible. Among the horrors they witnessed was the aftermath of an attack on Agate Street Infants School in Canning Town, which had been hit by a bomb on the night of 10 September when 500 homeless people were sheltering there, awaiting evacuation. The building collapsed on them; some 200 people were still under the rubble when the royal party arrived. 'The damage there is ghastly,' the Queen wrote to Queen Mary. 'I really felt as if I was walking in a dead city . . . It does affect me seeing this terrible and senseless destruction – I think that really I mind it much more than being bombed myself.' She ended her letter with a postscript: 'Dear old BP is still standing, and that is the main thing.'[95] The couple received an enthusiastic welcome. 'When we saw the Queen that day, everybody lost their downheartedness,' one local resident, Bill Bartley, recalled decades later.[96] 'There was still an air raid on when she walked through the rubble. I always thought the world of her. She doesn't sit back pompous-like. I remember her putting her arm round people covered in blood and grime and consoling them. I feel she knows what our lives were like. She could talk and she could listen, but above all, she cared. She would listen to a poor victim sobbing out their heart-rending story, and tears would well up in her eyes.'

The bombing of the Palace dominated the front pages the next morning, but it was not revealed how close the King and Queen had come to death until after the end of the war. Even Churchill claimed not to have known. 'Had the windows been closed instead of open, the whole of the glass would have splintered into the faces of the King and Queen, causing terrible damage,' he wrote. 'So little did they make of it that even I . . . never realised until long afterwards . . . what had actually happened.'[97]

On the day after the attack, Logue wrote to the King. 'It has been my great privilege to write you many letters,' he wrote, 'but never have I written one with such a feeling of thankfulness, and gratitude to the Most High, for your escape from the dastardly attempt on your life.'

It did not seem possible that even the Germans would descend to such depths of infamy but they little know the minds of the King and his peoples, if they imagine such an affront would deter us from the fixed determination to overthrow this horrible combination that threatens the world.

My own work is at a standstill as patients cannot travel to me on account of the constant air raids, and I cannot blame them for not wishing to come to London. Three nights a week I am on duty all night as an Air Raid Warden. Myrtle is very busy looking after Australian soldiers at Australia House. I would like the Queen to know how grateful we all are for her escape. My hope in life is that I am privileged to be present at the broadcast when 'Triumphant Peace' is the theme of your Majesty's speech.

Lascelles wrote back to Logue four days later, thanking him for his expression of concern, which the King and Queen had greatly appreciated. 'T.M. [their majesties] are none the worse for their experience,' Lascelles added. 'I hope you manage to get some sleep now and then.'

A few weeks later, the Logues, too, narrowly escaped with their lives. In early October, as Lionel wrote to relatives in Adelaide, 'a bomb landed at midnight in a neighbour's woodland, and did its worst: made his house uninhabitable, blew my chimneys down and my slate roof off, cracked the walls in one of the bathrooms, and brought the ceilings down, besides smashing innumerable panes of ¼-in plate glass'.[98]

The bombing of the Palace, and of other parts of the West End, did have one positive effect – on popular morale. The day before the second attack, Nicolson had written in his diary how 'everyone is worried about the feeling in the East End where there is much bitterness; it is said that even the King and Queen were booed the other day when they visited the destroyed area.'[99] As one London housewife from Kensington who had been bombed out of her home for a second time put it: 'It's all very well for them traipsing around saying how their hearts bleed for us and they share our suffering, and then going home to a roaring fire in one of their six houses.'[100]

Now, however, it seemed the royal couple were just as exposed as their subjects, prompting the Queen to claim, in what was one of the most quoted sayings of the war, that she was glad the Palace had been bombed since she could 'now look the East End in the face' – a feeling reinforced by the reception they received during their visits. The King agreed: 'I feel that our tours of bombed areas in London are helping the people who have lost their relations & homes,' he wrote in his diary, '& we have both found a new bond with them as Buckingham Palace has been bombed as well as their homes, and nobody is immune.'[101] As Mountbatten wrote to the King: 'If Goering had realised the depths of feeling which his bombing of Buckingham Palace has aroused throughout the Empire & America, he would have been well advised to instruct his assassins to keep off.'[102]

This was confirmed by the Mass-Observation organization, which, among other things, monitored the response of cinema audiences to national figures when they appeared in newsreels. 'Since the bombing of Buckingham Palace the King's popularity has risen, as instanced by one out of seven appearances applauded at the outbreak of war, to over one in three appearances applauded since the Blitz,' it found.[103] A report on 6 October noted that one speech by the King was clapped for seventeen seconds by the audience in a Gaumont cinema, the longest applause for one man ever recorded there. 'Now the King is clapped, not so much as a man, but as a symbol of the country,' the monitor, Mr England, wrote.[104] The newspapers, which since the abdication had been on a mission to boost the monarchy, also played their part, often exaggerating the numbers of people who turned out to greet the royal couple, who, for security reasons, usually arrived without warning. 'The King and Queen visited us in Liverpool on Wednesday,' wrote one shipping clerk, 'but as they came unannounced very few people saw them. I was talking on the phone yesterday and my friend told me that they were then visiting Lancaster, but as nobody was expecting them, very few people were congregated about. Last night the wireless announced that the crowds [in both cities] were so great that their car had to go at walking pace. One of us is wrong.'[105]

Yet there is no doubting the impact on the individuals whom the King and Queen encountered on their travels around the country – especially when the royal couple literally turned up on their doorstep. During a visit to Portsmouth, they asked to see a woman who had been bombed out of her first two homes and was now poorly housed in a third. A detective knocked on the door and the woman emerged with a baby in her arms.

'We heard of your misfortune,' began the Queen. 'May we come in and talk to you? The King and I would so much like to bring you such comfort as we can, and to hear your story.'

Though still doubtful of her visitors' identity, the woman let them in.

'I understand this is your third home,' said the King.

'That's right,' the woman replied. 'He burned us out of one and he flooded us out of another, but he'll never get us out of here.'[106]

Such visits were often lovingly recorded by those who came into contact with royalty. A nurse from Midlothian wrote in her diary how she had 'just been photographed beside the Queen when the Queen visited her canteen'; another woman showed one of the Mass Observation diarists 'a photo of her husband in uniform standing beside the Queen'. The King was in his element: he had always set great store by hard work, and the war gave him the opportunity to give his all, whether with such visits to bombed-out civilians or trips to inspect troops or factories engaged in military production. He also insisted on personally decorating all ranks himself with service medals – something none of his predecessors had done. Before the war, it had been primarily officers who received their decorations from the monarch's own hand; he extended the privilege to all the ranks and to the next of kin of those due to be decorated who had been killed while on active service. Such investitures, which took place week after week, could be monotonous occasions. For more than two hours, the King, standing on a raised dais, flanked by two gentleman ushers, would pin medals on as many 300 people at a time, shaking each by the hand and exchanging a few words. But as he saw it, this was a part of his duty.

At the same time, great play was made of the fact that the royal family were sharing the deprivations of their people: the heating at Windsor Castle and Buckingham Palace was reportedly turned down to conserve heat. The King was also said to go around the royal bathrooms, personally marking the hot-water limit – five inches from the bottom in each bath – which he measured with a foot ruler. Such deprivation was relative: it emerged decades later that the Queen and other members of her family each received twenty times more clothing coupons than their entitlement. The royal family also continued to eat well: game, fish, fruit and vegetables were never rationed and they had eighty rabbits sent to Windsor each week. Such details were not part of the official version of events. 'This war has drawn the Throne and the people more closely together than ever before recorded,' Churchill wrote to the King early in 1941. 'Yr Majesties are more deeply loved by all classes of your subjects than were any princes of the past.

*

While London continued to suffer a relentless battering, the King was preparing to address the nation again on 23 September 1940 – this time to announce the creation of a new decoration, the George Cross and Medal. Many such decorations had been created by previous monarchs to reward gallantry and meritorious conduct, but they were largely restricted to members of the armed forces; only one, the Victoria Cross, was open to all ranks. During his tour of the parts of London that were suffering most during the Blitz, the King had been struck by stories of exceptional courage, but also frustrated by his own inability to reward them because of the strict rules that governed the granting of decorations.

He had been especially impressed by the exploits of Temporary Lieutenant Robert 'Jock' Davies, the Commanding Officer of 16/17 Section, No. 5 Bomb Disposal Company Royal Engineers, who had successfully defused a 1,000kg bomb that failed to go off after being dropped close to the steps below the south-west tower of St Paul's Cathedral on 12 September. Davies's team had shown great skill and courage, first in extracting the bomb and then taking it to the Hackney Marshes, where it was detonated in a controlled explosion that made a crater a hundred feet across. Like other bomb disposal officers, he and George Wyllie, the sapper who had found the bomb, were not deemed by the War Office to qualify for the Victoria Cross because they were not 'working in the face of the enemy'.

A few days earlier, Logue had received a telephone call from Hardinge inviting him to lunch at Windsor on the Sunday, the day before the broadcast. He and Myrtle had just got back home: the air raids in south London had been especially fierce and they had left the city to stay with friends for the night. Lionel slept in the billiard room. 'It was very peaceful and gave us some necessary rest,' he wrote.

On Sunday, Logue set out early in the pouring rain, arriving at the Castle at 12.40. He met Hardinge, who handed him the speech, which Logue proclaimed 'quite good'. He was then put in the charge of Commander Harold Campbell, an equerry to the King with the ancient title of Groom of the Robes, who gave him a sherry and took him up the Long Room, where they waited for the King and Queen. The royal couple came in punctually at 1.15, the King dressed in his Field Marshall's uniform. They were joined by the two princesses, who were wearing powder blue. After a few minutes of bright conversation, the King declared himself to be hungry and led them through to lunch in the drawing room, with its long window looking out onto Home Park and Slough.

'It was such a happy little lunchroom, and everyone was happy,' Logue recorded in his diary. 'It seemed as if war was far away, for a time anyhow. After lunch we came back to the lounge and after some talk, their Majesties went. As he was going the King said: "Will you come along with me Logue."

'I said goodbye to the Queen in the long passage and thanked her for having me to lunch. She gave me her lovely smile and I went off with the King. Went through the speech: 12½ minutes 3 times. It was written by the Prime Minister and is quite good stuff.'

The next day Logue arrived at Buckingham Palace at 4 p.m. and Lascelles showed him the craters the bombs had made in the courtyard. Fifteen minutes later, the King sent for him, and they went down together to the dugout beneath the palace from which he would make the broadcast. It took them time to get used to the new location with its low ceiling, but Logue proclaimed the room's acoustic properties just about perfect. After a time, Wood came down and reported the King had been speaking at eighty words a minute, which meant the speech had taken twelve minutes. They made a few alterations, and when they were done, the King proposed a cup of tea. They went upstairs to the old broadcasting room, where the Queen was waiting. They drank China tea. It was from this room that they had seen the bombs hit the courtyard but, looking out, Logue couldn't help but marvel at how little destruction had been caused. 'A dreadful noise, but not much damage,' was the Queen's verdict on the raid. Laughing, she described how a police constable, a former soldier, had said to her: 'What a magnificent bit of bombing, Ma'am, if you'll pardon my saying so.'

At 5.40, they went down to the dugout for another run-through. Logue thought it had gone very well, although they had to take precautions as the air raid siren was sounding. When the all-clear came, bells rang out all over the Palace, among them one outside the door of the dugout, which had to be put out of order.

As they were waiting the last few minutes, the King began to laugh and said: 'I little thought that I would broadcast from the Housemaid's sitting room. I must write a book called "Places I've Broadcast from".'

At one minute to six he was in his armchair, waiting, which was always the hardest part. Then at the top of the hour, three red lights came on and he stood up, walked to the microphone and gave a little smile.

'It is just over . . . a year since the war began,' the King started, pausing uncomfortably between 'over' and 'a'. 'The British peoples entered it with open eyes recognising how formidable were the forces against them, but confident in the justice of their cause.' He went on to describe how much the situation had changed in the meantime: 'Great nations have fallen. The battle which at that time was so far away that we could only just hear its distant rumblings is now at our very doors. The armies of invasion are massed across the Channel, only twenty miles from our shores.'

The King also described the achievements and sacrifices of the

British people, their allies and of the Commonwealth, and talked of the Blitz and the 'honourable scars' Buckingham Palace had suffered when it was bombed. 'The walls of London may be battered, but the spirit of the Londoner stands resolute and undismayed,' he added. 'As in London, so throughout Great Britain, buildings rich in beauty and historic interest may be wantonly attacked, humbler houses, no less dear and familiar, may be destroyed. But "there'll always be an England" to stand before the world as the symbol and citadel of freedom, and to be our own dear home.'

The King then reached the main point of his speech: 'Many and glorious are the deeds of gallantry done during these perilous but famous days. In order that they should be worthily and promptly recognised, I have decided to create, at once, a new mark of honour for men and women in all walks of civilian life. I propose to give my name to this new distinction, which will consist of the George Cross, which will rank next to the Victoria Cross, and the George Medal for wider distribution,' he declared.

The King concluded on an upbeat note. 'We live in grim times, and it may be that the future will be grimmer yet. Winter lies before us, cold and dark. But let us be of good cheer. After winter comes spring, and after our present trials will assuredly come victory and a release from these evil things. Let us then put our trust, as we do, in God, and in the unconquerable spirit of the British people.'

After the end of the speech, the all-clear could just be heard. Logue was delighted at how well the King had performed. 'Despite the unpredictable conditions, he spoke splendidly – in a dugout, with an Air Raid warning on, after having been bombed the week before – a stout effort,' he wrote in his diary. 'He was very tired and pleased when he left for Windsor with the Queen at 6.30.'

A few weeks later, on 13 October, Princess Elizabeth, then aged fourteen, had the chance to follow in her father's footsteps by making a radio address of her own: during *Children's Hour* on the BBC, she made a five-minute broadcast to 'the children of the Empire'. She approached the task seriously, modifying the prepared text to add phrases of her own and practising breathing and timing. At the end, she invited Princess Margaret to join her in wishing their listeners good night. The next day, Logue wrote to the future queen to add his 'sincere and humble congratulations' to the many he expected her to receive for her performance.

'I am sure your royal parents will not mind my writing you, to say how splendidly your broadcast came through today,' he wrote:

It is always an ordeal to do anything public for the first time, but you spoke it so efficiently and your voice was under such excellent control, that I am sure you will never be worried in the future when you have to approach the microphone, and that is a very comforting thought for in your life you will have to do it many many times.

I am afraid I was far more nervous than you were over it, for there was not a tremor in your voice and the inflection was perfect.

On 17 October, one of the Queen's ladies-in-waiting wrote back to Logue to say she appreciated his letter and had been 'so glad to hear that you enjoyed listening-in'.

Although Britain continued to brace itself for the expected invasion, Hitler had now given up on the idea. During a meeting on 17 September with Göring and *Generalfeldmarschall* Gerd von Rundstedt, he became convinced that the operation was not viable given that the *Luftwaffe* had still not managed to gain control of the skies. Later that day he formally postponed Operation Sealion and ordered the dispersal of the invasion fleet that had been assembled in order to avert further damage by British air and naval attacks.

The relentless air assault on London nevertheless continued through the autumn of 1940. The south-eastern suburbs, where the Logues lived, were not the main focus of the German attack, but they, too, suffered considerable destruction, much of it visible from the clubhouse of the Dulwich & Sydenham Golf Club, where members of Logue's Home Guard unit continued their lookout duties.

On Monday, 9 September, when an air raid sounded soon after eight o'clock, Dr Bousfield wrote in his log:

Many heavy air attacks from W by N to N.E. along a line across the Thames. Heavy fires apparently beyond Blackfriars, Tower Bridge, and over docks caused at intervals and blazing till dawn. At 03.55hrs a very violent but short conflagration occurred in N.E. illuminating whole sky, suggestive of large gasworks. Batteries came into action against enemy aircraft caught in searchlights on several occasions. The shooting was very accurate.

The following Sunday came an attack closer to home:

21.15 hrs unexploded bombs dropped direct hit Dulwich College – 23.25hrs unexploded bomb to ½ to 1 mile away – 23.30hrs 'Molotov Bread Basket' [a large bomb containing numerous incendiary bombs] W.N.W. – 23.40hrs same again S.W. far off – 23.44hrs same again S.W. by W. far off – 23.58 brilliant flashes illuminating sky behind fires N.W. lasted 3–4 minutes – 00.23hrs bomb fairly near Post.

Hostile plane activity during night; very active AA (anti-aircraft) fire. Dug-out sump had to be pumped out. Water coming in down wall near telephone.

The same day, a Dornier was shot down over London and crashed onto Victoria Station. Two of the airmen died but one parachuted out successfully, landing in Wells Park in south-east London. First on the scene was the local butcher, William Wellbeloved, who, armed with his meat cleaver, took the German prisoner. Logue described the incident in a letter to relatives in Adelaide: 'From our front lawn we have seen some great fights, and had the satisfaction of seeing a Spitfire shoot down a Dornier about two miles from the house,' he wrote.[107] 'It was marvellous to hear the machine-gun fire, and then the German slowly turn and glide down head first.'

Initially, like its counterparts across the country, Logue's Home Guard unit struggled to get sufficient weapons. In the weeks that followed more were issued, together with bayonets, and a demonstration was given of a Browning automatic rifle. The unit's members soon had plenty of opportunities to make use of their newly issued weaponry, as the clear moonlight nights provided perfect conditions for enemy bombers. One of their most important tasks was shooting out the flares that were dropped by the *Luftwaffe* to illuminate potential targets and identify barrage balloon. On one occasion a parachute mine was seen falling close to the seventh green, followed by a large explosion that damaged the clubhouse. The volunteers blamed the owners of the Grange, a house near the course, which was not properly blacked out and leaking light, and which, it was felt, must have been seen by the German bomber. Two members of the unit were dispatched, who then shot out the offending lights. There was no mention in the log of the owner of the house's reaction.

On 14 October, two bombs exploded within a mile to the south; soon afterwards, a Messerschmitt 109 dived low over the clubhouse. There was considerable enemy activity that night and a barrage balloon came down on the thirteenth fairway, which the Home Guard had to secure. A week or so later, another 'Molotov Bread Basket' exploded on the golf course, scattering some hundred incendiaries over a wide area, several of which they put out. An entry in the log, echoing Alfred, Lord Tennyson, read: 'H. G. Welsh, with fires in front of him – fires to the right of him – and fires to the left of him, rushed forward carrying two buckets of sand, jumped a ditch and fell into a bunker straining both ankles severely. After receiving First Aid he carried on conscientiously with his turn of duty'. On the evening of 9 November, a few hours before Logue reported for his 00.30 to 02.30 shift, a plane was seen crashing, apparently in Bromley, five or so miles to the south-east. The Home Guard log reported that its three crew members had bailed out; one had been caught but two Germans were still at large. It was not recorded whether they were eventually apprehended,

Some of the German bombs nevertheless found their mark, among them one on 25 October that hit Cobbs Department Store on Kirkdale Road, Sydenham, the most prestigious establishment of the sort in south-east London. About three-quarters of the building was destroyed by the bomb and the ensuing fire, which needed twenty-five fire crews to put it out. The area suffered an even deadlier attack on 8 December, when a parachute mine fell on Elsinore Road in Forest Hill, to the east. Often exploding as they drifted down to earth, such bombs were capable of enormous damage since the blast spread out over a wide area. This particular one killed two people and injured 144, destroyed or damaged 370 houses and put Kilmorie Road School out of commission for the rest of the war. So many incendiaries were dropped that several targets including St Giles Hospital in Camberwell were hit; at one point twelve separate fires were burning. The volunteers recorded plenty of enemy aircraft on 23 December, too, with bombs dropped on the golf course. After a pause for Christmas, heavy raids resumed on 27 December.

In addition to his duties with the Home Guard, Logue also

worked three times a week as an air raid warden. He approached the job with his characteristic humour. Digging a woman out of the ruins of a bombed-out building, he asked: 'Was your husband with you?'*

'No, he enlisted,' the woman replied.

'The bloody coward!' Logue shot back.

The Germans, meanwhile, had been shifting their strategy to attack industrial centres outside London, mounting a devastating raid on Coventry on the night of 14/15 November. More than 500 tons of high-explosive bombs and 30,000 incendiaries were dropped over the course of 13 hours, turning the centre of the city into a sea of flames and killing nearly 600 people. Told of the scale of the attack, the King visited the next day. He arrived to find the city's fifteenth-century Gothic cathedral almost completely destroyed and spent hours tramping through the rubble, overwhelmed by the scale of the destruction. 'What could I say to these poor people who had lost everything, sometimes their families, words were inadequate,' he asked Logue a couple of weeks later when they were going through the speech he was due to make during the State Opening of Parliament. In the weeks that followed, the Germans turned their attention to Southampton, Birmingham, Bristol, Liverpool, Portsmouth and Manchester.

Amid the misery and destruction there were some lighter moments too. When the King arrived at the Palace from Windsor on his way to deliver the speech, he greeted Logue with a big grin. 'Logue, I've got the jitters,' he declared. 'I woke up at 1 o'clock after dreaming I was in parliament with my mouth wide open

---

* Logue described the incident to Valerie Robinson, the daughter of a friend while she was visiting London for the Festival of Britain in 1951 (letter to author).

and couldn't say a word.' The two men had a good laugh and went through the speech three times. Logue was pleased by the result, but it brought home to him how heavily the King's speech impediment still weighed on him despite all the years they had spent working together.

Because of the Blitz, parliament was meeting not in the Palace of Westminster, but in nearby Church House, which was being tried out as an alternative venue. As was the case the previous year, it was a simple ceremony: the King, in the uniform of an Admiral of the Fleet, did not put on the Imperial Crown, which was carried on a purple-covered salver by a member of the House of Lords, but instead wore his service cap. In his speech, he spoke of the close and cordial relationship between Britain and the United States, saying: 'It is good to know in these fateful times how widely shared are the ideals of ordered freedom, of justice and security.' That afternoon at four o'clock, Hardinge called Logue to tell him the King had accomplished his task 'splendidly'.

That year's Christmas card sent by the King and Queen to those, including the Logues, privileged to be on their list showed them standing in front of a bombed-out section of Buckingham Palace. By contrast, Queen Mary chose a picture of a rustic flower garden and quaint cottage, but with the greeting: 'There'll always be an England.' While the Blitz raged on, Britons were preparing to celebrate as best as they could what was the first real wartime Christmas. Carol singing was abandoned because of the blackout and the bombing, while many had to make do with 'Empire' beef and mutton rather than turkey or goose. For the first time, all heavy industry and many offices and stores had to work on Boxing Day. Yet theatres continued to stage pantomimes and churches put on nativity plays, while many of the big shelters where as many as a million Londoners were now forced to spend the night were decorated with Christmas trees.

The King was preparing to make his broadcast to the Empire. Christmas Day fell on a Wednesday, and the previous Friday Logue had a call from the Palace instructing him to hold himself in readiness. It was agreed he would be there at 1.15 on the Monday. Logue arrived fifteen minutes early, and Hardinge gave him a copy of the speech. Logue 'didn't like it a bit'. As far as he was concerned there was nothing for the King to get his teeth into and he thought the Princess Elizabeth had 'done the same thing so well a few weeks earlier'. The King was having lunch with Churchill and so Logue ate instead with Commander Campbell.

'When I went into the King, I found him looking very fit, and we had a go at the speech,' Logue recalled. 'The Prime Minister had had a go at the speech as well and during lunch marked it in his own illegible writing. The King and myself had a go at translating and at last fixed it up. It took bit of altering and even when finished I still didn't like it.'

The next day, Christmas Eve, Logue met Wood at Broadcasting House and they drove down together to Windsor, to which the royal family had decamped for the holiday. As they passed Runnymede, Logue 'thought of King John and all we are fighting'. They arrived and had a drink with Miéville before going up to the Long Room to wait for the Royal party.

Logue always knew when the King and Queen were coming, as first their dogs ran into the room barking. Then in walked the royal couple, smiling.

'Well, I'm hungry, let's have lunch,' said the King and they trooped into the dining room, with its long corridors looking over the garden and the home park. They went through the speech, but Logue still didn't like it. The King had refused to broadcast from his dugout and so had all the recording equipment put back into the study from which the Princess Elizabeth had made her broadcast. Logue was struck by how bare the rooms looked now that most of the good furniture had been put into storage. The King was not very well as he had eaten something that disagreed with him, so they only went through the speech once. Logue then drove back to London with Wood. They ran into a terrible fog after leaving Kingston but eventually reached Wimbledon and then it was on to Herne Hill and home.

The weather on Christmas morning was cold but cheerful. Logue did not want to chance the trains so took the Green Line Coach to Windsor instead. 'It had been standing in the cold all night and when the door was opened, and we got in, the cold hit you,' he wrote. 'It was like getting into an ice house. I got colder and colder and when I reached Windsor, I fell out of the bus a frozen mass.' The walk up to the Castle warmed him up a little; a glass of sherry with Miéville after he arrived helped further. 'The beautiful coal fire, still further thawed me out so when the King and Queen with the Princess and Duke and Duchess of Kent came in, I was almost human,' he wrote. At 1.10 they went upstairs in front of the lavishly decorated Christmas tree. The royal family had 'worked wonders' since he left the day before, he thought. They sat down to a Christmas Dinner of boar's head and prunes, which, according to Logue, 'looked and tasted marvellous', adding: 'I have rarely had such a beautifully cooked and served meal.'

Afterwards they all pulled crackers and the King wanted to know what the message in Logue's had said. Logue read it out loud: 'What is a pedestrian? One of those things motorists run over.'

The King thought for a minute before saying: 'No, I don't think we can interpolate it with the broadcast.'

After the meal, they went back to the Long Room, and the Queen took an object off the tree. 'Mr Logue, please keep this as a memento,' she said, handing it to him. It was a gold cigarette case. 'It was a beautiful gift, and I was overwhelmed and I am afraid I stammered out my thanks,' Logue recalled. Then the King said 'Come on let's do our work' and they went to his study and had a run-through of the broadcast, after which they moved to the Broadcasting Room. Wood joined them briefly, they synchronized their watches and he went back to his room and his equipment. The King and Logue were left alone chatting, as they waited for the three flashes of the red light to announce the start of the broadcast.

'In days of peace the feast of Christmas is a time when we all gather together in our homes, young and old, to enjoy the happy festivity and good will which the Christmas message brings,' the King began. 'It is, above all, children's day, and I am sure that we shall all do our best to make it a happy one for them wherever they may be.'

Many children, he continued, were separated from their parents, either because their fathers had gone away to fight or because they had themselves been evacuated – whether to the countryside or to temporary homes in Canada, Australia, New Zealand, South Africa or the United States. At the same time, in contrast to the First World War, where 'the flower of our youth was destroyed, and the rest of the people saw but little of the battle', the adults at home were this time 'in the front line and the danger together, and I know that the older among us are proud that it should be so'.

If war brings its separations, it brings new unity also, the unity which comes from common perils and common sufferings willingly shared ... Time and again during these last few months I have seen for myself the battered towns and cities of England, and I have seen the British people facing their ordeal . . . Out of all this suffering there is a growing harmony which we must carry forward into the days to come when we have endured to the end and ours is the victory . . .

We have surmounted a grave crisis. We do not underrate the dangers and difficulties which confront us still, but we take courage and comfort from the successes which our fighting men and their Allies have won at heavy odds by land and air and sea.

The future will be hard, but our feet are planted on the path of victory, and with the help of God we shall make our way to justice and to peace.

The text of the speech had not grown on Logue, but he was nevertheless pleased with the way in which the King delivered it. Afterwards, Wood came in to congratulate him on his performance. That evening Logue picked up Myrtle and they went down to dinner with John Gordon at his home in Croydon.

For their part, the King and Queen set off the day after Boxing Day to Sandringham for a few days. The big house had been closed since the start of the war and surrounded by barbed wire, and they stayed instead in Appleton House. It was hoped it would be a less obvious target for German bombers, but the King and Queen were nevertheless still protected by an armoured car unit and four Bofors guns. Among the trees nearby was a reinforced concrete air raid shelter. Despite the thick snow on the ground, the King went shooting every day. Writing in his diary, he began by describing 1940 as 'a series of disasters' but then went on to set out the positives of the previous twelve months, from the formation of the new government under Churchill – which 'stopped the political rot' – to the 'splendid' civilian defence services and morale of the people. 'Hitler has not had everything his own way,' he added.[108]

On New Year's Day Lionel was pleased to receive a letter from Hugh Crichton-Miller, a leading physician and psychiatrist who had been based for some time in the same building as him in Harley Street, and was now in charge of Stanborough Hospital, Watford.

'My dear Logue,' he wrote. 'I must send you a line to congratulate you on the success of your treatment, which was more obvious at 3.00 p.m. on Christmas Day than it had ever been before.'

Logue drafted his response on the back of the letter: 'Am so glad you like the effort. It was a very happy broadcast & did not cause the slightest worry or trouble. I only wish every patient would work as hard as he has, what splendid result one could obtain.'

CHAPTER SEVEN

No Longer Alone

1941 was to bring a dramatic change to Britain's fortunes. At the beginning of the year, the country stood virtually alone against the Nazis. By its close Britain had been joined by both the United States and the Soviet Union.

Roosevelt, re-elected for a third term as President in November 1940, was sympathetic to Britain's plight, and the American people were impressed by the country's brave resistance to Hitler. But they were still resistant to being dragged into a European war, and Britain was running out of money with which to buy the American goods it needed for the war effort. A solution was found when Roosevelt sent Harry Hopkins, a foreign policy advisor and one of his closest confidants, to London in January 1941 to get the measure of Churchill and assess the extent of Britain's determination to fight on. The two men quickly hit it off and Churchill agreed with Hopkins a new basis for the purchase of oil, equipment and other supplies on credit that would not have to be repaid until after the end of the war.

The Blitz, meanwhile, had raged on relentlessly through the winter. One of the most devastating attacks began on the evening of 29 December. From 6.15 p.m. until the all-clear sounded three and a half hours later, 100,000 incendiary bombs and another 24,000 high-explosive devices rained on the heart of the City. As it was a Sunday and the commercial areas were largely unoccupied, there were not the usual fire watchers on every rooftop, and the flames spread quickly. A low ebb tide on the Thames made it difficult for firemen to draw water. At one point some 1,500 fires were raging in a strip of land that stretched from St Paul's Cathedral to the edge of Islington to the north, forming the largest continuous area of destruction in any Blitz attack on Britain. It became known as the Second Great Fire of London. The Guildhall was hit, as were several Wren churches and railway and Underground stations. Miraculously, St Paul's Cathedral itself survived the destruction: twenty-eight incendiary bombs fell on the building, including one that just penetrated the dome, which, being a mainly wooden structure covered with lead, was highly combustible. Fortunately, the bomb, having lodged in the roof, fell outwards rather than inwards and was swiftly dealt with.

Herbert Mason, chief photographer of the *Daily Mail*, recorded the destruction from his vantage point on the roof of Northcliffe House on Tudor Street, close to Fleet Street. His photograph, *St Paul's Survives*, published on the front page of the *Daily Mail* on New Year's Eve, showed the cathedral wreathed in smoke while everything else around it burned. The image became emblematic of the message that 'Britain can take it' and helped bring worldwide attention to London's position on the front line of the battle against the Nazis. It was not until the next morning that the last of the fires could finally be brought under control.

The area around the Logues' home continued to take a battering in the early months of 1941: in what was one of the deadliest attacks in south-east London, a pair of parachute mines hit Dartmouth Road, at the junction with Cheseman Street, just under a mile south of Beechgrove on 16 April. Twenty-one people were killed – six of them policemen on duty at the police station – and twenty-five were injured. Among those hurt was Charles Jennings, a policeman who lived with his family at 7 Cheseman Street and had been on fire watch on the roof of the station His wife and daughter were sheltering in a Morrison shelter in the back garden, and although their house was badly damaged, they survived.

The war was also hurting Logue's business. Many of the young men who constituted the majority of his clients had been called up by the armed forces and were unable to come for consultations. The relentless aerial bombardment also discouraged others who lived outside London from venturing to the city. To add to his woes, Beechgrove had been damaged by the bomb the previous October that landed in their neighbour's woodland. In a spirit of despair, Logue wrote on 11 January to the charity that owned the freehold of the house, asking for a suspension of his £102 8s-a-year ground rent for the duration of the war.

'Up to the present, I have been able to meet all my obliga-tions at a very great sacrifice to myself and my family,' he wrote, 'but the time has come when I am no longer able to do this, and I must ask to be allowed freedom from my ground rent until my practice resumes its flow, or until the War is ended, when I hope that I shall be able to earn a living again.'

Logue also pointed out that the house was damaged, with the loss of the chimney stacks making the lighting of fires 'a most uncomfortable business, the rooms being filled with smoke for some hours'. Could anything be done to repair at least one stack to make the one living room they were using habitable, he asked. He also claimed that the battery of 4.5 inch anti-aircraft guns in the golf links at the bottom of his garden that made the ground shake every time it was fired was slowly 'disintegrating' Beechgrove and other nearby houses. 'How long will one be able to stand this bombardment?' he asked.

The charity replied to Logue that, as an emergency measure, it was prepared to half his annual payment to £52 8s, with him owing the remainder, which would accrue interest at a rate of four per cent. Though grateful for any relief, Logue was shocked by the interest rate, which, as he pointed out when he wrote back, was considerably higher than that paid on war loan.

Then, on 30 January, apparently out of the blue, Logue received a letter from Sir Ulick Alexander, Keeper of the Privy Purse, together with a cheque for £500 – the equivalent of more than £20,000 in today's money. 'I am commanded by the King to send you the enclosed cheque for Five hundred Pounds, this being a personal present from his Majesty in recognition of the very valuable personal services you have rendered,' Alexander wrote. 'The King is well aware that in these times everyone is suffering to some extent from financial distress, but feels that you cannot well have escaped the conditions that are so generally prevailing, and his Majesty hopes that you may find this gift a useful one at the present time.'

On 1 February Logue wrote back to Alexander: 'Your letter containing his Majesty's most generous gift which arrived today has touched me more that I can say. I have been so happy working with the King, that is reward enough and now to have the unexpected recognition of my service is indeed wonderful.'

Nine days later, Logue followed up with a letter to the King himself, who was at Windsor. 'It would be impossible for me to say on paper, how deeply troubled I am with Your Majesty's kindness and generosity in making me a gift of Five Hundred Pounds,' he wrote:

As you so well know, the majority of my work is done with young men, and they of course have been joining the forces ever since the war began. I have seen them go joyfully, but my practice is suffering more and more, and that you with all your great responsibility and worry should thank me and help me so naturally has overwhelmed me. My humble service has always been at your disposal, and it has been the great privilege of my life to serve you.

Your kindly thoughtfulness has touched me many times, and my sincere and heartfelt wish is that I may be spared to serve you for many years.

May I again say how grateful I am.

Work did not dry up completely, however, and Logue acquired some new patients – among them Nicholas Mosley, the second child of the fascist leader by his first wife, Lady Cynthia Curzon. Mosley's description of his treatment decades later, by which time he was a successful novelist, provided an insight into Logue's technique. Mosley's impediment emerged when he was a young boy, though he became aware of it only when he went to prep school at the age of nine and found himself having to stand up and talk to the class. As he grew up, the young Mosley was told the way to get over his problem was to talk more slowly and carefully. This only served to make things worse by making him more self-conscious and desperate to choke back his stammer. His mother died in 1933, a few weeks before his tenth birthday, and Mosley was taken under the wing of his aristocratic aunts. By the time he was seventeen, they decided something had to be done. 'I was due to go into the army and my aunts thought my terrible stammer would be an enormous obstacle to getting on,' Mosley recalled decades later.[109] 'So in my last year at Eton I was allowed to go up to London once a week after morning work. I had an hour with Logue in his Harley Street rooms.'

Logue, Mosley recalled, was 'charming to me as a 17-year-old. He was very still and very authoritative. He tried to make me speak in a sing-song voice because he said stammerers don't stammer when they sing or act. He encouraged me to talk like someone singing, my voice going up and down in cadences. He got me reading by heart a famous speech by William Pitt the Younger which I still remember. It included the phrase: "I am accused of the atrocious crime of being a young man". He told me to speak it as though I were addressing Parliament. So I put in a few Churchillian inflections.

'I could talk all right in sing-song mode when I was with him but when I went out to get a taxi to Victoria station I sounded completely half-witted,' he added. 'I thought: "Oh hell, what's the difference between feeling like an absolute ass and stammering." I couldn't go home and talk like this to my family.'

Mosley was still stammering badly when he left Eton for the Rifle Brigade in 1940, so the army allowed him to travel from the brigade's Winchester depot to see Logue for more treatment. He still struggled: although he could bark orders on the parade ground, at other times his stammer was worse than ever – though this did not prevent him from earning his commission. Mosley's impediment was to be with him for the rest of his life, but he remained grateful to Logue. 'He gave me confidence. He gave me hope.'

The German attacks on London continued, reaching a climax on the night of 10–11 May, which was to be the deadliest since the beginning of the campaign the previous September. In the course of just under seven hours, the *Luftwaffe* flew 571 sorties and dropped 800 tons of bombs, causing 2,000 fires; 1,436 people were killed and 1,792 seriously injured. The orgy of destruction began at 11 p.m.

and the all-clear did not sound until 5.50 the next morning. This time almost the whole of London was hit: German bombers targeted all the bridges west of Tower Bridge, factories on the south side of the Thames, the warehouses at Stepney and the railway line that ran northwards from Elephant and Castle. Westminster suffered especially badly: the Abbey and the Law Courts were damaged and the House of Commons caught fire, bringing its roof down.

'In the morning there was nothing left of the famous House but a charred, black, smouldering, steaming ruin,' recalled the writer William Samson, who worked during the war as a fireman. 'The Bar no longer stood to check intruders. The Speaker's chair was lost. The green-padded leather lines of seats were charred and drenched. The ingenious, ingenuous, most typical gothic innovations of the old period had gone for ever; and with them the Chamber, its Press Gallery, its Strangers' and Ladies' galleries.'[110] One-third of London's streets were impassable and all but one railway station line was blocked for several weeks. By the following month, more than two million British homes had been destroyed, more than half of them In London.

On 16 May, the King was visiting Sandhurst. As he glanced through the list of cadets, he spotted a familiar name: that of Antony Logue who, after two years of medicine in Leeds, had suspended his studies and in November 1940 received a commission in the Scots Guards. The King asked for him to be presented and they spoke for ten minutes. The encounter was reported in the Australian press, by the *Adelaide Advertiser*, which explained to readers he was the son of a famous Adelaide-born Harley Street specialist in speech defects 'with world experience in curative speech work' who had 'attended his Majesty'. The next day, Second Lieutenant Antony Logue was posted to the Scots Guards training battalion in Pirbright, Surrey.

Laurie's military career was also progressing. By now a lance corporal in the 1st Holding Battalion of the Royal Corps of Signals, based at Catterick Camp in North Yorkshire, he was being considered for officer training. Among those who vouched for him was an old family friend, Lieutenant Colonel Arthur Waite, an Adelaide-born Anzac war hero and director of the Austin Motor Company, who had won the first Australian Grand Prix in 1928. Laurie, Waite wrote, was 'an excellent type of man for commissioned rank and for any duties he may be called upon to do in the Service ... and his personal integrity is beyond doubt'. Laurie's application was approved in June, and in September he was sent for officer training to the Royal Armoured Corps Training Unit in Sandhurst, from which he would graduate and be commissioned as a second lieutenant the following February. May 1942 was also to see the birth of his and Jo's second child, Robert.

Valentine, by contrast, had yet to sign up but was confronted daily with the effects of German bombing through his work at St George's Hospital, where he was now chief of the orthopaedic department. While he was there he met Wylie McKissock, one of the pioneers of the emerging field of neurosurgery and decided to go and train under him at Leavesden Hospital near St Albans.

In mid-May the Blitz abruptly stopped; although London and other parts of Britain continued to suffer air raids in the months that followed, the country was never again to suffer a continuous bombardment of the scale it had undergone during the previous eight months. The reason for the respite lay in events about to unfold thousands of miles to the east. Hitler's decision to conclude an alliance with Stalin in 1939 had been inspired not by a desire for peace with his eastern neighbour, but rather to buy him time. On 22 June 1941 this 'devils' alliance' came to an abrupt end when German troops, along with other European Axis members and

Finland, invaded the Soviet Union in Operation Barbarossa. Three army groups with more than 3 million soldiers, 150 divisions and 3,000 tanks smashed their way across the border into Soviet territory, taking Stalin completely by surprise. The aim was to eliminate both the country and communism, providing Germany not just with *Lebensraum* but also with access to the strategic resources that Hitler required to defeat his remaining enemies.

When Colville broke the news of the attack to Churchill that morning, the Prime Minister responded with a 'smile of satisfaction'. Despite Churchill's long history of opposition to communism, he had no doubt as to where Britain's interests lay. 'If Hitler invaded Hell I would at least make a favourable reference to the Devil in the House of Commons,' he told Colville. That evening he made a special radio address to the nation. 'No one has been a more consistent opponent of communism for the last twenty-five years. I will unsay no word I have spoken about it,' Churchill declared. 'But all this fades away before the spectacle which is now unfolding. The past, with its crimes, its follies, its tragedies, flashes away.' On 13 July Britain and the Soviet Union signed an agreement in which they mutually undertook 'to render each other assistance and support of all kinds in the present war against Hitlerite Germany'. On 21 August, a British supply convoy set off for Murmansk, the first of what would be seventy-eight such convoys to be dispatched between then and May 1945; in all some 1,400 merchant ships would be involved, escorted by ships of the British, Canadian and US navies.

After entering Soviet territory, the German forces advanced rapidly, covering a front from the North Cape to the Black Sea, thousands of miles to the south. Within the first month they had encircled large Soviet forces at Minsk and Smolensk, while armoured spearheads reached two-thirds of the way to Moscow and Leningrad. By the end of September, they had taken Kiev and advanced eastwards

and southwards towards the industrial Donbass region of eastern
Ukraine and the Crimean peninsula. They also had their sights on
the main prize, Moscow. But the onset of the Russian winter began to
take its toll; although the Germans struggled on towards the gates of
capital – and were so close some officers claimed to be able to see the
spires of the Kremlin – they were stopped by Soviet counterattacks
in early December and forced to conduct a slow retreat. A defeat
reminiscent of that suffered by Napoleon's Grand Army more than
a century earlier loomed.

On 22 October, Lionel received a letter from Hardinge on Buckingham Palace-headed paper. The envelope was marked 'secret'. 'I
have not heard anything of you for a long time I am afraid, but I
hope that all goes well with you,' Hardinge wrote. 'This is a line to
say that your services may possibly be needed here before very long,
as, for your private information, the King will have to make a speech
at the opening of Parliament.'

The speech was set for 12 November and Logue went to the palace
two days earlier. After lunch with Hardinge and several others, he
sat down with the King at 2.30. 'He was looking younger & his voice
has deepened & he was standing much straighter,' Logue noted in
his diary. 'He said that the deep therapy on his back & between the
shoulder blades had done him a lot of good.' They went through the
text, which, according to Logue, contained the 'usual stereotyped
sentences which had to be used'. He contented himself with making
some minor changes. 'The word apprehension had to come out,' he
wrote, presumably because the King would have struggled over it.
As Logue was about to leave, the King sat down and began to talk,
quizzing him about Australian politics.

When Logue returned to the palace on the day of the State
Opening, the King described how, the previous day, he and the
Queen had narrowly avoided being caught up in a bizarre incident

as they drove through Chiswick: Gunner Philip Joseph Ward, who served in an anti-aircraft unit battery, had gone on a three-hour shooting spree through west London, killing three people in cold blood and injuring several others. Ward, who had a history of mental illness, was still bitter over his expulsion from the Brentford & Chiswick Junior Conservative Association in 1937 over his treatment of a female member, and was out to get revenge. His first victim was the solicitor who had formerly chaired the Conservative committee; the others were strangers unfortunate enough to find themselves in his path. 'We had a bit of luck,' the King told Logue. 'The madman who shot up the unfortunate people at Chiswick High St did it about 30 mins before the Queen and I drove through.'

The King's speech was again brief, in accordance with wartime tradition, at just over 300 words. 'The developments of the past year have strengthened the resolution of My Peoples and of My Allies to prosecute this war against aggression until final victory,' he began. 'I well know that My People will continue to respond wholeheartedly to the great demands made upon them to furnish My Forces with the instruments of victory, and that they are determined to meet, to the utmost of their power, the needs of the Soviet Union in its heroic conflict.' The King went on to note that America was providing supplies 'on a scale unexampled in history', to praise relations with Turkey, welcome the restoration of Haile Selassie as Emperor of Ethiopia that May and to admire the fortitude with which the people of Malta were enduring the assault from the air. 'The fulfilment of the task to which we are committed will call for the unsparing effort of every one of us,' the King added. 'I am confident that My People will answer this call with the courage and devotion which our forefathers have never failed to show when our country was in danger.'

*

Then came the second dramatic development of 1941: on 7 December, the Japanese attacked the American fleet at Pearl Harbor and in the Philippines, finally bringing the might of the United States to the Allied side. It was a Sunday and the Queen was listening to the radio in her room in Windsor. She went through and told the King. 'I've just heard the most extraordinary thing on the wireless,' she said. 'The Japanese have bombed the Americans. It can't be true.'[111] They also attacked British-ruled Malaya and Hong Kong. Churchill gave the King more details at their regular Tuesday lunch.

The next day the King and Queen set off on a prearranged visit to the mining villages of South Wales. They were in Bargoed on 10 December when Lascelles was called to the telephone. He was told that the battleship, the *Prince of Wales*, had been sunk in a Japanese air attack off the coast of Malaya. The battle cruiser *Repulse* was also lost. Many on board both vessels had been saved but more than 800 lost their lives. It was a massive blow to the British presence in the Far East, since there were no spare ships to replace the two lost. The King described the sinkings as a 'national disaster'. 'I thought I was getting immune to hearing bad news, but this has affected me deeply as I am sure it has you,' he wrote to Churchill from the Royal train.[112] The next day, 11 December, in what was probably his worst strategic error, Hitler declared war on America. Hours later Washington reciprocated.

The tragedies of Pearl Harbor and Malaya were in the King's mind that Christmas when he made his broadcast, Logue at his side as ever. 'The range of the tremendous conflict is ever widening. It now extends to the Pacific,' he said. 'Truly it is a stern and solemn time.' The focus of his broadcast, though, was on our 'one great family'. '[It is] in serving each other and in sacrificing for our common good that we are finding our true life', he said, going on to praise the men fighting by sea, land and air, and the women in the services or working in factories or hospitals. He concluded:

We are coming to the end of another hard fought year. During these months our people have been through many trials, and in that true humanity which goes hand in hand with valour, have learnt once again to look for strength to God alone.

So I bid you all be strong and of a good courage. Go forward into this coming year with a good heart. Lift up your hearts with thankfulness for deliverance from dangers in the past. Lift up your hearts in confident hope that strength will be given us to overcome whatever perils may lie ahead until the victory is won.

If the skies before us are still dark and threatening, there are stars to guide us on our way. Never did heroism shine more brightly than it does now, nor fortitude, nor sacrifice, nor sympathy, nor neighbourly kindness, and with them – brightest of all stars – is our faith in God. These stars will we follow with His help until the light shall shine and the darkness shall collapse.

God bless you, everyone.

Above: The Logue family (from left: Laurie, Antony, Myrtle, Lionel, Valentine) relaxing at their summer house on Thames Ditton island, Surrey, *c.* 1932.

Right: Myrtle on Thames Ditton island, *c.* 1932.

Lionel at work, with the same photograph of Myrtle on his desk, *c.* 1936.

The Logue family on the steps of Beechgrove, before Laurie's wedding in summer 1936.

Above: An official photograph of Lionel, *c.* 1937.

Left: Laurie in his Royal Corps of Signals uniform, June 1940.

Above: Myrtle on the lawn of Beechgrove, 1940. With petrol rationed, the Logues used sheep rather than a lawnmower to keep the garden grass in check.

Left: Lionel and Myrtle with Tov, their cairn terrier, in 1940.

Beechgrove under snow during the 'big freeze' of early 1940.

WITH BEST WISHES FOR
CHRISTMAS AND THE NEW YEAR
from

George R.I.   Elizabeth R

SEPTEMBER 10TH 1940

Buckingham Palace.

The Christmas card sent by the King and Queen to the Logues, 1940, showing
the Royal Family in the bombed part of Buckingham Palace.

Left: Lionel in his ARP uniform and gas mask in September 1940.

Opposite top: St Paul's Survives, published on the front page of the *Daily Mail* on New Year's Eve 1941, showed the cathedral wreathed in smoke while everything around it burned after heavy bombing.

Opposite bottom: The King, making his annual Christmas Day broadcast, 1944.

Below: The King meets residents during a visit to Bristol following an air raid, December 1940.

WITH BEST WISHES FOR
CHRISTMAS AND THE NEW YEAR
from

George R.I.   Elizabeth R

V.E.-DAY TUESDAY MAY 8TH 1945.

Above: The Christmas card sent by the King and Queen to the Logues, 1945.

Right: Lionel looking frail on his way to a Buckingham Palace garden party with Laurie and Joe, *c.* 1950.

CHAPTER EIGHT

Letter to Rupert

When Churchill returned to London in January 1942 after more than a month in America and Canada – including his first meeting with Roosevelt since the United States' entry into the war – he was understandably upbeat. With its attacks on Pearl Harbor and on Manila, Japan had achieved at a stroke what Roosevelt's powers of statesmanship had failed to do: it had brought a united America into the war on the Allied side. As Churchill told the King, 'he was now confident of ultimate victory, as the United States of America were longing to get to grips with the enemy and were starting on a full output of men and material; the UK and USA were now "married" after many months of "walking out".[113]

In the ensuing months the Allies nevertheless suffered serial setbacks as Japanese forces swept through Asia. On 15 February 1942, Singapore, a great island fortress with a garrison of 60–70,000 men, surrendered to the Japanese after a two-week siege. Churchill described it as 'the greatest disaster to British arms which our history records' and, for the first time since taking office almost two years earlier, found himself under attack from the press and the public and in the House of Commons. The King resented the harsh treatment being meted out to his Prime Minister. 'I do wish people would get on with the job and not criticise all the time, but in a free country this has to be put up with,' he wrote to his uncle, the Earl of Athlone, the Governor General of Canada.[114]

Although Churchill was widely seen as the only person who could win the war for Britain, he was also criticized for having taken on too much by insisting on combining the roles of Prime Minister and Minister of Defence. When the matter came up during their weekly lunch on 17 February, Churchill made clear to the King he would not give up the defence portfolio. He did, however, say he was prepared to reshuffle his government; two days later he did so, and on 25 February won a vote of confidence. Yet the military reverses continued: on 9 April, combined American and Filipino forces on the Philippines' Bataan peninsula finally surrendered to the Japanese after a three-month siege. By the end of the month, British and Dutch possessions in the East Indies had been overrun by the enemy, and Allied opposition to the Japanese in the South Pacific had completely broken down. By May, British and Chinese forces had been driven from Burma, and Japan was beginning to turn its attention towards India. The Germans, meanwhile, continued to ravage Allied shipping off America's Atlantic coast, and in June launched an offensive in the Soviet Union to seize the oilfields of the Caucasus and occupy the Kuban steppe.

Nor was Britain itself spared: at the end of April, the Nazis began a series of bombing raids on historic cities such as Exeter, Norwich, Bath, York and Canterbury, killing more than 1,500 people and causing serious damage to their ancient buildings. Known as the Baedeker Raids, after the travel guide, they were thought to be intended as reprisals for the RAF's bombing of Lübeck and other historic towns in Germany, their targets chosen for their cultural and historical significance, rather than for any military value. 'We shall go out and bomb every building in Britain marked with three stars in the Baedeker guide,' Baron Gustav Braun von Stumm, a spokesman for the German Foreign Office, is reported to have boasted on 24 April, the day after the first attack, which was on Exeter. The King and Queen toured the devastated cities, listening to stories of civilians killed and of homes destroyed. When, in Exeter, the King suggested that a piece of bomb be sent for scrap, the Queen shot back: 'Let's send it back to the Germans.'[115]

There were momentous developments, too, in North Africa where Axis and Allied forces had been pushing each other back and forth across the desert since Italy's declaration of war against Britain and France in June 1940. Despite some initial successes, Italy's Tenth Army had been all but destroyed by early the following year, prompting Hitler to dispatch a German expeditionary force under Lieutenant General Erwin Rommel. Known as the Afrika Korps, it was given the task of reinforcing the Italians and blocking Allied attempts to drive them out of the region. By spring, Rommel's forces were threatening to reach the gates of Cairo. Rommel opened his attack on 26 May, forced the evacuation by the French of Bir Hachim on June 11 and a week later laid siege to Tobruk, which surrendered on 21 June. Rommel then swept eastwards out of Libya into Egypt, reaching El Alamein, a small railway town on the Egyptian coast, sixty miles west of Alexandria, on 1 July.

The fall of Tobruk was a bitter blow to the Allies. Rommel captured 32,000 Allied defenders, the port and huge quantities of supplies, and was promoted by Hitler to Field Marshall. Churchill was visiting Washington at the time and suffered the embarrassment of having the news broken to him by Roosevelt. The Prime Minister described the fall of Tobruk as 'one of the heaviest blows I can recall during the war . . . defeat is one thing, disgrace is another'. He flew back to face a censure motion in the Commons but had little difficulty in facing down what he described to the King as 'the weaker brethren' in the House of Commons, winning the vote by 475 to 25.

On 3 June, during a gap between seeing patients, Lionel wrote a letter to Myrtle's brother, Rupert Gruenert, back in Perth. 'Dear Rups,' he began:

It seems many moons since I wrote you, but really there has been so little to write about, in these times of restriction. The only subject you can let yourself go on is the war, and that alters so quickly that before the ink is dry on your letter, the situation has changed. The only thing I will say is that everything you have ever said about those lousy little bugs, the Japs, has come true. Things with us are much happier, we have not had any extensive raids since May 1941 (on London) I think that they are a bit afraid to try anything whereby they might lose a lot of planes. Myrtle has just had a delightful week at Torquay and come home looking in grand form, despite air raid warnings. Laurie is a Lieutenant in the R.A.S.C. and should be a Captain very shortly. His wife has just had a baby son, and they have named it after you. Doesn't give the kid much of a start, does it?

Val has left St George's Hospital, and is now at the hospital at St Albans. He is specializing in head injuries, and will be there for another six months when he goes on to Edinburgh. After that (if the war is still on) he will go into the air force as a specialist, and begins with the rank of Major, so he is all right.

Tony is in the Scots Guards, and is close to home so is able to slip in and have a meal with us very often. He should be a second lieutenant in 3 months' time. They are grand fellows, and I am a very proud man to think I am their father.

Beechgrove has been terribly hard to keep going, as there is no labour. Myrtle has no servants at all, and we cannot even get a man to help with cutting the lawns, so a house with 25 rooms and 5 bathrooms these times is a bit of an incubus, and as I am not allowed to use the motor mower but have to use the heavy old 'push' one, I would not like to say how big the corns on my hands are.

There is plenty of work for everyone, but there is a hell of a time in front of Europe when the mess is over.

We are all in great form, and making the most of everything. Have not seen a lemon or a banana since the war began, but our ration is good and quite sufficient for everyone.

I have just been elected a member of the Savage Club [one of London's most venerable gentlemen's clubs] and also the representative of the British Society of Speech Therapists on the board of the British Medical Association, rather a big honour. I only wish these things had come 20 years ago, when one could enjoy them so much more. I am 62 and find I cannot do the things I once could.

Do hope everything is going well with you and yours. Have not heard from, or about you for over 12 months.

This letter has been written between patients, hence its disjointed appearance. Anyhow it lets you know just how things are.

Love from us all,

Lionel

That summer brought personal tragedy for the King. On 25 August, his youngest surviving brother, George, Duke of Kent, was killed, aged forty, in an air crash. Kent had begun the war at the Admiralty, but in April 1940 transferred to the RAF. In July the following year, he assumed the rank of Air Commodore in the Welfare

Section of the RAF Inspector General's Staff and, in this role, went on official visits to RAF bases to help boost wartime morale. Tragedy struck shortly after he took off on board a Short Sunderland flying boat from RAF Invergordon bound for Iceland. Flying through a dense mist at an altitude of just 700 feet, the plane hit a hill on the Duke of Portland's Langwell estate, bounced, turned over and burst into flames. Help took a long time coming, and when it arrived it was too late for all but one of the eleven men on board, a gunner in the rear turret. The Duke must have died instantly.

The King and Queen were at Balmoral at the time of the crash, after having been joined the night before by the Duke and Duchess of Gloucester. As they were having dinner, the King was called to the telephone. Realizing the interruption meant something serious, the rest of the company assumed it was to announce the death of Queen Mary, who was then seventy-five. The truth, broken to the King by Archie Sinclair, the Secretary of State for Air, was even more devastating. Princess Marina, the Duke's Greek-born wife and mother of his three children, was at Coppins, their country house in Buckinghamshire. Unconsolable, she refused to leave her room for days afterwards, alternating between bouts of uncontrollable weeping and complete apathy.

Two days after the crash, Logue wrote to Hardinge asking him to pass on to the King his condolences: 'I nearly called on you today, but after thinking it over realized that you must be grossly overworked in these grievous times & so I decided to write instead & ask if you would be so kind, at an opportune moment, as to convey to the King my humble sorrow, at the tragic blow that has fallen on him,' Logue wrote. ' I am not writing directly to the King, as I do not desire to add even one extra letter to the great mass of correspondence he is bound to receive, but I would like him to know how deeply I feel for him in this tragedy & I know of no one who can convey this message better then yourself.' Logue received a letter back on black-edged paper. 'His Majesty . . . greatly appreciates your sympathy in the tragic blow which has befallen his family,' it read.

The Duke's funeral was held in St George's Chapel, Windsor on 29 August. 'I have attended very many family funerals in the Chapel, but none have moved me in the same way,' wrote the King.[116] 'Everybody there I knew well but I did not dare to look at any of them for fear of breaking down. His death and the form it took has shocked everybody.' The Duke of Windsor, now settled in his new role as Governor of the Bahamas, was unable to attend. The tragedy nevertheless appeared to open the prospect of an improvement in his strained relations with his family. 'My thoughts go out to you, who are so far from us all,' wrote Queen Mary in a letter in which she acknowledged how devoted he and his dead brother had been to each other. The Duke's reply to his mother's 'sweet letter' was just as warm, and he promised to write regularly in future, saying how much he longed to see her again. Yet it proved a false dawn: as far as the Duke was concerned, there could be no reconciliation until the Palace agreed to his long-running demand that his wife be styled 'Her Royal Highness' – something the King remained determined not to accept.

After returning to Balmoral following the funeral, the King visited the crash scene on what he described in his diary as a 'pilgrimage'. 'The remains of the aircraft had been removed, but the ground for 200 yds long & 100 yds wide had been scored & scorched by its trail & by flame,' he wrote.[117] 'The impact must have been terrific as the aircraft as an aircraft was unrecognisable when found.'

Despite the crucial rule he had played in helping the future King since their first meeting in his Harley Street consulting room in

1926, Logue had been careful to maintain a low profile over the years. For those who served royalty, discretion was vital. Logue never gave interviews and was largely successful in keeping his name out of the newspapers. An exception to this had come with the publication in 1929 of an authorized biography of the Duke of York, as he was then, by Taylor Darbyshire, a journalist from the Australian Press Association, who had accompanied the royal couple on their high-profile trip to Australia and New Zealand in 1927. The book, which was widely quoted from by the British press, went into great detail about all aspects of the Duke's life, but it was the pages that Darbyshire devoted to his stammer and Logue's work in tackling it that were of most interest to the newspapers. Under headlines such as 'How the Duke Won Through', 'Defect in Speech Overcome by His Pluck' and 'Man who Cured the Duke', they ran details of what one paper called his 'youthful struggle to fit himself to take his place in public life'.

Describing the Duke as 'cured' of his stutter was wishful thinking – as was clear to anyone who listened to him struggle his way through a speech or a broadcast a decade later. Yet such was the deference that continued to be shown towards the royal family by the press that his affliction – and Logue's continued work to help him tackle it – remained largely out of bounds. This became even more the case after he succeeded to the throne, even though the newspapers back in Australia could not resist publishing occasional titbits about the life of one of their most famous sons.

In September 1942, however, Logue allowed himself a rare moment in the limelight when he appeared on a BBC radio programme called *On My Selection*. The weekly show featured an Australian or New Zealander living in Britain who was asked to choose the records they would take back home with them to remind them of their time in the mother country. Its format was similar to that of *Desert Island Discs*, which debuted that January and was still running more than seven decades later.

Because of the time difference with Australia, the programme, which went out live, was to be broadcast very early in the morning. A few days earlier, Logue received a letter from Cecil Madden, an executive from the BBC's External Services, with an unlikely offer: would he like to spend the night before in Madden's box in the Criterion Theatre in Piccadilly Circus? The theatre had been requisitioned during wartime by the BBC; its auditorium, being underground, was an ideal studio safe from the Blitz. From there it was only a short walk to Broadcasting House, which would ensure Logue would be in the studio in good time for the broadcast. 'It's a bit unusual and has a mattress and sheeting in it and is in the Upper Circle,' Madden wrote of his box, 'but the attendants would look after you very well and call on you with tea in a most baronial manner. It would mean that you would be on the spot.' It is not clear whether Logue took him up on his offer.

The programme's presenter, Joan Gilbert, did not attempt to explain to her Antipodean listeners her guest's connection with the King, describing him merely as 'Lionel Logue of Adelaide and for many years of London'. Logue did not refer to the nature of his work either. Instead, in introducing his choices that included 'Bird Songs at Eventide' (set by Eric Coates), *O Mimì, tu più non torni* from *La bohème* and Bach's 'Jesu, Joy of Man's Desiring', he spoke about the 'delicious music' made by birds in his garden at Beechgrove, his love of opera at Covent Garden – sadly closed for the duration of the war – and his growing taste for the simple music that he had disdained when young. His last choice was 'I'll Walk Beside You', a sentimental ballad that had become hugely popular during the war, sung by the Irish tenor, John McCormack. The song, he said, was intended 'as a tribute to the lass who has stood by my side for thirty-six happy years, and helped me so valiantly over the rough places'. Logue ended the broadcast with a few words to family and friends back in Australia: 'To my sisters and my brother Herbert, and our multitude of friends under the Southern Cross, our love and regard. And to all those mothers and fathers, whose fighting sons we love to entertain over here and whom we are proud to hail as our kinsmen, our good wishes are with you.'

Logue seems to have enjoyed his encounter with Gilbert but complained in his diary that making the programme had wasted hours of his time, obliging him to spend the following weekend catching up on his correspondence. 'The last letter I am writing is to a most charming girl to say how much I appreciated her kindly help last Thursday – and if there was any success it was entirely due to her, and I made my bow and say Thank you very much Miss Gilbert.'

By summer 1942, the tide of war was beginning to turn in favour of the Allies. Convinced that one more push eastwards would get him into Cairo, Rommel launched an offensive, but was stopped in his tracks by Claude Auchinleck, the British Commander-in-Chief of the Middle Eastern theatre, who had created a formidable defensive barrier around El Alamein. There was good news for the Allies elsewhere too: the Soviet Red Army began a summer offensive that would take them from the Don to the Elbe, while the Americans began to stay the Japanese advances in Asia and the Pacific. On 17 October, Roosevelt wrote to the King: 'Perhaps I can sum it up by saying that on the whole the situation of all of us is better in the Autumn of 1942 than it was last spring, and that, while 1943 will not see a complete victory for us, things are on the up-grade, while things for the Axis have reached the peak of their effectiveness.'[118] The President's optimism proved well-founded. The appointment of Lieutenant General Bernard Montgomery as head of the Eighth

Army in August in place of Auchinleck, who had lost Churchill's confidence by failing to follow up his success at El Alamein, gave new impetus to the Allied effort in North Africa. Montgomery, who vowed to 'hit Rommel for six out of Africa', restructured his force and did wonders for morale. 'I want to impose on everyone that the bad times are over, they are finished!' he told his troops. 'Our mandate from the Prime Minister is to destroy the Axis forces in North Africa . . . It can be done, and it will be done!'

After beating off a German attack soon after his appointment, Monty, as he was universally known, on 23 October launched a successful counter-attack. The Allies had 200,000 men and 1,100 tanks ranged against the Axis's 115,000 men and 559 tanks, and also benefitted from 300 Sherman tanks that had been hastily shipped to Egypt from America. Rommel was back home in Germany on sick leave, but hurried back to Africa to lead his men. Heavily outnumbered, he warned Hitler on 2 November that his army faced annihilation. The Nazi leader would not tolerate any talk of surrender: 'It would not be the first time in history that a strong will has triumphed over the bigger battalions,' Hitler told him the next day. 'As to your troops, you can show them no other road than that to victory or death.' The *Panzerarmee* had already begun to retreat by the time the order was received, however, and at midday on 4 November, Rommel's last defences had caved in. His remaining forces retreated to Tunisia. Montgomery's victory proved a turning point in the North African campaign and indeed the Second World War. It was said, with some exaggeration, that before El Alamein the Allies had never won a victory, but after El Alamein they never suffered a defeat.

Logue was one of the first to hear the good news. That afternoon he was at Buckingham Palace with the King going through the speech he was due to give at the State Opening of Parliament, set for 12 November, when the telephone rang. The two men looked at each other. Such sessions were considered sacrosanct; the King had given orders that he was not to be disturbed unless he was needed urgently.

'Well, this must be important,' the King said, walking to the table and picking up the receiver. He immediately became excited.

'Yes! Yes! Well read it out, read it out,' he said, before adding 'The enemy is in full retreat. Good news, thanks,' and hung up.

Smiling, he turned to Logue.

'Did you hear that?' he asked, and repeated the gist of the news from El Alamein. 'Well,' he added. 'That's grand.'

By the time Logue returned home, news of the victory had reached the newspapers; vendors had drawn red, white and blue frames around posters announcing Rommel's retreat. That evening the King wrote in his diary: 'A victory at last, how good it is for the nerves.'[119]

The Allies kept up the momentum: four days later, on the morning of 8 November, a combined Anglo-American force of more than 70,000 men landed on the coast of north-west Africa, launching what was known as Operation Torch. Planned and supervised by General Dwight D. Eisenhower, newly appointed as supreme commander of North African operations, it consisted of three task forces intended to seize the key ports and airports in Morocco and Algeria, both of which countries were nominally in the hands of the Vichy France regime. The Western Task force targeted Casablanca; the Centre Task Force aimed at Oran, over the border in Algeria, and the Eastern Task Force went for Algiers. Successful completion of these operations was to be followed by an advance eastwards into Tunisia.

Intended to open a second front in North Africa, this was the first major offensive undertaken on Allied initiative rather than in response to enemy action. It was quickly rewarded with success:

Oran surrendered on 9 November and Casablanca on the 10th. The same day Eisenhower struck a deal with Admiral Francois Darlan, the pro-Vichy commander of all French forces in North Africa, making him French High Commissioner. In return Darlan ordered his men to cease resistance and to cooperate with the Allies. Joining forces with such a notorious collaborator with the Germans was hugely controversial, but Eisenhower defended the move as 'a temporary expedient, justified only by the stress of battle'; the Germans responded by occupying Vichy France. Few tears were shed when Darlan was assassinated a few weeks later by a French monarchist.

An elated King sent a generous tribute to Churchill: 'When I look back and think of all the many arduous hours of work you have put in, and the many miles you have travelled, to bring this battle to such a successful conclusion you have every right to rejoice, while the rest of our people will one day be very thankful to you for what you have done,' he wrote. Churchill responded in equally effusive manner: 'No minister in modern times, and I daresay in long days past, has received more help and comfort from the King, and this has brought us all thus far with broadening hopes and now I feel to brightening skies.'[120]

The tide was turning, too, in Russia. In August 1942 the Germans launched an offensive to capture Stalingrad and scored initial gains, pushing the Soviet defenders back into narrow zones along the west bank of the Volga River. On 19 November, however, the Red Army launched Operation Uranus, a two-pronged attack that targeted the weaker Romanian and Hungarian armies protecting the flanks of the German Sixth Army. These forces were overrun and the Germans cut off and surrounded. Ordered by Hitler to remain, the remnants of the Sixth Army fought on but in February 1943 finally surrendered. Taken together, Stalingrad and El Alamein were to prove a turning point in the war.

*

As 1942 drew to a close, Logue's three sons were all involved in the war effort in different ways: that November, after almost a year based in Wanstead, in north-east London, the 1st Battalion of the Scots Guards in which Antony was serving was finally mobilized for service overseas and moved north by train to headquarters in Ayrshire. It was not clear where they would be deployed, but North Africa or India seemed most likely.

Valentine, meanwhile, was continuing his training as a neuro-surgeon and had been promoted to assistant to Wylie McKissock. That November their unit was moved out of Leavesden Hospital and transferred to Atkinson-Morley, a convalescent home in Wimbledon that was part of St George's which had been equipped with a new operating theatre and lent to them. It was a curious experience for Valentine to return to his former hospital. As he wrote to Laurie: 'It sounds a fair proposition but I don't know how long I can stomach walking in the shadow of St George's.'

Laurie, himself, had set off at the end of September with his unit for Nairobi – although strict censorship rules prevented him from revealing his destination to his family, whose letters to him were full of speculation about where it might be. They knew it must be warm – which, stuck as they were in grey, wintery London, made them jealous – but nothing more than that. 'The old lady is still speculating on your whereabouts,' Valentine wrote to him on 5 December. 'We have come to the conclusion that the only place you can't be is Australia . . . I must say I find England rather dull at the moment, but I hope to see the world myself in the not too distant future.'

For her part, Myrtle was continuing to help the troops passing through Australia House: by 1942 the social centre had grown into what became known as the Boomerang Club: spread over two floors, it was a place where Australian servicemen could obtain advice about accommodation, have a drink, meal or haircut, play billiards or the piano and catch up with friends – or with news of those who had been killed. The BBC made weekly broadcasts from the club featuring personal messages from servicemen to their relatives back home. Myrtle helped out with the lunches; sometimes they fed between 300 and 400 men a day. She wondered where they all came from.

Myrtle's letters to her sons provide an insight into life on the home front, with both its ups and downs. 'Our poor little sheep was chopped today,' she wrote to Laurie that November. 'As you may have noticed, he was a ram and recently has been feeling rather alone. As he is very strong I have been frightened he might bull me from the top slopes. I have to sell him to the Pool and will be able to have a joint off him.' The other animals she kept at Beechgrove were about to suffer the same fate. 'The geese are all being chopped for Christmas, probably to feed the hospital opposite – 50% of my rabbits go to the Pool, and I shall be glad to get rid of them, it's no joke in the winter to find food for them all, and the work is considerable.'

Christmas meant another royal broadcast. A couple of days before, Logue rehearsed it with the King, whom he found to be in excellent form. The speech itself required a little surgery: Logue didn't like passages that the Prime Minister had written into the text as they didn't seem right coming out of the King's mouth. 'It was typical Churchill and could have been recognised by anyone,' Logue complained in his diary. 'With the King's help, we cut out adjectives and the Prime Minister.'

The weather was fine, despite a touch of fog, and, unlike the previous two years, there was no snow. Logue was again summoned to join the royal family for the festivities. The Christmas tree looked much nicer and better decorated than the year before; to his doting eyes a decoration sent by Myrtle had made all the difference. When the Queen came in, she walked over to Logue and told him how pleased she was to see him. To his surprise, she then asked him to repeat a trick he had been showing a couple of the equerries before lunch: how to breathe using only one lung. Logue happily performed his party piece, during which only one side of his chest expanded as he inhaled, but then warned her and the two princesses not to attempt to imitate him.

Lunch was a fairly simple affair: turkey, plum puddings and grapes, washed down with beer rather than wine. Just after 2.30, Logue followed the King into his study for a final run through of the speech. At 2.55 they entered the broadcasting room, he and Wood synchronized watches, and at 2.58 the Queen came in to wish her husband good luck. A few seconds later the three red lights went on and, with a glance in Logue's direction, the King began.

'It is at Christmas more than any other time, that we are conscious of the dark shadow of war,' he said. 'Our Christmas festival to-day must lack many of the happy, familiar features that it has had from our childhood ... But though its outward observances may be limited, the message of Christmas remains eternal and unchanged. It is a message of thankfulness and of hope – of thankfulness to the Almighty for His great mercies, of hope for the return to this earth of peace and good will.' Logue followed the printed text for a couple of paragraphs, but then stopped doing so because it was going so well; it seemed all the work he and the King had done together was 'bearing fruit'.

The King went on to speak of the great contribution being made to the war effort by the other members of the Empire – and also by America. He ended with a story Abraham Lincoln once told about a boy who was carrying a much smaller child up a hill. 'Asked whether the heavy burden was not too much for him, the boy answered, "It's not a burden, it's my brother". The King concluded his speech: 'So let us welcome the future in a spirit of brotherhood, and thus make a world in which, please God, all may dwell together in justice and peace.'

After twelve minutes it was over. Logue was delighted by what he had heard. 'It is a grand thing to be the first to congratulate a King, and letting a few seconds go by to make sure we were off the air, I grabbed him by the arm, and in my excitement said "splendid",' Logue wrote in his diary. 'He grinned and said, "I think that's the best we have done, Logue. I will be back in London in February, let us keep the lessons going"'. The Queen came in, kissed him fondly and said, "That was splendid, Bertie". Logue left for John Gordon's house, where he had more turkey, only this time accompanied by champagne.

The newspapers were impressed, too. 'Both in manner and in matter, the King's broadcast yesterday was the most mature and inspiring that he has yet made,' commented the *Glasgow Herald*. 'It worthily maintained the tradition of Christmas Day broadcasts.' Churchill, the greatest orator of them all, called the King to congratulate him on how well he had done.

On Boxing Day, the King sent Logue a handwritten letter: 'My dear Logue, I'm so glad that my broadcast went off so well yesterday,' he wrote. 'I felt altogether different and I had no fear of the microphone. I am sure that those visits that you have paid me have done me a great deal of good & I must keep them up during the new year. Thank you so very much for all your help. With all good wishes for 1943.'

Logue wrote back, full of enthusiasm:

Your Majesty,
    You certainly have the nicest, and most human way of doing things, as nothing in the world could have been appreciated

more, or given me greater happiness, than your most welcome letter.

To-day my telephone has been beating a tattoo, all manner of people have been ringing to congratulate you, saying how they wished they could write & let you know how much they enjoyed the broadcast. As I said on Friday, you approached the microphone in quite a different spirit, almost as if it were your friend and never looked like being held up.

I will be honoured to help the appointments going, and will get in touch when you return to London. In the excitement of Christmas Day, it slipped my memory to say Thank You to the Queen & Yourself for your card & to say how much I appreciate & value it. I thoroughly enjoyed my whole day at the Castle & think it is a wonderful augury for 1943.

Myrtle was not there to share her husband's triumph. On 22 December, she had set off for a week's holiday in Torquay with Valentine, who had been given some free time by McKissock, who was concerned at how hard his protégé was working at the hospital. 'We had the most lovely weather, warm with no wind, we wore neither coat nor hat and did long walks over the beautiful country,' she wrote to Laurie on her return:

It is so lovely down there, very reminiscent of Capri and the French Riviera minus their smells. He [Valentine] danced each night, whilst I played bridge or danced also. I made him visit the spa and have Vichy Baths and a Sun Ray afterwards. And on other days we swam in the indoor pool, which is slightly heated. Tony has written us a good many letters over Christmas but it seems that he will not be home for some time. I am sending on your letter to him to read. I am enclosing one result of his visit to the photographer, not bad is it?

We killed four geese . . . the fifth I am keeping until Tony can get home. But she is becoming so tame and follows us around like a dog, so it will be difficult to kill her. We sent a hen and a rabbit to the Waites for Christmas. Did you hear H.M's broadcast, it was easily the best ever, and your father got the most delightful letter of thanks from him after it was all over. Also got a letter from the Queen's Lady-in-waiting, thanking me for some decoration I had sent to the princesses for their Christmas tree.

CHAPTER NINE

Cutting the Gordian Knot

It was 12.30 on 20 January 1943, and the younger children in Sand-hurst Road School in Catford, south-east London, were sitting down for lunch. Their older schoolmates were getting ready for a trip to the theatre to see *A Midsummer Night's Dream*. A seven-year-old in the playground looked up after hearing what sounded like the roar of an RAF bomber and waved. Seconds later, the plane's pilot, Hauptman Heinz Schumann, cut her down with a round of machine-gun fire. Then, turning his Focke-Wulf FW 190A-4 and diving again, he released a single 1,100 pound bomb into the school building. The air raid warning had sounded far too late for the children and their teachers to take cover. In a serious failure by London's air defences, no barrage balloons had gone up.

Molly Linn, who had just turned twelve, looked out of the window moments before Schumann unloaded his deadly cargo. 'The pilot was wearing a leather helmet and goggles, but it didn't occur to me that he was German,' she recalled more than six decades later, the memory of the day's horrors still fresh.[121] 'His mouth was drawn back and for a few seconds I thought he was grinning. Then I realised he was snarling, and I saw him reach forward and do something with the controls. He was probably releasing the bomb at that very second.'

The carnage was appalling: thirty-two children and six staff were killed; sixty were hurt, many buried for hours under the rubble. 'It was a terrible sight,' one man who had been cycling nearby and rushed to the scene told *The Times*.[122] 'We started dragging the debris aside and pulling the kiddies out, handing them out on boards through the window. Most of the children were badly wounded. Two were jammed in the fireplace.' Six children later died in hospital, while hundreds of parents hunted desperately for the missing. The girl in the playground was never identified.

Schumann's plane was one of twenty-eight Focke-Wulf fighter-bombers that had taken off at noon from an airfield in German-occupied France. Escorted by Messerschmitt Bf 109 fighters, they were on a mission to attack any large targets of opportunity in what the Germans called a *Terrorangriff* (terror attack). It is not known whether the pilot had realized that his target, which was several storeys high, was a school rather than a block of flats or factory – though the raid was apparently intended as a retaliation for the RAF bombing of Berlin three days earlier. Schumann himself was killed in action that November.

The devastation was not confined to the school. According to reports in newspapers the next day, nine or ten people were killed by bombs dropped on a bank and public house, while three women and six young children died when another bomb hit a café. The raiders, flying at roof-top height, also machine gunned a train approaching London as well as a railway station, killing several people, including children and, in another district, shot at shoppers and at men working on their allotments. A team of girls were hoisting a barrage balloon when it was hit, caught fire and fell blazing, trapping them beneath. Several were taken to hospital with serious burns.

In accordance with the rules of British wartime censorship, the precise location of each incident was not given, for fear the enemy could use the information to fine-tune future attacks. German broadcasters nevertheless seized on the day's attacks as proof of their ability to cause the kind of damage to London by day that the RAF could manage against Berlin only at night. *The Times* was having none of it. 'Yesterday's daylight raid by a small number of fighter bombers was, among other things, a revelation of German reactions to the increasing inferiority of the *Luftwaffe* to the air strength arrayed against it in and around Europe,' a leader thundered.[123] 'No military damage worth mentioning was done by the attack. None indeed could have been inflicted by so small and lightly armed a force; and the killing of school children and the machine-gunning of suburban streets make up the sum of the raiders' achievement. As a sequel to the two recent British attacks on Berlin this raid may be described as both retaliatory and propagandist.'

The school, in Minard Road, was just four miles east of Beech-grove, but Lionel and Myrtle had been out at the time of the attack. Although minor compared with the relentless bombardment London had suffered during the Blitz, the raid served as a reminder that the Germans were still capable of striking at the heart of their enemy. 'I returned home to find we had been machine gunned,' Myrtle wrote almost matter-of-factly to Laurie on 8 February. 'The Huns just came over at treetop height, then flew up and down the hill gunning the houses. Nobody hurt, but one of our attic windows was smashed. We had had a nasty raid on the previous Sunday, which was just like old times and I did my dodge under the table.'

Myrtle's mood nevertheless remained remarkably upbeat. In late January, she received a telegram from Antony, announcing he was coming down from Scotland for a belated Christmas celebration.

'Kill the fatted goose,' he wrote. When he arrived at Beechgrove, the family sat down to a dinner of Australian ham followed by a plum pudding. Myrtle made the most of her youngest's brief stay; most days the two of them went out to the cinema or to see a show, and Valentine came round to visit almost every night after work.

The weather was also smiling on them, allowing Myrtle to busy herself in the garden and look after their growing collection of animals. 'We are having the most divine winter: warm with lovely sunshine. The best ever,' she wrote to Laurie. 'I have three young families of bunnies, which is rather unusual and they are all about 14 days old. My hens [are] laying bigger and better eggs upon minced raw potato peelings and minced acorns for their night meal . . . How I wish you were home to disbud the Azalea from last year's flowering. I am afraid my blooming this year may be scant, however it will be interesting to see . . . We are all well darling and so is your family, so don't worry about any of us. Val envies you tremendously, he's working so hard at getting wonderful experience.'

In the same letter, Myrtle told Laurie they had finally solved the mystery of his location: 'We have just received an aerogram from you in which you describe the marvellous view of Mount Kenya and Kilimanjaro,' she wrote. 'So it must be Nairobi.'

Antony, meanwhile, was about to leave the peace and quiet of Scotland for his first taste of war. His destination was North Africa. Although Operation Torch had got off to a strong start, Eisenhower had not been able to achieve his goal of taking Tunisia. His forces had instead been halted in the bleak, bare hills a day's march from Tunis, the capital. Therefore, while the British Eighth Army pushed westwards from El Alamein, it was decided to assemble a far larger force than had been initially dispatched to attack from the west. The British element in this force was the First Army, within which was the 24th Guards Brigade, which included the 1st Battalion, in which Antony was serving.

Since moving to Ayrshire the previous November, the battalion had been in a state of readiness for what was expected to be a rapid deployment; instead it remained in Scotland. Finally there came the order to move: on 26 February, after a brief train journey to Gourock, they boarded a coastal steamer that took them to the SS *Samaria*, a former ocean liner, moored about three miles out in the Clyde. The ship lay at anchor until the night tide of 1 March and then set sail; the *Samaria* was accompanied by six other vessels and an escort of three destroyers and three corvettes. On the afternoon of 9 March, the *Samaria* docked in Algiers rather later than planned after an enforced detour to avoid U-boats. As the men waited to disembark, they came under attack from German fighters, but two of the planes were shot down. From there they moved on by boat to Bône and then had a long drive westwards to Bej, before moving off again and taking up defensive positions between there and Medjaz-el-bab. No sooner had they got themselves settled than they were on the move again, this time to relieve the Coldstream Guards, who were being sent to the rear for training. The Scots Guards formed the centre battalion of the brigade, with the Irish Guards on their left and the Grenadier Guards on their right. Their main activity was patrolling, but it was a perilous business: they were almost completely surrounded by minefields and most days came under attack from Stuka dive-bombers.

Over the following few weeks Antony and his fellow Guards were involved in fierce fighting, some of the bloodiest of which was on 28 April when they launched an attack on the Bou, a hill on the east of the River Medjerda. Their objective lay about two miles away through cornfields; the Guards were told to deploy to a distance of ten feet between men. A vivid account was provided by a Guardsman named Spencer. 'From the moment we started until the time we were held up we were under heavy machine-gun and mortar fire,' he wrote:

> We hadn't advanced far before we had casualties. A mortar bomb fell in the midst of No. 16 Platoon H.Q., injuring four men. One man Guardsman Doherty died shortly after through his wounds. This did not deter the other men, who kept the three lines as if they were on a parade ground. Captain Stockton, who up to this time had shown no fear at all and was a shining example to the other men in the company was killed by a mortar bomb which fell right in front of him. This was a sad blow.

Other casualties swiftly followed. 'By this time we were a very depleted force, and wounded were lying all over the place,' Spencer continued. 'Practically all the N.C.Os were wounded and we had only one stretcher bearer with us – Guardsman McDonald – who was doing the work of four men.'

Antony was among the wounded, having been hit by shrapnel from a mortar bomb. He was roughly bandaged but warned that there were no medics nearby and told to hold on to his side. He was then pulled under a jeep, where he had to wait for some time before help came. He was unconscious for four days.

While Antony was being treated in hospital for his injuries, the Guards pressed on. On 7 May, the British 7th Armoured Division captured Tunis, while the US II Army Corps took Bizerte, the last remaining port in Axis hands. Six days later, the Axis forces in North Africa surrendered. 'It is an overwhelming victory,' the King recorded in his diary.[124] In a telegram to Churchill, he spoke of the campaign in North Africa reaching a 'glorious conclusion,' attributing its success to the Prime Minister's 'vision and unflinching determination in the face of early difficulties', adding: 'The African campaign has immeasurably increased the debt that this country, and indeed all the United Nations, owe to you.'[125] Churchill replied in similar fashion.

The victory was seized on by the King as a reason to visit his armies in North Africa and to share with them his pride in what they had achieved. He knew his presence would not just boost the morale of the British and Imperial troops of the First and Eighth Armies; it would also be good for relations with the Americans and the French. There was a personal motivation too; it was three years since his last visit abroad, to the British Expeditionary Force in France, and he was desperate for a break from the daily routine of working at his desk, granting audiences and holding investitures.

The King had first raised the idea with Churchill in March, by which time it was clear that it was no longer a matter of *if* but *when* the Allied forces in North Africa would prevail. Churchill was supportive and, a few days later, the war cabinet gave the King the necessary assent for the trip when he dined with them at 10 Downing Street. Plans were drawn up under conditions of extreme secrecy; it was decided the King would travel incognito as 'General Lyon'. Although he was looking forward to being with his troops again, he had last-minute doubts as to whether he should leave Britain at such a critical moment. A nervous flyer, he was also not looking forward to the journey. The day before his departure, the King summoned his solicitor and put all his affairs in order. 'I think it is better on this occasion to leave nothing to chance,' he wrote in his diary.[126]

The trip was set to begin on 11 June. That morning came news that the Italians had surrendered the heavily fortified island of Pantellaria, described by Mussolini as 'the Gibraltar of the Central

Mediterranean'. The King flew off from Northolt airport that evening aboard a specially fitted York transport aircraft accompanied, among others, by Hardinge, his private secretary. The original programme had called for a refuelling stop in Gibraltar, but the Rock was shrouded in dense fog and they had to continue straight to North Africa. In the light of the misgivings the King had expressed about the flight, the change of plan caused alarm in London. The Queen told Queen Mary she had experienced an 'anxious few hours', in which she 'imagined every sort of horror & walked up & down my room staring at the telephone'.[127]

The King's plane finally landed in Algiers shortly after noon the next day. In the two weeks that followed, he travelled more than 5,000 miles across Algeria, Tunisia and Libya in the stifling heat, meeting the British commanders, Generals Alexander, Montgomery and Wilson, and their divisional and corps commanders, as well as Generals Eisenhower and de Gaulle, who had moved his head-quarters from Britain to Algiers in May so as to be again on French territory. The King also made a point of visiting his troops, not just on the parade ground but also at play, turning up unannounced on a beach where 500 of them were bathing – earning him an ovation and a rendition of 'For he's a jolly good fellow'. At his villa in Algiers he hosted a garden party for 180 British and American soldiers. The future Prime Minister, Harold Macmillan, recently appointed Minister Resident to Allied Forces Headquarters, proclaimed it a 'tremendous success . . . H.M. did very well and was most gracious to everybody. The Americans were really delighted, and letters about it will reach every distant part of the U.S.A.'[128] In Tunisia, the King watched a performance by an Entertainments National Service Association (ENSA) troupe on a white marble terrace in the grounds of a villa in Hammamet. Among those performing was the actress Vivien Leigh. 'It was a night of perfect beauty with a huge moon which shone on the sea only about 30 yards behind where the audience was sitting,' she recalled. Afterwards she and other members of the cast were presented to the King. 'He was looking extremely well and never stuttered once the whole time,' she noted.[129]

The stress, coupled with high temperatures and an upset stomach, also brought out the less pleasant side of the King's character. Macmillan found him often difficult and uncooperative. Sometimes he snapped: when one of the commanders, Brigadier Robert Hinde, was presented to him, the King asked if they had met before.

'I don't think so,' replied Hinde.

'You b-b-b-bloody well ought to know,' the King spluttered back.[130]

On his way to Britain, the King made a brief visit to the 'island fortress' of Malta whose highly strategic position in the Mediterranean had earned it a battering from the Germans. It was a risky undertaking: the island was still being subjected to enemy air raids, and Sicily, sixty miles to the north, remained in the hands of Axis forces. Nevertheless, on the night of 19 June, in conditions of extreme secrecy, the King set off from Tripoli abroad the cruiser *Aurora*. Shortly after eight the next morning, in brilliant sunshine, the King, in his white naval uniform, stood on a specially constructed platform in front of the bridge as the ship slowly made its way into the Grand Harbour at Valletta. He had a lump in his throat as he lifted his hand in salute to the thousands of islanders who had turned out to cheer him. He spent the whole day touring the island and received an enthusiastic reception from crowds lining streets that had been hastily decorated with flags and flowers. 'You have made the people of Malta very happy today, sir,' the Lieutenant Governor told him as he prepared to board the Aurora back that evening.

'But I have been the happiest man in Malta today,' the King replied.[131]

He landed back at Northolt aboard a four-engine bomber, escorted by a squadron of Spitfires, at 6 a.m. on 25 June. Tanned and dressed in the tropical uniform of a Field Marshal, he was met by Churchill at the airport and they talked about his trip as they drove back together to Buckingham Palace.

Two weeks later, Logue was summoned by the King for what would be their first meeting of the year. The hiatus in their relationship was not for want of trying on Logue's part. That March, he had sent the King a note suggesting they recommence their sessions. 'Your Majesty,' he wrote. 'In your greatly valued letter to me on December 26th last, you were gracious enough to say that you would like to continue our weekly appointments about March as they had been of value to you. This letter is to say that I am at your command & will be only too pleased to make any appointment you desire.'

The King did not take up the offer, but he did have another pleasant surprise for Logue: on the eve of the Coronation in 1937, he had been made a Member of the Royal Victorian Order. Now, in the 1943 Birthday Honours, published on 2 June, he was promoted to the rank of Commander in the order. 'I am deeply grateful and very touched at your Majesty's thought for me, and I hope to be a loyal commander of the order,' Logue wrote back. He was formally confirmed on the King's official birthday, celebrated on the second Thursday of June, though the investiture was not held until just over a year later.

During their meeting, the King told Logue about his experiences in North Africa. 'He apologized for not seeing me the day he got back, but the War Cabinet came along at my time and he had meant to ring me up all morning,' Logue recorded in his diary. 'He said the trying part of the trip is the vibrations in the plane – which gets on your nerves. The water and food had affected them all and they all had tummy troubles. He had loved the swimming and the climate.

When he got back he had changed and put on heavy clothes, only to have to change again as he was too hot.' As Logue went to leave, the King surprised him with an unexpected – and candid – tribute to the importance of the help he had given him over the years. 'I wonder where I would have been now, if I never met you, Logue,' he said. 'In a mad house, I should think.'

A major upheaval, meanwhile, was brewing in the royal household, even though Logue did not appear to have been aware of it. At its centre was Hardinge. As loyal a servant to George VI as he had been to Edward VIII and George V before him, Hardinge was admired by those who worked with him for his serious-mindedness, great administrative and executive talents and his highly developed sense of duty. But he was also arrogant, aloof and an often impossible colleague. Macmillan, who met Hardinge during the royal tour of North Africa found him 'idle, supercilious, without a spark of imagination or vitality', adding damningly: 'He just doesn't seem to live in the modern world at all. He would have been out of date in the 1900s.'[132]

It was Hardinge's increasingly fraught relationship with the King and Queen that proved his undoing. As principal private secretary, he was meant to be the main channel of communication – in both directions – between the monarch and the outside world. But their disagreement over appeasement, with Hardinge unhappy at the unwavering support the King had given Chamberlain over his attempts to do a deal with Hitler, had cast a shadow over their early relationship and things had continued to deteriorate in the years since. After having been allowed considerable freedom of action over state business by the two former monarchs he had served, Hardinge resented George VI's insistence on seeing everything for himself – and even more so the Queen's determination to become involved in matters he did not consider were anything to do with her.

He was also uncomfortable with the more informal atmosphere that prevailed under the King and was driven mad by the Queen's lack of punctuality. 'He and the King were so temperamentally incompatible that they were driving themselves crazy,' wrote Lascelles, who as Hardinge's deputy could see at close hand the deterioration of the relationship between the two men. "The situation had become so bad that something had to be done about it.'[133]

Lascelles believed it was down to the royal family to 'cut the Gordian knot', but despaired of them actually doing anything: Bertie Clarendon, the Lord Chamberlain, 'who should properly have wielded the scissors, could not be trusted with negotiating a change of scullery maids, let alone of private secretaries', he felt. So it fell to Lascelles himself to act. The moment came after the King returned from North Africa. Lascelles was angry that Hardinge had not briefed him properly before leaving and protested to him. Hardinge responded by sending back Lascelles a note 'so impertinent that I had no alternative but to write out my resignation to the King'. Then, in a further bizarre twist, Hardinge himself offered his resignation, too, and his was the resignation that the King accepted – apparently without hesitation. When Lascelles suggested they give his boss six months' leave before reaching a decision, the King replied emphatically: 'Certainly not – he might come back.'[134] And so it was Lascelles, a more genial figure, who took his place at the King's side. The official version, as reported by the 'Court Circular' in *The Times*,[135] was that Hardinge had tendered his resignation after being ordered by his doctors to 'take a prolonged rest' and that this had been accepted by the King 'with great regret'.

Logue had also had his disagreements over the years with Hardinge, who, he felt, had never appreciated the importance of his work and would insert phrases in the King's speeches that Logue knew would prove problematic. 'It is astonishing that I cannot get them to understand that a speech may read very well, but be a perfect devil to deliver,' Logue wrote in his diary after one such clash:

> They rejoice in alliteration, surely the hardest things to say. Hardinge's statement to me, that, as long as the King's speeches read well in the papers, it doesn't matter how they are delivered, is so absurd that it hardly require an answer.
>
> But Hardinge is essentially a secretary used to the written and not the spoken word. When the people hear the King broadcast they know it is the King and hear what he says – but when they read a speech by him in the newspapers – they know that he did not write it.

Logue nevertheless had the good grace to write to Hardinge to wish him well. 'In the papers yesterday I read the, to me, unwelcome news that you had resigned from the position of secretary to the King,' he wrote. 'This took some digesting, as I have got so used to seeing you & consulting with you . . . I am going to miss you more than I can say. I could not let you go, without thanking you, for your great courtesy & many acts of kindness extending over many years, & it would hurt me to even think that I would not contact you again. I do hope that you are soon in much better health.'

Just over a week later, Hardinge replied: 'Thank you so much for your most kind letter of July the 19th. The strain of the last seven years has proved too great, and I just could not go on any longer. You and I have managed to get over some pretty awkward obstacles together, and I should hate to think that we should not see anything of one another in the future.

'I hope after some months of complete rest to be fit again, but during this time I shall not be showing up very much.'

Logue, now in his sixties, was also beginning to suffer from poor health. After several months during which he felt increasingly unwell, he was diagnosed with a stomach ulcer. In August 1943, he went into hospital for an operation. The King, who was having his traditional summer break at Balmoral, was kept informed of Logue's progress. A letter that Miéville sent Logue on 26 August showed the affection in which he was held in the Palace. 'I was delighted to get a letter from your good lady this evening telling me the glad news that the operation was successfully completed & that all was going as well as could be hoped,' he wrote:

That is just fine & I am wasting a shilling on a telephone call up North, as unaccountable as it may seem, I know that H.M. will want to know as soon as possible & that he will quite likely be pleased to hear that all is well! It beats me!

Well! I suppose you have got the prettiest nurse in the hospital looking after you! I only wish that I could come & see, but I am very much tied up here & cannot get away for a minute. I am alone in my glory. I came down South yesterday, & Tommy Lascelles went up North.

H.M. was in grand form with the fleet. He is always at his best and happiest when he is with the Navy. He is completely at ease. He knows their drill and talks their language & I must say that they are a remarkably fine lot of men. So cheery & good natured. It is a tonic to be amongst them . . .

Do let me know how you get on & what your plans are. The party will not return here anyway till towards the end of next month. I go back North in about ten days' time. They can't do without me! Says you!! Buck up & get well. We want you back.

Yours Ever,

Eric

Such was the seriousness of the operation that Logue remained in hospital for several weeks, though his stay was enlivened by the arrival on 11 September of a consignment of grouse from the Palace, prompting him to write a thank you letter to the King.

By Saturday's post, 2 brace of Grouse arrived, I am deeply grateful for this Royal Gift. Myrtle and my son are coming to the hospital on Wednesday evening, as also are my surgeon & house doctor, and all hope to do full justice to your present.

I am progressing slowly but safely & everyone who counts seems to be satisfied. As a reward, I am now allowed to write in ink & this is my first letter so written.

Thank you so much for your thoughtful conclusion.

On 15 September, Miéville wrote back from Balmoral to discuss plans for Logue's convalescence. 'I am afraid you have had a bad time, but it is splendid news that you are really on the mend & that you will soon be out and about again,' he said:

Before I came up here for my second spell (damn it!) nearly a week ago, your good lady rang me up & I put the machinery in motion to get you away to the sea. If there is any hitch, get on to Tommy Lascelles at B.P. Our plans are to come South during the middle of next week, but only to be in London for a day or two before visiting Norfolk for ten days or so in order to slaughter as many birds as possible there! It is a very bloodthirsty business this shooting game & I am glad that I do not indulge! Anyway, we do not really return to London until about the middle of next month.

All folk well here, H.M. is in good health, except when the weather is bad & he cannot shoot. He then takes the line that the Almighty is deliberately opening the heavens & letting out the well known Scotch Mist just to annoy him personally. I try to point out that other people also are involved & are equally annoyed, but he does not seem to see it that way! . . .

The best of luck, old chap. Keep smiling & come back to us soon. We all miss you & none more than me.

Your ever,

Eric

In a note at the end of the letter, Miéville warned Logue that his services would soon be required again to prepare the King for his next major speech, at the opening of parliament, which would be 'probably Nov 17th, not before'.

Logue was discharged soon afterwards and, thanks to the arrangements made for his convalescence by the Palace, was able to spend time in Westgate-on-Sea on the Kent coast. By the autumn he was finally getting back on his feet. 'I rejoice to say that I am quite recovered,' he wrote to the King on 23 October. 'And I am looking forward to attending on you on your return. It has been a long three months. As it is the first ulcer I have ever had, I did not take to it too kindly, but I thank the Good Lord that everything has been a great success.'

Logue continued to receive comfort from the expressions of gratitude he received from his patients, some of whose letters are included among his papers. A fifty-three-year-old civil servant named C.B. Archer, from Wimbledon, wrote in November 1943[136] to thank Logue for completely curing him of the stammer from which he had been suffering since the age of eight, apparently through teaching him to breathe abdominally. 'It was a lucky day for me a little over six months ago when I first got into touch with you,' Archer wrote. 'I think only a stammerer can really appreciate what a different world I live in now. It is as if a load has been lifted from my mind.' The letter, running to five hand-written pages, gave an insight into the blight that the speech impediment had cast over Archer's professional as well as his private life.

'My stammering has been a terrific drawback to me in the civil service,' Archer continued. 'Otherwise I should probably have been an assistant secretary by now. All promotions are as a result of interviews by a Promotion Board and you imagine what a sorry show l made in front of them.' He vowed that when he retired from the civil service he would 'join a political party, stump the country and put up for Parliament. I think I must be a born orator! Questions & interruptions don't worry me in the least now & in fact I welcome them. You must come and hear my maiden speech in the House of Commons. You mustn't mind if it is from the Labour benches, as I think the Labour party will give me more scope for public speaking.'

The following month, Logue received an especially effusive letter from a Tom Mallin, in Sutton Coldfield, Birmingham,[137] noting how both his mother and his friends had noticed the difference since he had started consulting Logue. 'My friends all say I have "changed" – yes – but for the better,' Mallin wrote:

> Now I begin to realise that the voice can be so beautiful, satisfying and expressive, it is a wonder I haven't stumbled to it before. The words that underline all my feelings, and those that you offered before me. A thing of beauty is a joy forever! Sir, how can I ever thank you for making me happy? If you have made happy all those you have taught you should not die unforgotten.

Mallin said he was duc to go to an interview a couple of weeks later, 'and I will remember everything you have taught me. I will be sure of impressing them.'

That December brought a cause for celebration of a more personal nature: Valentine had proposed to Anne Bolton, a consultant child psychiatrist at the Middlesex Hospital, and their forthcoming marriage was announced in *The Times* on 9 December. The ceremony took place on 8 Jan 1944 at Hampstead Parish Church, close to Anne's parents' home on The Bishop's Avenue in north London. Although both Lionel and Myrtle were there, their other sons' postings abroad meant they were unable to attend. The couple then set off for a short holiday in Devon. Six months later, the surgical unit at Maida Vale Hospital, where Valentine was now working, was transferred to Bath. This coincided with a major increase in his responsibilities as he gained in experience: he was now operating on patients under general anaesthetic, concentrating almost exclusively on the skull and brain and on spinal injuries. Many of his patients were soldiers who had been hastily patched up in the field and sent home for specialist treatment in Britain, but there were a number of civilians too.

In a letter dated just over a week after Valentine's wedding, Antony sent his brother his best wishes. 'My very heartiest congratulations and best wishes etc., etc. and infinite regrets that I was not at the altar steps to lose the ring,' he wrote:

Did you remember your lines? Do write & tell me all about it (with pictures) and I hope you had a lovely honeymoon. Mother said you would be spending it in Devon, I can't imagine a better place.

As I am the only bachelor of the family, I hope you are looking out for a very beautiful wife for me. I am afraid she will have to have a great deal of money & be able to do 14 hours of work a day, but you might find one. If so, lock her in the wine cellar until I get back.

Antony also mentioned that he had seen John Gordon, who had been visiting British forces to write a series of stories for the *Sunday Express* and had taken him out for a 'most entertaining evening', during which he introduced him to Alan Moorehead, a celebrated Australian-born foreign correspondent who wrote for the *Daily Express*, and Cyril Falls, a military historian. 'It was so good to see him again, he brought back many happy memories,' Antony wrote. Somehow, Gordon also managed to give him a bed – presumably one that the British military authorities had provided for his own comfort.

Victory in North Africa was followed in the summer of 1943 by the opening of a new front: on 10 July, the British Eighth Army under Montgomery (and the US Seventh Army under General George Patton) began their combined assault on Sicily. A fortnight later Mussolini was deposed, and on 3 September, the government of Pietro Badoglio agreed to unconditional surrender. The same day, the first of the Allied forces landed on the Italian mainland. On 13 October Italy declared war on Germany.

There were other causes for celebration elsewhere: the *Tirpitz*, a 35,000-ton German battleship that had posed a serious threat to the Allied Arctic convoys, was crippled in September 1943 while at anchor off the coast of northern Norway. The daring attack was carried out by newly designed X-Craft midget submarines that dropped powerful two-ton mines on the seabed beneath their target. Then, on Boxing Day, the 26,000-ton battle cruiser *Scharnhorst* was sunk nearby. The battle of the Atlantic had effectively been won by the Allies.

Yet the wider war was far from over. There had been a hope that, following the Italian government's surrender, the Germans would withdraw northwards, given that Hitler had been persuaded that southern Italy was strategically unimportant. This proved to be little more than wishful thinking. The German forces instead put up fierce resistance along a line of defences running across the full width of the country, eighty or so miles south of Rome known as the Gustav or Winter Line, which Field Marshal Albert Kesselring, the German commander in the Italian theatre, vowed to make so strong that the Anglo-American forces would 'break their teeth on it'. The King monitored events with alarm. 'Fighting in the mountains is hopeless,' he wrote in his diary on 21 December. 'The men are in good heart but the conditions are dreadful. Mud, rain, and cold for weeks now.'[138] Fierce battles were also raging in Russia, while the Japanese were far from being vanquished. The King's mood was further darkened by news that Churchill, who had been attending conferences in the Middle East, had been taken ill with pneumonia in Tunis, the second time that year he had been laid low by the disease.

The Christmas break, which the King spent at Windsor with his family, provided some respite. Among the guests was a young Royal Navy lieutenant, Prince Philip of Greece and Denmark. Philip had first been introduced to the royal family in June 1939 when the King had visited the Royal Naval College at Dartmouth; at the time Philip was eighteen and the future Queen just thirteen. Someone had to look after Elizabeth and Margaret while their parents were engaged in their official duties, and Mountbatten made sure that his nephew, Philip, a tall, strikingly good-looking man who had just graduated as the top cadet in his course, was given the task. Elizabeth (who was Philip's third cousin through Queen Victoria, and second cousin, once removed, through Christian IX of Denmark) was smitten. 'She never took her eyes off him,' observed Marion Crawford, her governess, in her memoirs.[139] Philip, by contrast, was 'quite polite to her, but did not pay her special attention', instead spending a lot of time 'teasing plump little Margaret'.

Elizabeth had been in love with Philip 'from their first meeting', according to George VI's official biographer (whose manuscript was read and approved by her after she became Queen), and the two of them kept in touch in the intervening years, writing what were described as 'cousinly' letters to one another. Elizabeth was excited to learn that Philip would be spending the Christmas of 1943 with them and, before that, attending the annual royal pantomime that she and Margaret had begun staging a couple of years earlier at Windsor and in which they took the starring roles.

'Who do you think is coming to see us act, Crawfie? Philip,' Elizabeth said to her governess 'looking rather pink'.[140] Philip sat in the front row alongside the King and Queen and Marina, the Duchess of Kent, who was his cousin. The pantomime went well, with Philip entering in the fun and laughing at all the bad jokes. Crawford had never seen Lilibet, as the future Queen was known in the family, more animated. 'There was a sparkle about her none of us had ever see before. Many people remarked on it,' she noted.[141] Philip then stayed the Christmas weekend at Windsor; the high point was on Boxing Day, when 'after dinner and some charades, they rolled back the carpet in the crimson drawing-room, turned on the gramophone and frisked and capered away till near 1 a.m.', presided over by the King dressed in his tuxedo of Inverness tartan.[142]

In his Christmas broadcast, the King struck a tone of what his official biographer described as 'mingled gratification and warning'.[143] 'In this year that is almost passed, many things have happened, under God's providence, to make us thankful for His mercies,' he said.

The generous strength of the United States of America, the tremendous deeds of Russia, the endurance of China under her long ordeal, the fighting spirit of France re-born, and the flower of the manhood and womanhood of many lands that share the burdens of our forward march – all these have played their part in the brightening of our fortunes on sea, on land, and in the air.

Since I last spoke to you many things have changed. But the spirit of our people has not changed. As we were not downcast by defeat, we are not unduly exalted by victory. While we have bright visions of the future we have no easy dreams of the days that lie close at hand. We know that much hard working and hard fighting, and perhaps harder working and harder fighting than ever before, are necessary for victory. We shall not rest from our task until it is nobly ended.

In private, the King allowed himself some wishful thinking. In his diary entry on Christmas night, he wrote simply: 'Let us hope next Christmas will see the end of the War.'[144]

CHAPTER TEN

The March on Rome

Just after 2 a.m. on 22 January 1944, 40,000 Allied troops of the American Fifth Army, VI Corps and the British First Infantry Division swarmed ashore on a fifteen-mile stretch of Italian beach near the resort towns of Anzio and Nettuno, taking the Germans almost completely by surprise. The British forces included the Scots Guards, among whose number was Antony Logue, who had finally returned to his unit after a long recovery from the injuries he had suffered in North Africa.

Operation Shingle, as the landing was known, was a bold attempt to circumvent the Gustav Line, which was still preventing the Allied troops from advancing northwards through Italy. Under the plan, General Mark Clark, the commander of the American Fifth Army, would outflank the German army by landing on the coast north of the line, about thirty miles from Rome, and then advance northwards on the capital. The operation was championed by Churchill, who had consistently argued the case for attacking Germany through its Mediterranean 'underbelly'. He prevailed despite resistance from the Americans and the Russians, who saw the operation as a sideshow that risked distracting attention and military forces from the

184

main event: the planned invasion of continental Europe across the Channel.

Among the sceptics was the American Major General John Lucas, whose VI Corps, made up of British and US divisions, was to lead the assault. Lucas had been left out of the planning of the operation and did not think the forces he had been given were sufficient to achieve the goals he had been set – with good reason. 'I felt like a lamb being led to the slaughter,' he wrote in his diary, comparing Churchill's role in devising the plan with the ill-fated Gallipoli campaign of the First World War with which the then First Lord of the Admiralty had been closely associated. 'This whole affair had the strong odour of Gallipoli and apparently the same amateur Churchill was still on the coaches' bench.'

Despite Lucas's misgivings, the operation got off to the best possible start. The Allies had expected they would have to fight their way in from the coast. Instead, the American forces landed without trouble of any kind. Although their British comrades had to contend with mines and barbed wire, they suffered only minor casualties. German aircraft did not appear until 8 a.m. and no sign of enemy opposition was reported until 10 a.m. – eight hours after the initial landing.

The newspapers back home were understandably jubilant. 'It was so easy and so simply done,' wrote Don Whitehead, of the Combined United Press, who rode ashore with the second wave at 2.10 a.m.[145]

It caught the Germans so completely by surprise that, as I write this dispatch, six hours after the landing, American troops are literally standing with their mouths open and shaking their heads in utter amazement.

We began walking, expecting each moment that the enemy would open fire, but we just walked. Nothing happened in my sector. There were only a few scattered shots fired and most of them came from our troops to the north.

At this early stage there is every indication that General Clark's Fifth Army has pulled off a brilliant manoeuvre to knock the enemy from the flank and open the road to Rome.

Yet despite this auspicious start, Lucas failed to capitalize on the element of surprise – and decided instead to delay his advance until he had sufficiently consolidated his position. His caution was partly down to his conviction that he did not have sufficient forces; he had also apparently taken to heart advice from Clark who told him on more than one occasion: 'Don't stick your neck out.' Whatever the reason, it proved to be a serious miscalculation. Kesselring took advantage of the pause to form a defensive ring around the beachhead, trapping the Allies inside. Within days, almost all the German reserves had arrived to support the counter-attack. Rather than facing a force of 20,000, Lucas's men soon found themselves up against 120,000 Germans, 70,000 of whom were combat soldiers.

The Allied operation degenerated into the kind of trench warfare the combatants' fathers would have known on the Western Front during the First World War. During daylight the frontlines were quiet, except when a sudden movement on one side provoked a sniper's bullet or a burst of machine-gun, mortar or artillery fire. When darkness fell, the beachhead came to life as patrols went out, ammunition and supplies were brought forward and the dead buried. There could also be lighter moments, though, as was revealed in a bulletin by one of Antony's fellow Scots Guards, Lieutenant H. Brooking Clark, of the 2nd battalion, dated 1 February and marked 'CONFIDENTIAL'. Clark described how he presided over a headquarters of four – comprising a golf pro, a Blackpool football star, a keen amateur cyclist and his former servant, known throughout the battalion as 'Flash Harrington', who scrounged and cooked the 'most amazing things', including pancakes and jam tart, baked over a hole in the ground and using Andrews Liver Salts in place of baking powder. Also sharing their dugout was a white rabbit and a 'bomb happy hen' that hopped from bed to bed and became such a nuisance they eventually bundled her off to rear command head-quarters. At one point, the relative calm was shattered by the noise of pneumatic drilling: the commanding officer was so impressed with the lieutenant's dugout that he had a similar one carved out of the rock for himself next door.

Antony also seemed to be having a fairly quiet time of it. In a letter to his family written five days later, there was no mention of fighting. Instead he asked his parents to thank John Gordon for the bed that he had left him which was 'serving its purpose now in no mean fashion', and for a fleece jacket that was keeping out the strong winds. He reminisced about life back home. 'The garden will be beginning to look wonderful again very shortly,' he wrote:

Did you have any snow at Beechgrove over Christmas? The first Rhododendron will be showing again soon.

I am so glad to hear also that my nephew & niece are in the best & most resplendent spirits. Has Alexandra quietened down yet? Believe Robert is even noisier that she is, practically impossible. The next sight I suppose will be that of Val pushing a pram, you can tell him that I am going to stay away long enough to miss that phase!

Such relative calm was not to last, however. Ordered by Hitler to 'lance the abscess south of Rome', Kesselring unleashed a series of attacks aimed at driving the invaders off the narrow semi-circular beachhead to which they were clinging. 'The fighting we have been in has been described as the most bitter fighting in the war, wrote Lieutenant Colonel D.S. Wedderburn in a bulletin dated 12 February. 'The battalion is said by everyone to have fought absolutely wonderfully ... We have made successful attacks and fought off, practically to the last round and last man, the most desperate counter-attacks.'

A crucial phase began in the early hours of 16 February with the German launch of Operation *Fischfang* (Fishing), which was intended to drive a wedge into the Allies' left flank. Waves of tanks and infantry hurled themselves at the American and British defenders. Reynolds Packard, a reporter with the British United Press, who watched the assault from the roof of a barn, saw tank battles and infantry fighting stretching out along the skyline. 'The enemy has been exposing himself to our fire as never before,' he reported. 'German wounded and dead are so numerous that they are hampering the infantry attacks. In some sectors the Germans attack over a carpet of their own dead.'[146] Another reporter on the beachhead, Basil Gingell, was also staggered by the enemy's determination. 'With a disregard for life that one could scarcely believe, the German units have been formed up and flung into battle across low-lying plains into the very mouths of our artillery,' he wrote. 'They attempted a "Light Brigade" charge without horses and were mown down by the huge weight of shells flung against them.'[147]

Like everyone else in Britain, Lionel and Myrtle were following the progress of Allied forces through reports in the newspapers, but they did not immediately realize their own son was among them. In the letter sent eight days before the landing in which he had congratulated Valentine on his wedding, Antony described his own news as 'negligible'. And then it had gone quiet.

Although Myrtle correctly guessed her son's location, confirmation did not come until a month after the landing: 'The censorship bar now having been lifted we are now able to say what you have already guessed, that we are in the Anzio Bridgehead,' Antony wrote in a letter home, dated midnight 19 February and penned by torchlight. 'So I hope you will understand the scarcity & incoherence of my correspondence, during the last month.'

> You can tell Val that, until last night I had not taken off my boots or my coat, or removed a stitch of my clothing for 19 days, a very different figure to the debonair figure of peacetime. Still, it has been a classic show and one that I feel should live in history forever. I am very proud to have been here and to have participated in my tiny way. The fellows have fought as only the Brigade of Guards can, more than that I cannot say.
>
> Pardon that handwriting, I am writing this on my hand, by the aid of a torch & it is raining like hell, oh the glories of battle!

Despite the wretched conditions, Antony still found time to tease his newlywed elder brother. 'Anne seems, by all accounts, to be kicking Val into shape as the model husband,' he added. 'I do not really believe that she can make him clean his own shoes. If she has, it is a very gallant effort and bravo Anne!'

The determination shown by Kesselring's forces prompted fears that the Allied offensive might end in a second Dunkirk. Miraculously, such a disaster was averted, but criticism was mounting of Lucas, who rarely left his underground headquarters in Nettuno and failed to inspire the confidence of either his own men or his superiors. On 22 February he was dismissed. 'I had hoped we were hurling a wildcat onto the shore, but all we got was a stranded whale,' was Churchill's damning verdict. Lucas was replaced by Major General Lucian Truscott, who had been appointed his deputy six days earlier. One of the American army's most able commanders, the square-jawed, rough-hewn Truscott brought a dramatic change of style, visiting every unit on the beachhead within his first twenty-four hours and inspiring fierce loyalty among those under his command. Yet it took time for him to restore the Allies' fortunes.

When Antony wrote another letter home on 4 March, he began by apologizing for not writing before, 'but things have been a little hectic'.

I hear that the Grenadiers are getting a bit of publicity in the big city just now, thank god the Brigade is getting written up at last even only 1st battalion of it! Most of the stories I have heard over the wireless and in the papers about the fighting here are all nonsense, but it has been a most remarkable affair from beginning to end, & which I feel sure will leave its mark on the history of the war. The story of it can never be told in a letter, it will have to wait until I can tell it to you myself.

Antony wrote home again several times in the ensuing weeks, though censorship meant he was not able to go into detail. His letters instead included more mundane matters, such as requests to help manage his financial affairs. He also made his usual quips about his eldest brother's exploits in Africa. Writing on 14 April, he said the letters he had received included 'a rather more pathetic one from Laurie, saying that having tracked a miserable green river in the heart of God knows where, to its final disappearance into the sand, (infuriating!), he now struggled on to Mogadishu (wherever that may be) and is now in bed with the doctor (metaphorically) with Amoebic Dysentery (whatever that is) and will be in bed for at least three weeks. This last is the only piece of good news in the epistle, it will keep him out of trouble!' A few weeks later, Antony wrote home to announce his own promotion: 'His Majesty has realized that my talents have been ignored for too long and his government have seen fit to make me a Captain!'

As Antony noted in his letter, the achievements of the British forces in Italy were finally receiving some praise in the newspapers back home. A piece in *The Times* that March headlined 'Scots Guard in the Beach-Head: Valour against Odds', described in glowing terms a battle on the Anzio beachhead that ended with twenty guardsmen taking eighty Germans prisoner at the point of a bayonet.[148] Recognition of what they were up against went down well with Antony and his comrades. 'I am glad that you read the tribute to the Regiment in *The Times*,' he wrote to his parents on 5 May. 'I had heard that it was very good, and as you say, much overdue.'

Then, on 23 May, after several months of bloody stalemate, the Allied forces finally attempted a breakout offensive. The first day's fighting was intense: the 1st Armored Division lost 100 tanks and the 3rd Infantry Division suffered 955 casualties, the highest single daily tally for any US division during the war. The Germans took heavy casualties too: the 362nd Infantry Division lost an estimated half of its fighting strength. But as the VI Corps broke free of the Anzio beachhead, German opposition began to collapse. Rome now lay within the Allies' sights – although such was Clark's determination to be the first to take the city that he allowed the retreating German Tenth Army to escape unscathed – to fight again.

Allied forces entered Rome in the early hours of 4 June. Later that morning, Clark held an impromptu press conference on the steps of the city hall on the Piazza del Campidoglio. Leaning against the stone railing and looking out over a sea of British, American and Italian flags, he proclaimed it a 'great day for the Fifth Army and for the French, British and American troops of the Fifth that have made this victory possible'. Below the terrace, the hill swarmed with jeeps, command cars and light armoured vehicles.

The capture of the first of the three Axis capitals was a major symbolic victory for the Allies. The *New York Times* struck a suitably portentous note: 'With some twenty-seven centuries looking down upon him, an American general, crowned not with the laurel leaves of the Caesars but with a simple overseas cap over a simple field uniform, and riding not in a chariot but in a jeep, drove up to Campidoglio of Rome yesterday and formally proclaimed the occupation of the Eternal City by his troops,' it said of Clark. 'This campaign not only accomplished what Hannibal had failed to do – namely, capture Rome from the south – but also so outmanoeuvred the enemy that he had to leave the city intact to save himself.'[149]

Antony recounted his experiences in a letter dated 15 June. 'I apologise most abjectly for the lapse of time preceding this letter but the reason is obvious. I have not travelled so fast or so far willingly for some considerable time,' he wrote:

Well, what price the beachhead now, eh! It proved its worth during the last few days of its life all right. Unfortunately, we were not there to break out of the never to be forgotten country north of Anzio, but as you know in the terrific shuffle round, we had come out for some rest and came up from Canino, so I have seen both sides of the battle front now.

As you may well imagine, we were tremendously bucked at getting into Rome. I was in it in a Jeep on the second night, one of the most beautiful cities I have ever seen, all was completely quiet and orderly, people enjoying their ordinary lives without disturbance and except for the stream of the convoys, no soldiers to be seen. It was the finest occupation I have experienced. We were in a wood north of Rome when we heard of the second front, and since then we have not stopped. I have had enough ecstatic welcomes during the last fortnight to last me all my days. These northern Italian cities, amongst the most beautiful in the world, have welcomed us right royally, and in most cases the Germans fires have not yet gone out. A most exciting time.

Yet the battle for Italy was still far from over: 'Our last month has been indescribable,' Antony continued five days later:

We have been in the forepart of this great tidal wave, and although on the BBC one hears all about these simple operations of 'winkling out' Germans and 'mopping up' and 'patrol activity' it is a very different proposition when you come to do these 'routine' operations. You will be hearing a lot now that the Western front is open again about the glorious feats of the fancy supporting armies. They are great performers, for a short time, but it is the old infantryman who takes the damned objective and (what is more) holds it.

I must say it has been a most satisfying chase with the Germans getting just a taste of what we have been receiving for the last 4 years.

This letter has been written spasmodically and I am nearly a hundred miles from the places where I started it. The weather, which has been terrible up to now, rain such as I have never seen before, which has slowed down our tanks and vehicles and enabled the Germans to get away time and time again, has now set fair and dusty and progress is, consequently, much more rapid and satisfactory. As you know one of the main troubles has been demolitions and the Sappers have been magnificent. We are all exhausted but they are dead on their feet, but still capable of putting up an astounding performance. Without them no advance is possible at any speed.

The beginning of 1944 saw Britain facing a new threat at home – from the air. British and American forces had mounted a punishing series of bombing raids by day and by night on Berlin and other German cities, including a devastating firebombing of Hamburg in July 1943 in which around 50,000 people were killed and large areas of the city destroyed. Later that year, as the Allies' Combined Bomber Offensive was gathering momentum, Hitler finally responded by ordering a series of retaliatory strikes on London. The Germans called it Operation *Steinbock* (Capricorn). With characteristic black humour, those at the receiving end quickly dubbed it the Baby Blitz.

This fresh assault came as an unpleasant shock to Londoners, for whom the relentless bombing they had suffered during the Blitz of 1940–1 was now a distant memory. Thanks to the Allies' military successes abroad, victory over the Germans seemed only a matter of time. Large crowds turned out to see in the New Year in Piccadilly Circus; if it had not been for the continuing blackout, London could have been a city at peace. The main concern of most Londoners was instead the bitterly cold winter, with its freezing fogs. Following a drought the previous summer and autumn, this also meant a shortage of vegetables, adding to the misery of rationing.

The arrival of the first wave of more than 400 German bombers (just after 8.40 p.m. on 21 January) shattered any feeling of complacency. The damage done by 269 tons of bombs was trivial compared with the destruction being wrought by the Allies on Germany almost every night, but by sunrise nearly a hundred Londoners were dead or wounded. Firebombs had struck parliament, the Embankment, New Scotland Yard and a host of other sites across the city centre. To emphasize the retaliatory nature of the raids, sections of the capital were given code names representing devastated German cities, such as Berlin, Hamburg and Hanover. The first target, Waterloo, was codenamed München (Munich).

There were more attacks on London in the weeks that followed. The Germans also carried out sorties against Hull and Bristol. Some 1,500 British civilians were killed and nearly 3,000 wounded, but the operation, predictably, did not succeed in ending the British and American attacks on Germany. Furthermore, the Nazis were squandering planes they could not afford to lose: of the 524 committed to the campaign, nearly 330 were downed. In May, they finally called off the raids.

Logue, meanwhile, continued to work as best he could. On 8 March, he wrote to the King in the hope of persuading him to take some more appointments. 'Now that the weather is showing a tendency to be kind to us I wonder if you would like to have one or two opportunities before Easter, just to keep your voice in working order,' he wrote. 'You know I will be only too pleased to wait on you at your convenience.' The King had other more urgent priorities, however. Since returning to London after his Christmas break he had been travelling up and down Britain inspecting troops and encouraging officers and men in the ordeal that lay before them. A new dramatic phase in the war, with which Lionel would be personally involved, was about to begin.

CHAPTER ELEVEN

D-Day

On 1 June 1944 at 9.30 p.m., Logue received a call from Lascelles. The message from the King's private secretary was short and to the point.

'My master wants to know if you can come to Windsor tomorrow, Friday, for lunch,' he asked. Logue was happy to oblige.

Logue took the 12.44 train. He found Lascelles in the equerries' room. He was in a serious mood. 'Sorry I cannot tell you much about the broadcast,' he said. 'It is, as a matter of fact, a call to prayer, and takes about five minutes, and strange as it may seem, I cannot tell you when it is, as you have probably guessed that it is to be given on the night of D-Day, at 9 o'clock.' It was not clear when that would be; it was expected to be in the next two or three days, but the precise timing depended on the weather.

Logue went to have lunch with the equerries, the ladies-in-waiting and the Captain of the Guard. Afterwards the King summoned him. Everywhere there was an air of great tension. The King was in his study; the blinds were drawn, but the room was still extremely hot. He looked tired and told Logue he hadn't been sleeping well. But when they went through the speech, Logue was charmed by it.

Lascelles had not needed to explain what he meant by D-Day. The military terminology for the day chosen for the Allied assault on Europe had long since passed into common parlance, and the Germans, too, knew an assault was coming. But when – and where – the Allied forces would land remained a closely guarded secret. The element of surprise was essential, and every trick was used to keep the enemy guessing – from inflatable mock tanks, dummy landing craft and parachuting mannequins, to fake radio traffic and a stream of disinformation fed through double agents.

It had been seventeen months earlier, at the Casablanca Conference in January 1943, that Roosevelt and Churchill agreed on a full-scale invasion of Nazi-dominated Europe using a combination of British and American forces. Churchill, who was determined to avoid a repetition of the costly frontal assaults of the First World War, had proposed invading the Balkans, with the aim of linking up with Soviet forces and then possibly bringing in Turkey on the side of the Allies. The Americans preferred an invasion of Western Europe, however, as did the Russians, who wanted a 'second front' – a major operation that would engage a significant portion of the *Wehrmacht* – and they, rather than Churchill, prevailed. The decision to launch what was named Operation Overlord was confirmed that August at a highly secret military conference in Quebec attended by Churchill and Roosevelt, and hosted by William Lyon Mackenzie King, the Canadian Prime Minister. By that winter the choice of landing point had been narrowed down to either the Pas-de-Calais area or Normandy. On Christmas Eve, Eisenhower was appointed Supreme Commander of the Allied Expeditionary Force (SCAEF).

The plans for the operation were outlined by Eisenhower and his commanders at a top-secret meeting on 15 May in the unlikely setting of a classroom in St Paul's School in west London. The pupils had been evacuated to Berkshire on the outbreak of war, and Montgomery, an old boy of the school, had turned its buildings in Hammersmith into the headquarters of the 21st Army Group, which he commanded. Besides the two men, also present were the King, Churchill, Jan Smuts, the South African Prime Minister, the chiefs of staff and more than 150 commanders of the land, sea and air units that would carry out the operation. As Lascelles later recorded: 'I could not help reflecting as I looked round the room that there had probably been no single assembly in the last four years the annihilation of which by a single well-directed bomb would affect more profoundly the issue of the war.'[150]

At the end of the meeting, the King unexpectedly stood up, mounted the platform and, talking without notes, made a short speech in which he wished success to those due to take part in the landings. Montgomery described his intervention as 'absolutely first class'.[151] For those present, it underlined the King's determination to be more than a mere figurehead and to be actively involved in decision making. Over the following few days, more and more forces were concentrated in southern England: by 22 May, the King had visited each of the assault forces in their ports of assembly. 'I have now seen all our troops who are taking part in Overlord,' he wrote in his diary.[152] The invasion was imminent.

As the preparations continued, the King found himself embroiled in a dispute with Churchill. On 30 May, during their usual Tuesday luncheon, the Prime Minister revealed his intention to watch the invasion from HMS *Belfast*, one of the vessels in the invasion force. The King replied that he would do the same, and Churchill did nothing to dissuade him. Nor did the Queen. 'She was wonderful as always and encouraged me to do it,' the King noted. Lascelles, by contrast, was appalled and shook the King by asking whether risking his life in this way would be fair to the Queen and indeed 'whether he was prepared to face the possibility of having to advise Princess Elizabeth on the choice of her first Prime Minister, in the event of her father and Winston being sent to the bottom of the English Channel'.[153] By the next morning, the King's usual common sense had reasserted itself and he accepted it would be too dangerous for him to witness the invasion from the Channel. It took more to convince Churchill, who to Lascelles was 'just like a naughty child when he starts planning an escapade'.[154] When Lascelles reminded him that a Prime Minister could not leave the country without the King's consent, Churchill dismissed the objection, saying that he would not technically be going abroad since he would be on board a British warship.

Churchill stood firm for several days, but by the Friday morning he appeared to be wavering. Lascelles thought a 'second barrel from the King might push him over, and at the same time give him a graceful excuse for changing his mind'.[155] And so the King wrote the Prime Minister a letter that was sent round by dispatch rider to Downing Street. 'I ask you most earnestly to consider the whole question again and not let your personal wishes, which I very well understand, lead you to depart from your own high standard of duty to the state,' he wrote.[156] Churchill received the letter just as he was about to set off for Eisenhower's headquarters near Portsmouth and did not immediately reply – leading the King to believe the only way he could ensure his Prime Minister did not set off with the invasion force would be to drive down to the coast to stop him personally. In the event, the King was spared the journey. When Lascelles got through to Churchill on the phone the next evening, the Prime Minister told him down a crackling line that he would heed the monarch's appeal, after all. 'He has decided not to go on the expedition, but only because I have asked him not to go,' the King wrote in his diary.[157]

There was a more fundamental question to be resolved: the timing of the invasion itself. The initial date set was for Sunday 4 June, when the tides would be most favourable. But the weather during the weekend was poor; it was cold and wet, and there were high seas and a gale blowing from the west, all of which would make it impossible to launch landing craft from larger ships. Low cloud would prevent Allied aircraft from finding their targets. The date was pushed back to the Monday, but that, too, seemed problematic, with storms forecast. The alternative was to postpone until the tides were good – which would have meant waiting another month. But sending the troops back to their embarkation camps would be a huge and difficult operation, and a July landing would allow only a few months of fighting before the unpredictable autumn and winter months. Advised by Group Captain James Stagg, chief meteorologist for the RAF, of a brief window in the weather, Eisenhower took the momentous decision to go for 6 June.

When the King was told of the delay, his first thought was for the troops. 'This added to my anxieties as I knew that the men were going on board the ships at the time, & that their quarters were very cramped,' he wrote in his diary.[158] On the evening of the 5th, Logue was summoned to help him go through the speech. He arrived as arranged at the Palace at 6 p.m. and was shown in to see the King fifteen minutes later. The atmosphere was tense, but there were also some comic moments. As the King was going through his voice exercises with Logue, they caught sight out of the window of a procession of five people in the garden of Buckingham Palace, among them a policeman. As they watched, the sole woman among them put a net over her head, which made Logue think they were trying to coax a swarm of bees into a box. 'The King got quite excited, and wanted to go out and give them a hand,' Logue recalled. 'It only wanted me to say yes, and he would have opened the window and gone on to the lawn – but it wouldn't do to have the King chance being stung by a bee just before a broadcast so, curious as I was, I had to pretend that I was not interested.'

After going through the speech once, they went downstairs to the air raid shelter and joined Wood of the BBC for another run-through. It went well: the speech ran to five and half minutes, and they needed to make just two alterations. The only problem was the loud clicking of a clock coming from the King's bedroom. 'That clock's got to be stopped,' he told Wood. 'We cannot have that coming through the speech.'

After the rehearsal they returned to the King's room – and he went immediately back to the windows to see what had become of the bees. The people had all gone; all that was left was a small box underneath the tree. As Logue was sitting making small changes to the speech, the Queen came in, and to his amusement, the King 'explained like a schoolboy, what had happened about the bees, even going down on his knees to explain the detail of the capture'. The Queen also became excited, exclaiming: 'Oh, Bertie, I wish I had been here.'

In the early hours of 6 June, Operation Neptune (the name given to the first, assault, phase of Operation Overlord) began. Shortly after midnight, 24,000 British, American, Canadian and Free French airborne troops landed. Then, beginning at 6.30 a.m. British Double Summer Time, the first Allied infantry and armoured divisions embarked along a fifty-mile stretch of the Normandy coast. Three hours later, the BBC's John Snagge broadcast a brief communiqué announcing the operation. 'Under the command of General Eisenhower, Allied naval forces, supported by strong air forces, began landing Allied armies this morning on the northern coast of France,' he said, repeating the announcement for emphasis.

Despite the dramatic events on the other side of the Channel, Logue went to work in Harley Street that morning as usual, though the King's broadcast due that evening was never far from his mind. At lunchtime a message came through saying the King was touring military headquarters and wanted to postpone their final run-through from 6 until 7 p.m. Logue arrived at 6.45 and after a few voice exercises they went down into the dugout. The rehearsal went perfectly; the King then went off to have a sandwich while Logue had dinner with the equerries – 'a very jolly one,' Logue wrote in his diary. 'Everyone seemed very pleased with the invasion as far it had gone and Eisenhower said it was 80% successful.' At 8.30, he returned to the dugout in readiness for the broadcast.

As people across Britain gathered around their radios, the King spoke: 'Four years ago our nation and empire stood alone against an overwhelming enemy with our backs to the wall, tested as never before in our history. In God's providence we survived that test,' he began.

> The spirit of the people, resolute and dedicated, burned like a bright flame, lit surely from those unseen fires which nothing can quench.
>
> 'Now once more a supreme test has to be faced. This time the challenge is not to fight to survive, but to fight to win the final victory for the good cause. Once again, what is demanded from us all is something more than courage, more than endurance.

The King went on to call for 'a revival of the spirit, a new unconquerable reserve' and a renewal of 'that crusading impulse on which we entered the war and met its darkest hour'. He concluded with a quote from verse 11 of Psalm 29: 'The Lord will give strength unto his people, the Lord will give his people the blessing of peace.'

The tone of the speech matched the national mood. The front pages of the following day's newspapers carried graphic accounts of the Normandy landings: 'We Hold Beachhead' proclaimed the *Daily Mirror*, describing the initial success. 'Allied Invasion Troops Several Miles into France', said the *Daily Telegraph*, which noted the speed with which the Allies had taken control of the beaches. The King received a number of letters praising his performance, including one from Queen Mary. 'I am glad you liked my broadcast,' he wrote back.[159] 'It was a great opportunity to call everybody to prayer. I have wanted to do it for a long time.'

The landings themselves were only the beginning, though. The King and Queen monitored the next few critical days anxiously. 'We spent a quiet week-end, though not in our thoughts,' he wrote in his diary.[160] Though he had been denied the opportunity of watching the D-Day landings from on board ship, the King remained determined to visit the troops himself as soon as possible. This was not just to see at first hand the conditions in which they were fighting, but also because he knew his presence would symbolize the wholehearted support they were receiving from the nation at home. On 12 June Churchill travelled safely over to Normandy for the day, and when the two men met for their regular Tuesday lunch the next day, the King expressed the desire to do the same. Churchill had no objection. The cabinet, he wrote, felt no doubt that 'a visit of the King to the armies in France would be an encouragement to the Allied forces engaged and also make an impression upon our Allies throughout the British Empire and Commonwealth which would be favourable to our cause'.[161]

The King left London by train on the night of 15 June and, after spending the night at Horsley in Surrey, set off from Portsmouth at 8 a.m. aboard the cruiser *Arethusa*, which was flying the Royal Standard. The Channel was choppy, and the crossing to Normandy took four and half hours, an hour longer than expected. The sea was full of shipping: strings of landing craft coming and going, the huge concrete units that made up the Mulberry artificial harbours set up by the Allies along the coast and a host of small vessels of every type. The fighting was still not over, though; *Hawkins*, a heavy cruiser, was firing in support of an attack as the King was deposited by a landing craft on the beach in front of a waiting Montgomery. Lunch, at his headquarters in a small chateau at Creully, noted Lascelles, who accompanied the monarch, included 'genuine Camembert cheeses – a thing we've not seen in London since 1940'.[162]

During the afternoon, the King spent several hours inspecting the terrain and decorating some of the officers and men who had taken part in the operation. Montgomery would not let the party go anywhere nearer the front line, which was just six miles away, for fear of German snipers, who were continuing to pick off Allied forces. To the King's disappointment, they also had to abandon plans to cruise along the coast to see the Mulberries being constructed, because the Germans had dropped a number of mines there the night before. They arrived back safely at Portsmouth that evening at nine o'clock, reaching Windsor two and a half hours later. 'A long and interesting day,' the King noted in his diary that evening with customary understatement. 'It was most encouraging to know that it was possible for me to land on the beaches only ten days after D-Day.'[163]

On the morning of 4 July Logue had been due to attend his investiture as a Commander of the Royal Victorian Order. A week before the ceremony, he received a letter from the Central Chancery of the Orders of Knighthood advising him that the formal investiture had been cancelled. No reason was given, but he was told he should nevertheless still come to the Palace, but that afternoon instead. Logue remained pleasantly surprised by his award: 'I was under the impression that no honours could be given to common civilians like myself during war time,' he wrote to Sir Ulick Alexander. The ceremony coincided with a further recognition of his professional achievements: his election as a fellow of the College of Speech Therapists. It is not clear which of the two made him prouder: he promptly wrote to *Who's Who*, asking for his entry to be updated with both.

Rejoicing over the success of Operation Overlord was tempered by a new threat to Britain. The days after the D-Day landings saw the deployment by the Hitler of his long-rumoured secret weapon, the V-1 or *Vergeltungswaffe* (vengeance weapon). Pilotless planes that were filled with explosives – doodlebugs, as they became known – rained down on London and south-east England during that summer, shattering the brief calm that had followed the end of the Baby Blitz.

The first V-1 struck the East End of London at 4.25 a.m. on 13 June, a week after D-Day, hitting a bridge across Grove Road that carried the Great Eastern Railway from Liverpool Street to Essex and East Anglia. The track and bridge were badly damaged, and a number of houses demolished. Six people were killed. It was followed five days later by what was to be the deadliest attack of the campaign when a V-1 hit the Guards' chapel on Birdcage Walk, close to Buckingham Palace. A mixed military and civilian congregation gathered for Sunday worship had just begun the Sung Eucharist when the craft nosedived, destroying not just the roof but also the supporting walls and concrete pillars and the portico of the chapel's western door. Tons of rubble fell onto the congregation, killing 121 soldiers and civilians and seriously injuring 141. The victims included the officiating chaplain, the Reverend Ralph Whitrow, several senior British army officers and a US army Colonel. It took two days to dig out the dead and injured. News of the tragedy was suppressed, but rumours soon spread across London.

The King was deeply shocked. Many of the worshippers had been friends and acquaintances of the royal family. 'A change to our daily routine will be needed,' he said. All investitures were cancelled for the time being and, just to be on the safe side, for the next few weeks he and Churchill held their traditional Tuesday luncheon in the air raid shelter of Buckingham Palace. The Palace itself did not suffer a direct hit, but the glass in its widows was repeatedly blown out and a bomb that fell in Constitution Hill destroyed a seventy-five-yard stretch of its boundary wall. 'There is something very inhuman about death-dealing missiles being launched in such an indiscriminate manner,' the Queen wrote to Queen Mary the following month.[164]

The V-1s were principally a terror weapon. Londoners became used to the characteristic buzzing sound of their pulse jet engine and knew to fear for their lives when it cut out: there followed a few heart-stopping seconds of silence after which the device would hit the ground or the top of a roof, detonating its payload of a ton of high explosives. In total, 2,419 reached the capital, killing 6,184 people and injuring 17,981, the majority of them civilians, and causing widespread damage to London's infrastructure. The V-1s' gyroscope-based targeting systems were hugely inaccurate: although aimed at Tower Bridge, they did not succeed in taking it down, although one passed through the central arch and sank the tug on the other side. There were further misses, but the remaining hits were scattered across London and beyond, with areas to the south and east of the capital suffering particularly.

The most serious attack near Beechgrove was on the afternoon of 5 August when a V-1 hit a Co-op on Lordship Lane, less than a mile to the north of the Logues' home, demolishing the shop and six others near it and damaging an area within a radius of 700 yards. Twenty-three people died and forty-two were seriously injured. Rescue squads worked round the clock for two days in the attempt to recover victims. The greatest density of hits – more than 140 – was on Croydon, to the south, which lay on the V-1s' flight path; three out of four homes in the borough were damaged and a total of 211 residents killed.[165]

As they had done during the Blitz, the King and Queen toured the bombed areas. 'I do feel so proud of the way our people are going through this terrible ordeal, for it is very hard to be bombarded once again,' the Queen wrote. 'It is cruel to lose everything, but the amount of times I have heard people say "Ah well, mustn't grumble, must we" and in a philosophical way after escaping with just their lives! It's a great spirit and they deserve many years of real Peace.'[166] The King also made a point of visiting anti-aircraft batteries and fighter squadrons to see for himself the measures being taken to shoot down the V-1s, though he was taken aback by the inarticulate modesty of many of the young pilots. 'I find it so difficult to talk to them as they will never say what they have done, and they have all got stories to tell,' he wrote after a visit to RAF stations near Chichester that July.

Like many Londoners, Lionel and Myrtle were desperate for a respite. When the attacks were at their height, they left Beechgrove for the relative safety of Worcester, which was well beyond the range of the V-1s. They stayed with Richard Bettinson, Lionel's solicitor. Bettinson was normally based in Birmingham but after the outbreak of war, in order to escape the bombs raining down on Britain's second city, he had moved his family to Worcester. After a time Lionel had to return to London to continue his work, but Myrtle stayed on. With the tide of war beginning to turn in the Allies' favour, Bettinson decided it was safe to return to Birmingham and began house hunting. Myrtle went with his wife to look at some properties and suggested they might share one. 'But my mother was not very keen,' her son, John, recalled years later.[167] 'You will have gathered Myrtle was a very strong character!' That summer, Lionel and Myrtle also managed to spend some time on the west Wales coast.

Antony, who was continuing his progress through the Italian countryside with the Guards, was aware of his parents' travels when he wrote to them on 31 August. His letter was written in his usual affectionate, mocking tone. 'Well, me dears, how is life gadding about central England?' he began.

Where are you resting the old head now, the Palace in Brum, or the Castle in Wales? Tell that bum of a brother of mine in Bath to write to me, I suppose he is ignoring me because I am not in Normandy, the sod!

One hardly dare open the papers these days, it is so good. It may mean a lot to you in England this French news but you have no idea how wonderful it is to the exiles down here.

Have you heard from Laurie (the Pride of Lyons) recently[he added, in a light-hearted jibe at his elder brother's job at the catering company]? Has he recovered from his dysentery? I have been very lucky here. Apart from a slight touch of dysentery in North Africa, I have escaped all the ills that flesh is heir to out here. Are you both in good form still? It can't be long now before these bloody flying bombs are scotched at source, and then you will sail back to Beechgrove, just in time to get a party laid on for my return (whoopee!).

The V-1 attacks on Britain came to an end in September after their launching sites in northern France and Holland were overrun.

Yet a team headed by Wernher von Braun, the rocket scientist, was already close to developing an even more terrifying weapon, the V-2, the world's first long-range guided ballistic missile. The first test flight had been carried out in October 1942, but there were considerable technical problems to overcome. Allied intelligence had been aware of the plans and disrupted the rockets' development by mounting an attack the following August on Peenemünde, on the Baltic island of Usedom where they were being developed by a group of scientists in great secrecy. The attack killed some of the key personnel and forced production to be shifted to the underground Mittelwerk plant to the south, near Leipzig. Von Braun and his team pressed on, however, and by the end of August, the V-2s were ready to go.

Just before noon on 8 September, a first rocket was launched from a battery in occupied Belgium at Paris, killing six people and injuring thirty-six. The same afternoon, one was fired at London, from Wassenaar in Holland. The V-2 took just seven minutes to cover the two hundred or so miles, crashing to earth at 6.43 p.m. in Staveley Road in Chiswick, killing two adults and a three-year-old girl and injuring nineteen. The blast demolished eleven houses, seriously damaged many more and made a crater thirty feet deep. Seconds later, another V-2 landed harmlessly in Epping Forest. Over the following seven months, the Nazis launched more than 500 V-2s at London. Again, the south-east of the capital suffered badly: the worst attack in the Logues' area took place on 1 November in Etherow Street, less than a mile south of the Co-op that had been demolished by the V-1 three months earlier. Striking just after 5 a.m., when most people were still asleep, it totally destroyed twenty-three houses and badly damaged eighty more. Twenty-four people died. However devastating, this paled in comparison with the deadliest V-2 attack on 25 November 1944, when a rocket hit a Woolworths department store in New Cross at lunchtime, killing 168 people and seriously injuring 108.

Worried about the potential effect of Hitler's 'wonder weapon' on civilian morale, the British government initially tried to conceal the causes of the explosions, which they blamed instead on defective gas mains – but the truth quickly got out, prompting beleaguered Londoners to nickname the weapons 'flying gas pipes'. On 8 November, the Germans finally announced their existence to the world and, two days later, Churchill confirmed to parliament that England had been under rocket attack 'for the last few weeks'. There was 'no need to exaggerate the danger', Churchill told MPs. 'The scale and effects of the attacks so far are not significant. Casualties and damage have not been heavy.'

In fact, an estimated 2,754 civilians in London were killed and 6,523 injured by V-2s, a relatively small number given the weapons' potential destructive power. Casualties were kept down by deliberate false reports fed by British intelligence to the Germans claiming that the rockets were overshooting their London targets by ten to twenty miles; subsequent weapons were recalibrated, with the effect that many then fell in rural Kent, where they did less damage. The final V-2 to hit Britain exploded in Orpington on 27 March 1945, killing one woman, Ivy Millichamp, the last civilian fatality caused by enemy action on British soil. Earlier that day, 134 people had died in the second worst V-2 incident of the war when a rocket hit a block of flats in Stepney, east London.

By the middle of 1944, the King was planning another foreign visit – this time to Italy. The fact he was able to contemplate such a trip was a reflection of the changing military situation. Although the north of the country – including Mussolini's 'Republic of Salò' – remained in German hands, the Allies now controlled the south. The King told Churchill he would like to spend a week with British troops, whose successes had been overshadowed by the D-Day landings. It was agreed such a trip would do much to boost morale. More contentious was the King's desire to also spend a day in recently captured Rome. The Foreign Office was alarmed at the prospect of the King meeting his Italian counterpart, Victor Emmanuel III, who was seen as tainted by his association with Mussolini. Nor were they keen on an encounter with the Pope, because of what Eden described as his 'very neutral record in this war'. The King complied with his ministers' wishes, and Rome was removed from his programme.

He flew out on 23 July 1944 for eleven days, travelling through Italy by road and by air. On the Bay of Naples, he stayed in Villa Emma, the house in which Lord Nelson first met Lady Hamilton, and visited the former royal palace of Caserta in which he was served lunch in the great baroque salon. After flying north towards the front, he spent two nights in a couple of caravans at the headquarters of General Sir Oliver Leese, overlooking Arezzo. As had been the case during his North African visit, there were plenty of opportunities for meeting British and Allied troops – not just formal reviews but also impromptu encounters with troops.

Glass of whisky in one hand and cigarette in the other, the King was in his element as he sat talking with military personnel late into the night. The visit appeared to have the desired effect on morale: General Sir Harold Alexander, who commanded Allied forces in Italy, told him 'he was particularly glad I had come out at that moment as the troops rather feared that their campaign had been put in the shade by the Press ever since the landing in Normandy,' the King wrote.[168]

Antony, meanwhile, was in touch with his family on 24 September with news of his promotion to Adjutant of the first battalion, the highest post that an officer of his rank and station of service could hold. 'I am more than flattered and as you may well imagine over-joyed,' he wrote:

> It is one of the most difficult jobs in the army, as one has to be a lawyer, doctor, commander, administrator, judge and advisor all in one – but a most satisfying job and one that gives me enormous experience for after life. In addition to the obvious advantages, there is the material one, of an increase in pay (adjutant's pay) of 3/6d per diem, at which I am last to sneeze!
>
> The war seems to be entering onto its final stages with the display of fireworks and everybody is most cheerful and opti-mistic and demobilisation schemes (rather premature this!) are on everybody's lips.

Yet conditions for the forces in Italy remained tough. 'Last evening we had the first rain of the winter,' Antony wrote on 11 October:

> A thunderstorm the like of which I have never, and hope never to see again, hailstones literally the size of your thumbnail, bouncing off the sand to a height of 6 feet, and so thick that the visibility through a clink in my small tent, issued the day before, thank God! was about 2 yards, quite impossible to go out.
>
> In about 20 seconds the water inside my tent was up to my ankles and rose about 1 foot in half an hour, then the storm subsided and we had bright sunshine.
>
> The tents were dug in and we had large trenches dug all around but it did not make the slightest difference, they filled in the matter of seconds and burst their banks and inundated

us, the most remarkable sight I have yet seen in this country of remarkable sights.

How is dad? Do keep me posted, and tell him to continue to write to me and I will answer. I do hope he's back home doing the 'Flying Jordans' [an Australian circus troupe known for their flying acrobatics] by now. Also tell that swine of a brother of mine to drop me a line and tell me all the scandal.

On 24 August, the King, who was taking a brief holiday in Balmoral, wrote to Montgomery, who was by then headquartered with the 21st Army Group in the Dutch town of Eindhoven. 'Ever since you first explained to me your masterly plan for your part in the campaign in western France, I have followed with admiration its day-to-day development,' he said.[169] 'I congratulate you most heartily on its overwhelming success.' Sensing an opportunity to bask in some reflected royal glory, Montgomery, who had been promoted to Field Marshall on 31 August, invited him to visit his group headquarters. The King was keen and, brushing away fears for his safety travelling so close to the front line, flew into Eindhoven on 11 October for a six-day stay.

Montgomery insisted this would be a working visit without formal parades and other such ceremony; the King was to stay in his own caravan as 'an ordinary soldier guest, with no formality at all'.[170] During his trip he also travelled 200 miles to Liège to the headquarters of Eisenhower, who, to Montgomery's displeasure, had recently taken over from him as Commander-in-Chief Allied Ground Forces. Eisenhower welcomed the King warmly, declaring: 'If there is ever another war, pray God we have the British as an ally, and long live King George VI.'[171]

The twenty-ninth of November meant a State Opening of parliament – so another speech. Going through the text with the King,

Logue played his habitual role of identifying awkward phrases that might trip him up. 'They seem to try to get tongue twisters in,' he wrote of those responsible for the speech. 'In an unbreakable alliance' looked like it was going to cause problems, as did 'fortified by constant collaboration of the governments concerned'– so both were replaced.

Despite all the progress he had made over the years with Logue, the King was still far from a flawless public speaker – as is clearly audible from recordings of his speeches that have survived in the archives. A contemporary analysis was provided in an unsolicited letter sent to Lascelles that June. It was written by the Reverend Robert Hyde, the founder of the Boys' Welfare Association, the organization of which the King had become patron more than two decades earlier when he was the Duke of York. Over the years, Hyde had plenty of opportunities to listen to the King at close quarters and was keen to share his impressions – although he didn't offer any solutions. Lascelles passed the letter to Logue.

'As you know, I have studied the King's speech for some years, so send you this note for what it is worth,' Hyde wrote. The hesitations, he said, seemed quite consistent. 'Apart from a slight lapse into his old difficulties with the c's and g's as in "crisis" and "give", the same two groups still seem to worry him': the 'a' vowel, especially when it was followed by a consonant, as in 'a-go' or 'a-lone', and a repeated sound or letter, as in the combination 'yes please' or 'Which we'.

The State Opening was followed the next Sunday by another royal broadcast. At 9 p.m. on 3 December, the King made a radio speech to mark the disbanding of the Home Guard. A Nazi invasion had seemed imminent when the force was set up in summer 1940. The decision to wind it up was a reflection of the extent to which the tide of war had by now turned in the Allies' favour. The occasion was marked by a review of representative units in Hyde Park at which the King took the salute. In his speech that evening, broadcast from Windsor, he expressed the nation's thanks to those who had served in the Home Guard for their 'steadfast devotion' that had 'helped much to ward off the danger of invasion'. Logue had worked with the King on the text and went to hear him deliver the speech. He was impressed to note he had only one problem with it: he stumbled over the 'w' in the word 'weapons'.

Afterwards, Logue shook hands with the King and, after congratulating him, asked why that particular letter had caught him out.

'I did it on purpose,' the King replied with a grin.

'On purpose?' asked Logue, incredulous.

'Yes. If I don't make a mistake, people might not know it was me.'

The Queen and the two princesses then came into the room and congratulated the King. Logue was struck by how tall Margaret had become. He then told Elizabeth how impressed he had been by the speech she had made when she launched her first warship – the battleship *Vanguard* – on Clydebank a few days earlier. The future Queen told Logue of her terror on walking out onto the platform and seeing the huge ship towering over her. Logue wanted to know why the name of the ship had been cut out.

'It is a fetish in Glasgow that no one mentions the name of a ship,' she replied.

Logue had dinner by himself, and as he made his farewells the King said: 'Don't forget the Christmas Broadcast.'

On 23 December, Logue made his usual trip to Windsor to run through the wording of his speech. The tone of the text was optimistic: in it the King expressed the hope that before the following Christmas 'the story of liberation and triumph' would be complete. 'If we look back to those early days of the war, we can surely say that the darkness daily grows less and less,' read the text.

'The lamps which the Germans put out all over Europe, first in

1914 and then in 1939, are slowly being rekindled. Already we can see some of them beginning to shine through the fog of war that still surrounds so many lands. Anxiety is giving way to confidence and let us hope that before next Christmas Day, the story of liberation and triumph will be complete.'

An annotated copy of the typewritten text, marked 'fourth draft' that was contained among Logue's papers, shows changes he made to eliminate words or phrases that could potentially catch out the King: 'calamities', with its difficult initial 'k' sound, for example, was replaced by 'disasters', while 'goal', with its tricky hard 'g' at the beginning was substituted by the much easier 'end'. The King, meanwhile, had made modifications of his own, adding at the end his yearning for the day when 'the Christmas message – peace on earth, goodwill towards men – finally comes true'. All in all, though, Logue was impressed by the text. 'They all have to be cut out of the same pattern, but I think we altered this particular one less than any other,' he wrote.

As they sat in the study in front of the burning fire, the King suddenly said: 'Logue, I think the time has come, when I can do a broadcast by myself, and you can have a Christmas dinner with your family.'

Logue had been expecting this moment for some time, especially since the Home Guard speech, which the King had delivered so confidently. The Queen agreed they should give it a try. So it was decided that, for the first time, she and the two princesses – rather than Logue – would sit beside the King while he spoke.

'You know, ma'am, I feel like a father who is sending his boy to his first public school,' Logue told the Queen as he went to go.

'I know just how you feel,' she replied, putting her hand on his arm and patting it.

*

While the King was preparing to make his broadcast, Logue was celebrating his first Christmas Day at home since before the war by throwing a house party; Gordon of the *Sunday Express* and his wife were among the guests. Logue was so busy with all the preparations that he scarcely thought about the speech, but at five minutes to three, he slipped off to his bedroom. After saying a silent prayer, he turned on the radio, just in time.

Logue was impressed by what he heard: the King sounded much better than he remembered from three years previously, the last time he had heard him on the radio. He spoke confidently and with good inflection and emphasis, and the breaks between words had all but disappeared. During the eight-minute broadcast, he hesitated badly only once, on the hard 'G' in 'God', but that was only for a second and then he continued even more decisively than before. All the while, Logue made copious notes.

Logue's guests were listening in the drawing room. When he went back to join them, they all congratulated him.

Lionel then tried a little joke: 'Would you like to hear the King speak?'

'Well, we've just heard him,' replied Gordon.

'If you go to the two extensions of the phone, you will hear him talk from Windsor.'

During their final run-through, it had been agreed that Logue would call the King after the broadcast; so he took the main phone and telephoned him, while his guests listened in on the two other phones. When the King came on the line a few seconds later, Logue congratulated him on a wonderful talk, adding: 'My job is over, sir.'

'Not at all,' replied the King. 'It is the preliminary work that counts, and that is where you are indispensable.'

Logue received a number of letters of congratulations – including one from the physician and psychiatrist, Hugh Crichton-Miller.

'That broadcast was streets ahead of any previous performance,' he wrote to Logue on Boxing Day. 'One heard the self-expression of a new freedom which was wholly admirable.'

A delighted Logue passed the message on to the King: 'Many letters of congratulations have come in over the Christmas Broadcast but the one I prize the most is from Crichton-Miller, a great psychoanalyst,' he wrote.

In his return letter a few days later, the King said it was 'certainly encouraging for both of us to get such a report from an expert', adding:

> I do hope you did not mind not being there as I felt that I just had to get one broadcast over alone. The fear of the 'mike' itself has really gone.
>
> The preparation of speeches & broadcasts is the important part & that is where all your help is invaluable. I wonder if you realise how grateful I am to you for having made it possible for me to carry out this vital part of my job. I cannot thank you enough.

Four days later, Logue responded: 'Your very gracious and very welcome letter has given me greater pleasure than I can ever hope to explain.'

> When we began years ago the goal I set myself was for you to be able to make an impromptu speech without stumbling and talk over the air without the fear of the microphone. We did not dream then that a yearly broadcast would be added to your manifold duties.
>
> As you say, these things are now an accomplished fact, and I would not be human if I were not overjoyed that you can now do these things without supervision.

When a fresh patient comes to me the usual query is – 'Will I be able to speak like the King?', and my reply is, 'Yes, if you will work like he does' – I will cure anyone of intelligence if they will only work like you did – for you are now reaping the benefit of this tremendously hard work you did at the beginning. I look forward to the initial preparation of your speeches with keen pleasure, knowing that the delivery will be all that is required, as the greatest pleasure in my life has been the honour of working with you.

CHAPTER TWELVE

Victory

It was one of the greatest – and certainly most joyous – street parties London had ever seen. On Tuesday, 8 May, tens of thousands of singing, dancing people gathered in the Mall in front of Buckingham Palace to celebrate victory over the Germans. Similar scenes were repeated across the length and breadth of Britain. 'The day we have been longing for has arrived at last, & we can look back with thankfulness to God that our tribulation is over,' the King wrote in his diary.[172]

Preparations for the celebrations had been going on for months: the balcony of the palace had been strengthened, the crimson and gold drapery readied. Loudspeakers and floodlights had been erected in the Mall. A team of bell ringers were on standby to ring in victory at St Paul's Cathedral, people stocked up on Union flags and houses were garlanded with bunting. The King had even recorded a version of the speech he was due to give and been filmed doing so. 'Victory in Europe to be declared to-day,' read the headline in that morning's edition of *The Times,* announcing that day and the next as holidays.

At 3 p.m. Churchill spoke to the nation. At 2.41 the previous morning, he announced, the ceasefire had been signed by Colonel

General Alfred Jodl, Chief of the Operations Staff of the German Armed Forces High Command, at the American advance headquarters in Rheims. In his speech, Churchill paid fulsome tribute to the men and women who had 'fought valiantly' on land, sea and in the air – and to those who had laid down their lives for victory. Fittingly, his broadcast was delivered from the War Cabinet Office, the same room in which Neville Chamberlain had announced six years earlier that Britain was at war with Germany.

When Churchill finished speaking, the crowds briefly fell silent before chanting: 'We want the King, We want the King.'

They did not have long to wait. Shortly afterwards, the King, bare-headed and wearing his habitual naval uniform, stepped out onto the balcony, to a chorus of: 'For he's a jolly good fellow'. For the first time in public, he was accompanied not just by the Queen, who was wearing powder blue, but also by the two Princesses – Elizabeth in the khaki uniform of the Auxiliary Territorial Service, which she had joined that February, and Margaret in a blue dress.

An hour or so later, they came out again, and then a third time at 5.30, now accompanied by Churchill, who stood between the King and Queen, waving his cigar to the crowd and giving the victory sign. Churchill left soon afterwards, but just before 7 p.m. the royal family appeared again. 'We went out 8 times altogether during the afternoon and evening,' the King wrote in his diary.[173] 'We were given a great reception.'

Logue's role, as ever, had been to help the King prepare for his speech that evening, which would be broadcast on the BBC and relayed to the crowds outside the Palace. The previous Saturday he had received a telephone call at 11.30 a.m. from Lascelles asking him to go to Windsor that afternoon: 'Peace Day V', as it was known, was in the offing, but Lascelles was still not certain of the exact date. Following Hitler's suicide in the *Führerbunker* on 30 April, Berlin had capitulated to the Russians, while Montgomery had received the surrender of all the German forces operating in north Germany, Denmark and Holland. This still left those in Norway, the Channel Islands and in some pockets still holding out on the French coast. Until they, too, gave up, the war in Europe was not over. Churchill nevertheless believed VE (Victory in Europe) Day could be celebrated by that Monday.

A car came from the Palace to Beechgrove to pick up Logue. He was at Windsor Castle by 4 p.m. 'Found him looking very tired and weary,' he wrote in his diary of the King. 'My heart ached for him.' They went through the speech, which Logue liked very much – although he did alter a few passages, including a line: 'We must go back to work tomorrow'. As someone pointed out, many people would interpret this as 'The King said there was no holiday tomorrow', which, thought Logue, showed how careful one had to be before making such statements.

On Sunday evening, the King and Queen drove up from Windsor in readiness for the announcement expected the next afternoon. On Monday at 3 p.m., the King had a further run-through with Logue, this time at the palace, and it was agreed that Logue should return at 8.30 that evening. He went home for a rest, but at six o'clock the telephone rang; it was Lascelles. 'Not tonight,' he said. 'Norway has not come into line.' Although Churchill was keen to announce the end of hostilities that evening, both Truman and Stalin wanted to postpone for a day, leaving him little option but to do as they wished. The cabinet met and decided to issue a statement proclaiming the following day and the Wednesday to be VE Day holidays. The King was frustrated: 'This came to me as a terrible anti-climax,' he complained.[174]

The delay in the official announcement did not prevent jubilant crowds from turning out in large numbers. Tens of thousands of people, carrying flags and sounding rattles and hooters, thronged the streets around Piccadilly Circus, clinging to cars and clambering onto the roofs of buses. Tugs, motor boats and other small craft raced up the Thames sounding their sirens, and bonfires were lit around London. That evening a crowd gathered outside Buckingham Palace and began to call for the King, but he declined to step out onto the balcony, 'not wishing to shoot his grouse before the Twelfth, so to speak', as Lascelles put it.[175]

VE Day dawned fine and warm after heavy thunderstorms overnight. That morning Logue received another message from the Palace. 'The King would like to see you at dinner tonight, and bring Mrs Logue' – to which an unidentified hand had added: 'Tell her to wear something bright'. When Lionel and Myrtle set off for Buckingham Palace at 6.30, they found the streets decked with flags but virtually deserted. It took them only a few minutes to drive the seven miles from Beechgrove to the centre of London. They encountered their first traffic barrier near Victoria Station, but Miéville had rung up Forest Hill police and asked them to organize a pass, which Logue had picked up. This got them through the barrier and on to the first gate of the Palace. Logue expected a hold-up, but the policeman there was an old friend and the gate swung open. As their car crossed the courtyard towards the Privy Purse entrance, a tremendous cheer broke out – the King and Queen had just come out onto the balcony again. Lionel and Myrtle joined other members of the royal household in wildly cheering and waving handkerchiefs.

Lionel made for the new broadcasting room on the ground floor, facing the lawn, and went through the speech with the King. They made a couple of minor alterations before the King declared, rather plaintively: 'If I don't get dinner before 9 I won't get any after, as everyone will be away, watching the sights.' This, coming from a man in such an exalted position, sent Logue into paroxysms of laughter

– so much that the King himself joined in, though after reflecting for a moment, he said: 'It's funny, but it is quite true.'

After they had eaten, they went back to the broadcasting room at 8.35. Wood, of the BBC, was there. He and Logue synchronized their watches and had another run-through. There were two minutes to go before the King, dressed in his naval uniform, was due to step out once more onto the balcony, but this time to make a speech. Another small further alteration, and then the Queen, now wearing a white ermine wrap over her evening gown and a diamond tiara in her hair, came into the room, as she always did, to wish her husband luck.

Once the floodlights were switched on, a mighty roar erupted from the crowd. 'And in an instant the sombre scene has become fairyland – with the Royal Ensign, lit from beneath, floating in the air,' Logue wrote in his diary. 'Another roar – the King and Queen come on to the balcony.' He was struck by the way the lights played on the Queen's tiara; as she turned, smiling, to wave to the crowd, the floodlights created what looked like a band of flame around her head.

'Today we give thanks to Almighty God for a great deliverance,' the King declared:

> Speaking from our Empire's oldest capital city, war-battered but never for one moment daunted or dismayed, speaking from London, I ask you to join with me in that act of thanksgiving.
>
> Germany, the enemy who drove all Europe into war, has been finally overcome. In the Far East we have yet to deal with the Japanese, a determined and cruel foe. To this we shall turn with the utmost resolve and with all our resources But at this hour when the dreadful shadow of war has passed far from our hearths and homes in these islands, we may at last make

one pause for thanksgiving and then turn our thoughts to the task all over the world which peace in Europe brings with it.

Continuing, the King saluted those who had contributed to victory – both alive and dead – and reflected on how the 'enslaved and isolated peoples of Europe' had looked to Britain during the darkest days of the conflict. He also turned to the future, urging that his subjects should 'resolve as a people to do nothing unworthy of those who died for us and to make the world such a world as they would have desired, for their children and for ours.'

'We may allow ourselves a brief period of rejoicing,' he concluded. 'But let us not forget for a moment the toil and efforts that lie ahead. Japan with all her treachery and greed, remains unsubdued.'

The King was exhausted – and it showed; he spoke slowly and stumbled more than usual over his words, but that didn't seem to matter. The crowd listened in silence, but at the end they raised a great cheer and sang the national anthem. 'We all roared ourselves hoarse,' recalled Noël Coward, who was among the crowd. 'I suppose this is the greatest day in our history.'

The King and Queen reappeared on the balcony together with the princesses at about 10.45 p.m., standing waving to the crowd for about ten minutes, and yet again just before midnight as searchlights flashed across the sky. This time, though, the two princesses were not with them. They had asked their parents to be allowed out to join in the celebrations. The King agreed: 'Poor darlings, they have never had any fun yet,' he wrote in his diary. And so, Elizabeth and Margaret slipped out of the Palace incognito, chaperoned by their uncle, David Bowes-Lyon, the Queen's youngest brother, and accompanied by their governess and a party of young officers. No one recognized the nineteen-year-old heir to the throne and her fourteen-year-old sister as they joined the conga line into one door of the Ritz and out of the other amid crowds that chanted 'We want the King! We want the Queen!' and sang 'Land of Hope and Glory'. Years later the future Queen was to describe this as one of the most memorable nights of her life.

At 11.30 the Queen sent for Lionel and Myrtle, and they said their goodbyes in the sitting room. Then the King's equerry, Peter Townsend, led them out through the gardens to the Royal Mews where their car was waiting. The crowds had thinned out considerably by then, but there were still plenty of people on the streets celebrating victory. The Logues gave a ride in the car to a soldier they saw standing in Horseferry Road, taking him as far as the Kennington Oval. After he had got out, they picked up a couple with a little girl, who wanted to go to Dog Kennel Hill, near Beechgrove. As they drove, they talked about the evening's events and about the King and Queen. The couple thanked the Logues warmly as they left.

The next afternoon, the royal couple drove through north-east London; the following day they headed south to New Cross, Greenwich and Streatham, where they were greeted by large enthusiastic crowds; at various points they would get out of their car and mingle with them. Both evenings they again appeared on the balcony of Buckingham Palace to an ovation from the revellers gathered below. National Services of Thanksgiving were held at St Paul's on 13 May and at St Giles' Cathedral in Edinburgh on 16 May. The following day, the King went to the Great Hall of Westminster where he received addresses from both Houses of Parliament. During his long response he made a prolonged hesitation on the word 'imperishable' and faltered when he spoke of the death of the Duke of Kent. 'We listened in silence to the King's speech,' wrote Harold Nicolson in his diary. 'He has a really beautiful voice and it is to be regretted that his stammer makes it almost intolerably painful to listen to him. It is as if one read a fine piece of prose written on a typewriter the keys of which stick from time to time and mar the beauty of the whole. It makes him stress the wrong word.'[176]

Exhausted, the couple went for a short rest at Windsor. 'We have spent a very busy fortnight since V.E. day & feel rather jaded from it all,' the King wrote in his diary. 'We have been overwhelmed by the kind things people have said over our part in the War. We have only tried to do our duty during these 5½ years. I have found it difficult to rejoice or relax as there is still so much hard work to deal with.'[177] The Queen put it more simply: 'We felt absolutely whacked,' she revealed later.[178]

Whacked or not, there was little time to relax: the war against Japan was still not yet won, while the situation in Europe remained tense following Stalin's insistence to Churchill and Roosevelt at the Yalta conference that February that Poland and the other countries of Eastern Europe should be part of a sphere of Soviet influence. On a personal level, the King was saddened by the sudden death in April of Roosevelt, whom he had regarded with genuine admiration, affection and gratitude since their meeting in America on the eve of war. The blow was even greater because Roosevelt had spoken of paying a return visit to Britain that spring and the King was looking forward to hosting him at Buckingham Palace.

It was instead Harry Truman, Roosevelt's vice-president and successor, who came to Britain that August, though for only a few hours on his way home to America from the conference in Potsdam on the future of Germany and Europe. The King had been determined to get to know the new American leader in the hope of establishing the same rapport with him as he enjoyed with Roosevelt and travelled down to Plymouth Sound to meet Truman on board the battle cruiser, HMS *Renown*, which was anchored alongside the USS *Augusta*. The two men hit it off. Truman proclaimed himself 'impressed with the King as a good man'.[179] Among the subjects discussed was America's atomic bomb, the first of which Truman would drop on Hiroshima on 6 August, four days later.

Domestic events, however, posed the greatest challenge to the King. It was now almost ten years since the last general election. While the all-party National Government had been united over the waging of war, it was divided on ideological lines when it came to determining the direction of domestic policy, which now moved to the fore. Churchill hoped his coalition could nevertheless continue in office until the defeat of Japan, but Attlee was pressing for an election. Faced with apparently insurmountable policy differences, Churchill eventually bowed to Labour's demands and on 23 May went to the Palace to request a dissolution. The election was set for 5 July, though counting was postponed for three weeks to allow time to get in the ballots from troops stationed overseas.

Churchill was confident of victory; on 25 July, the day before the count, he told the King he expected the Conservatives to be returned with a majority of between thirty and eighty.[180] Yet he had seriously misjudged the mood of the British people. Far from rewarding the Prime Minister for his wartime leadership, they seemed determined to punish the Conservatives for the failings of the inter-war years, during which they had run the country continuously with only two brief interruptions. The Conservatives lost 160 seats, while Labour gained 230, giving them a massive overall majority of 180. On the evening of 26 July Churchill drove to the Palace to offer his resignation and recommend the King send for Attlee. It was, according to the King, a 'very sad meeting'. The distrust that had characterized his relationship with Churchill when they first worked together five years earlier had long since been replaced by mutual admiration and what the King's official biographer described as a 'unique degree of intimacy'.[181] Indeed, the King felt towards his defeated Prime

Minister the same sympathy he had felt for Chamberlain when he was ousted five years earlier. 'I saw Winston at 7.00 p.m. and . . . told him I thought the people were very ungrateful after the way they had been led in the War,' the King noted in his diary.[182] 'We said goodbye & I thanked him for all his help to me during the 5 war years.' Half an hour later, the King received Attlee, who seemed as surprised by his own victory as Churchill had been by his defeat.

The King also faced a more personal problem: finding a potential role for the Duke of Windsor. The issue could be put on the back burner as long as Britain was at war, but as the end of the conflict loomed, the Palace became preoccupied with where the King's elder brother should live and what he could do. The Duke had effectively forced the issue in January by saying he would step down from the governorship of the Bahamas at the end of that April, a few weeks before the end of what was traditionally a five-year term of office. Various possibilities were discussed in the ensuing months: the two that most appealed to the Duke were another representational job abroad or returning to Britain. Both prospects were unacceptable to the Palace; Lascelles argued it would be best for him to live as a private citizen in the United States, but the Duke, who remained preoccupied by his finances, would do so only if he were given an official position – which would be the only way of obtaining relief from heavy American taxes. This, however, was ruled out by the Palace. Nothing had been decided when his resignation was formally announced except that he and Duchess would go first to Miami on holiday. In the end the former monarch had little alternative but to resume his pre-war exile in France.

Although Logue had celebrated his sixty-fifth birthday that February, he had no plans for retirement and continued to see other patients – among them Michael Astor, the twenty-nine-year-old son of Viscount Astor, the wealthy owner of the *Observer*, who wanted to follow his father into politics. On 3 June, Miéville, who had introduced them, wrote to Logue to thank him for 'what you did for young Astor' after he was adopted as the Conservative candidate for Surrey East. 'He ought to get in as it is a v. safe seat, but I fear he will not contribute much when he does arrive in the House of Commons,' he added. Miéville was right on both counts: Astor was duly elected, but served only until 1951 and made little impact on British public life.

For Logue, joy at the return of peace quickly became tinged with worries about his family. East Africa had not proved good for Laurie's health: the bout of dysentery he suffered in Mogadishu in April 1944, about which Antony had written mockingly, had actually been a serious one. In the course of the following few months he had been in and out of hospital there and in Nairobi several times. His parents were keen to get him home – which Logue achieved, by pulling a few strings at the Palace. Laurie left his unit at the beginning of December, with a medical classification of 'D' – temporarily unfit for medical service – and set off for Britain on 10 January. A few days later Logue wrote to Miéville to thank him for his help. Laurie, he wrote, had been 'nearly at the end of his tether, and could not have gone on much longer . . . I cannot tell you how grateful Myrtle and myself are to you.'

Once back in Britain, Laurie slowly recovered, but Logue's own health was deteriorating. Later in June he went into St Andrew's Hospital in Dollis Hill in north-west London, to have an operation on his prostate. The hospital was run by the Little Sisters of Mary, also known as the Blue Nuns, and Logue was treated in a new wing for private patients. While he was in hospital he spoke to the medical staff about his work. 'He was very modest but happy to talk,' recalled John Millar, one of two resident medical officers. 'His teaching methods were primarily concerned with breathing, control of the muscles of the chest and diaphragm. He demonstrated to me how he was able to contract individual chest muscles.'

While Logue was recuperating, Myrtle suddenly fell seriously ill and was taken to the same hospital. A few days later, on 22 June, she died of acute kidney failure. The shock was all the greater since a fortnight earlier she had still been working with her usual energy at the Boomerang Club. Its members expressed regret at the death of one of their 'most active voluntary workers'. Logue was heartbroken at the loss of the woman, who, as he had described in his BBC radio interview in September 1942, had 'stood by my side' for so many years 'and helped me so valiantly over the rough places'. Myrtle was cremated at Honor Oak Crematorium in south-east London, near their home.

The King sent a telegram of condolence as soon as he heard the news: 'The Queen and I are grieved to hear of Mrs Logue's death and send you and your family our deepest sympathy in your loss – George.' He followed up with two letters: one on June 27 and a second on the following day. 'I was so shocked when I was told because your wife was in such good form on Victory night,' he wrote to Logue. 'I do so feel for you as I know you had a perfect companionship with her . . . Please do not hesitate to let me know if I can be of any help to you.'

On 14 July, Logue wrote back to the King:

Your two letters gave both my boys and myself great comfort and I am deeply grateful to you.

Valentine [who had joined the Royal Medical Corps on 10 February] leaves in a few weeks for India with a neurosurgical unit. And Tony we expect to go back to Italy shortly.

Laurie I hope will be left in England. He has had a bad time in Africa and has not yet recovered. I don't know just what I would have done without him. I have not been very well but I am glad to say that I am back at work, the great panacea for all sorrow, and I am entirely at your Majesty's convenience. I expect there will be a Parliament to be opened shortly.

The State Opening, which took place on 15 August, saw a return to most – if not quite all – of the pomp of the pre-war years. Thousands of people lined the streets as the King, dressed in the service uniform of an Admiral of the Fleet, and the Queen, wearing her customary shade of light blue, travelled to parliament in an open landau. The ceremony had initially been scheduled for 8 August. But Attlee had had to take Churchill's place alongside Truman and Stalin at the Potsdam conference almost immediately after his election victory was announced. The State Opening was therefore postponed by a week to give the Labour leader more time to complete his government and formulate his programme. The day also brought another cause for celebration: a few hours earlier, Emperor Hirohito of Japan announced his country's surrender, following America's dropping of the second atomic bomb on Nagasaki on 9 August. The Second World War was finally over.

The King's speech reflected the momentous nature of the event: 'The surrender of Japan has brought to an end six years of warfare which have caused untold loss and misery to the world,' he said. 'In this hour of deliverance, it is fitting that we should give humble and solemn thanks to God by whose grace we have been brought to final victory.' The government, he continued, would work with the governments of the Dominions and with other peace-loving peoples 'to attain a world of freedom, peace and social justice so that the sacrifices of the war shall not have been in vain'.

The speech also concerned domestic policy. Attlee took Labour's massive majority as a mandate for a programme of sweeping social, economic and political change that aimed to transform Britain. Among the major reforms to which the new administration was committed was the nationalization of the Bank of England, the coal industry and the gas and electricity networks, as well as the creation of a National Health Service. 'It will be the aim of my ministers to see that national resources in labour and material are employed with the fullest efficiency in the interests of all,' the King declared. MPs were told money would be needed 'not, happily, for the continuance of the war, but for expenditure on reconstruction and other essential services'. The King delivered his speech well. 'His voice was clear, and he spoke better than usual and was more impressive,' wrote Chips Channon, the diarist. 'But they say that the word Berlin had to be substituted for Potsdam, which he could not have articulated.'[183]

As a constitutional monarch, the King had no alternative but to accept his new government. A natural conservative, he did think the government was pushing ahead too fast with nationalization programme, though, and expressed private concerns about the effect of heavy taxation and estate duties on the wealthy classes. When Vita Sackville-West told him that her family's home, Knole, had been given to the National Trust, he replied despairingly: 'Everything is going nowadays. Before long, I shall also have to go.'[184]

During the afternoon cheering crowds gathered around the Palace, and, that night, after they had changed into their evening clothes, the King and Queen went out repeatedly onto the balcony, just as they had done three months earlier on VE Day. The evening was perfectly clear, warm and still. The writer, John Lehmann, described making his way towards the Mall through streets that were brightly lit and bedecked with flags until he reached 'the great illuminated façade of the Palace, with an enormous, raw half-moon hanging over it.'

As we came nearer, the noise of singing increased. People were clustered as thickly as swarming bees. Every few minutes the singing would pause, and the chant would go up: 'We want the King . . . We want the King.' Until at last the French windows on the far, red-draped, fairy-tale balcony were opened, and the King and Queen, diminutive but glittering figures – the Queen's diamonds flashed into the night under the arc-lights – came out to wave and be greeted by cheer after cheer, waving of hands, and the singing of 'For he's a jolly good fellow'.[185]

That Christmas the King again spoke to the nation without Logue at his side. The tone of this, his first peacetime broadcast after six years of war, was suitably upbeat. 'By gigantic efforts and sacrifices a great work has been done, a great evil has been cast from the earth,' he said. 'No peoples have done more to cast it out than you to whom I speak. With my whole heart I pray to God by whose grace victory has been won, that this Christmas may bring to my peoples all the world over every joy they have dreamed of in the dark days that are gone.' Yet the joy was tempered by grieving for those who had given their lives in the war and a thought for those, 'still to be numbered in millions, who are spending Christmas far from your homes, engaged in East and West in the long and difficult task of restoring to shattered countries the means and the manners of civilised life'.

Peace may have come, but life in Britain remained tough. As *The Times* put it in its report of the King's broadcast: 'The continuing shortages in the supply of many necessaries, especially houses, food, clothing and fuel, will call for the same spirit of tolerance and understanding which the nation has displayed during the past six years of war.' Rationing, far from being ended, became stricter: bread, which had been freely on sale during the war, was rationed

from July 1946; in November the following year so, too, were potatoes after the crop was hit by spring floods followed by a summer
drought. The government came under intense criticism. 'So Britain
is now to face the winter with both bread and potatoes rationed – the
two commodities which during the war were considered unration-
able, the shock-absorbers of the rationing system,' commented the
Spectator. 'The position, of course, looks different according to the
comparisons made. If the comparison is with pre-war days it is
intolerable, if with Central and Eastern Europe at the moment it is
comfortable.'[186] The restrictions were gradually lifted in the following
years, but it was not until July 1954, with the end of controls on meat
and bacon, that food rationing in Britain finally ended – fourteen
years after it was introduced.

Logue, meanwhile, was left to grieve for Myrtle alone: Antony had
left the army and was continuing his studies at Queen's College,
Cambridge, after having managed to be transferred from London
University. Realizing his heart was not in being a doctor, he had
switched to law. Laurie was back working for Lyons at their headquarters in Nottingham, while Valentine was in Mandalay, where he
performed a brain operation – a first for Burma – that was witnessed
by doctors and surgeons from across the country.

Logue's own health continued to trouble him; in spring 1946
he had to go back into hospital. His growing world weariness was
evident in a letter he sent to Myrtle's brother, Rupert Gruenert,
that May. 'Life goes on, and I am working very hard, harder than
I should at my age 66, but work is the only thing that lets me
forget,' he wrote. He also expressed the hope that he could visit
Australia – in what would have been his first trip home since he
and Myrtle emigrated to Britain more than two decades earlier.
'As soon as the Commonwealth give over control of the shipping

lines, I am coming out for a six-month spell, but not under the present conditions, thank you. When I travel I like to do it in comfort. I am not allowed to fly, on account of my abnormal blood pressure.' He never made the trip.

CHAPTER THIRTEEN

Voices from the Other Side

In April 1947, with Myrtle gone and his sons far away, Logue sold Beechgrove. It was not just because the house was now far too large for him. As he wrote to the King that December when he sent him his annual birthday greetings, 'it held too many memories' of life with Myrtle. He moved to a 'comfortable little flat' at 29 Princes Court in the Brompton Road in Knightsbridge, just opposite Harrods. Beechgrove was bought by the Community of the Nursing Sisters of St John the Divine as a residence for its members.

Logue continued to teach, more often than not in his new home rather than Harley Street, even though he kept his practice there. After years in which he was careful not to speak about his royal connection, he now allowed himself to boast a little about his relationship with the King – or 'my king' – as he called him. This was especially the case when talking to his younger patients, who appeared suitably impressed. 'He showed us a letter he had got from the King, written in his own hand writing, thanking Mr Logue for some books he had given the King for his birthday,' Alan Elliott, a fourteen-year-old from Northern Ireland, whom Logue had begun to treat four years earlier, wrote to his family. 'Mr Logue says that if he puts: "The King, London" with his own initials in the bottom left hand corner [of the envelope], it goes straight to the King and no one dare touch it!'

David Radcliffe, who was in his second or third year at Oundle School in Northamptonshire when he was sent to see Logue, had a similar experience. 'I will always remember Logue saying, on one of my visits, "Did you hear my King's speech on the radio last night?",' he recalled more than half a century later. 'It was encouraging to think that King George, my king, and I had something in common, and that I too had been helped by one who I think was truly a national hero for helping George VI lead the country through so many difficult years.'

Of Logue's various cases in the immediate post-war years, particularly poignant was that of Jack Fennell, a thirty-one-year-old from Merthyr Tydfil in Wales, who had written to the King in September 1947 pleading for his assistance. Unemployed, penniless, and with one child, Fennell was despondent and suffered from an inferiority complex brought on by years of discrimination over his stammer. Lascelles forwarded Fennell's letter to Logue, asking him to take a look at him and give an opinion on his condition. Logue reckoned he might need as much as a year of treatment – which Fennell couldn't afford. After trying in vain to get help from the various welfare bodies, Fennell eventually found a sponsor in Viscount Kemsley, the newspaper baron who owned the *Daily Sketch* and the *Sunday Times*. Lodging in an army hostel in Westminster and with the offer of a job at the Kemsley newspaper press in London, Fennell began his treatment in January 1948. Kemsley paid Logue's fee, which he reduced from his usual three pounds three shillings a consultation to two pounds and ten shillings.

By April the following year, Logue wrote back to the newspaper baron boasting of the progress his patient had made. Fennell had grown in confidence and passed 'with flying colours' an interview to work at the Atomic Energy Research Establishment at Harwell, Oxfordshire. Logue continued to see him for another year, although their appointments were reduced to just one a month. By August 1949, things were going so well at work that Fennell had moved his family into a house in Wantage; in January the following year he enrolled at the Oxford College of Technology and by May was offered a permanent job at Harwell.

Logue's own youngest son, however, was in poor health. Antony was taken into hospital in the spring suffering from suspected appendicitis but then had to undergo four major operations within six days. In his customary birthday letter to the King that December, Logue blamed the dramatic turn of events on a delayed reaction to the injury Antony had suffered in North Africa in 1943. His son had been involved 'in a desperate fight for his life and is still in hospital', Logue wrote. 'He is at last making progress, and I hope to have him here for Christmas.'

The King wrote back two days later expressing sympathy. 'You have certainly had your share of shocks and sorrows,' he said. Rather touchingly, after their years of working together, he updated Logue with how his public speaking was going, noting how pleased he had been with a speech he had made at his father's memorial. He expressed concern, however, that his Christmas message would not be easy, 'because everything is so gloomy'.

Antony recovered and returned to Cambridge, graduating in law in June 1949. Logue was suitably proud. He also realized a long-standing ambition of his own: in January the previous year he wrote to the King asking him to become patron of the College of Speech Therapists, which now counted 350 members, was 'quite solvent' and was recognized by the British Medical Association. 'I am sixty-eight years of age and it will be a wonderful thought in my old age to know that you were the head of this rapidly growing and essential organisation,' he wrote. The King agreed.

Logue was nevertheless finding it difficult to adapt to life without Myrtle and was drawn to spiritualism in the hope of making contact with her on the 'other side'. In 1946 he got in touch with Lilian Bailey, a prominent 'deep trance medium' who over the years held séances for a number of prominent figures in Britain and abroad – among them the Hollywood actresses Mary Pickford, Merle Oberon and Mae West, and Mackenzie King, the Canadian Prime Minister. Born into a working-class family in Cardiff in 1895, Bailey worked as a secretary for the army in France during the First World War – for which work, she claimed, somewhat implausibly, to have been awarded the OBE – and then married William Bailey, a railway stoker with whom she went to live in his native Crewe. Mourning her mother, who died when she was eighteen, she drifted into spiritualism, which was enjoying a renaissance in the 1920s as women tried to contact the husbands they had lost in the war. Bailey soon made a name for herself and, after a few years, was travelling frequently to London to satisfy the growing demand for séances. Eventually she and her husband moved to the capital, settling in a luxurious home.

Bailey claimed as her spirit guide an ex-Grenadier Guards captain named William Hedley Wootton, who, so her story went, had been shot over one eye and killed instantly in France during the First World War. To those who questioned her, Bailey insisted that she had authenticated Wootton's service at the War Office, which had confirmed he had been killed in the First Battle of Ypres. She also claimed to have written to his mother, who by then had moved to Boston, after her spirit guide told her the address. Bailey's claims were accepted at first hand by her contemporaries, but Christopher Wilson, a historian, who researched Bailey decades later, found no trace of Wootton in military records. Nor could he find any record of Bailey having been awarded an OBE.[187]

Logue was introduced to Bailey by another colourful character, Hannen Swaffer, a prominent journalist and drama critic, who was both a militant socialist and the leader of a spiritualist home circle that followed the teachings of a Native American spirit named 'Silver Birch'. According to an account by Bailey's biographer, William F. Neech,[188] Logue told Swaffer that he had been left so grief-stricken by Myrtle's death that he had contemplated suicide. 'I am a broken man. I have lost my wife and I cannot go on,' he said.

A few days later, Swaffer and Bailey met at a spiritualist gathering.

'Can you come to my flat to help a man in grave trouble?' he asked her.

The medium said she was happy to help, and a few days later, Logue arrived at Swaffer's flat overlooking Trafalgar Square. The journalist had moved there some years earlier to have 'a front seat when the revolution came'. He was still waiting, the British proletariat having remained depressingly reluctant to rise up and overthrow their oppressors. The doorbell rang, and Bailey made her entrance. Logue recognized her, but she gave the impression of not knowing who he was – a tribute to his success in having kept his long relationship with the King out of the public eye. They sat down in a circle, but even before Bailey entered her state of trance, she looked embarrassed.

'I don't know why it is and I scarcely like to tell you, but George V is here,' she said, hesitatingly. 'He asks me to thank you for what you did for his son.'

To her surprise – and relief – Logue replied simply: 'I quite understand.' Bailey also announced that she could see Myrtle's spiritual form. 'But she is too excited to do more than send her love to her husband.'

A few days later they met again. Again, according to Neech's account, Myrtle this time 'communicated' with Logue, controlling Bailey's body and wrapping her arms around him. Myrtle, it was claimed, told him of changes he had made to his home since her death – things no one else could know. Wootton, her spirit guide, even told Logue that his pet name for his wife was 'Muggsy'.

Then Bailey invited Logue to ask any question.

'Does my wife want to say anything about the place where we first met?' he asked.

Bailey responded with a puzzled expression. 'She is referring to a bird named Charlie. It is not a canary. It looks like a sparrow.'

Logue was overwhelmed. Charlie Sparrow was his best friend and it was at his twenty-first birthday party that he and Myrtle met and fell in love.

From then on, Logue had regular séances with Bailey. Logue's sons were horrified, but there was nothing they could do to dissuade their father. Such was his gratitude towards Bailey that he even gave her the ornate wooden chair in which the King used to sit when, still the Duke of York, he had visited Logue's Harley Street consulting room. Valentine, well on his way to becoming one of Britain's leading neurosurgeons, had no time for what he considered nonsense. Nor did his wife, Anne: 'It was something we thought was really crazy and wished to goodness he wasn't doing it,' she recalled years later.[189] The King was more understanding; when Logue told him of his séances with Bailey, he replied simply: 'My family are no strangers to Spiritualism.'

Amid the gloom of the immediate post-war years, there was one glimmer of light: on 10 July 1947, it was announced that Princess Elizabeth and Prince Philip would marry. The two had remained in touch since their meeting at Windsor in Christmas 1943, prompting speculation of a possible future union – speculation that was encouraged both by Philip's 'Uncle Dickie' Mountbatten and by the exiled King George II of Greece. As long as the war continued there was little chance of their relationship going any further. That changed when peace came. The King was in two minds about the match, not least because he thought his daughter was too young and was concerned she had fallen for the first young man she had ever met. Philip was also seen by many at court – the King included – as far from the ideal consort for a future monarch, not least because of his German blood; the Queen was said to refer to him privately as 'the Hun'. In the hope that their daughter might find someone else, she and the King organized a series of balls packed with eligible men, to which Philip, to his great annoyance, was not invited. Yet Elizabeth remained devoted to her prince.

Eventually, in 1946, Philip asked the King for his daughter's hand in marriage. The King agreed – but still had one last trick up his sleeve: he insisted any formal announcement was postponed until after Elizabeth's twenty-first birthday in April the following year. In the meantime, at Mountbatten's suggestion, Philip had renounced his Greek and Danish titles, as well as his allegiance to the Greek crown, converted from Greek Orthodoxy to the Church of England and become a naturalized British subject. He also adopted the surname Mountbatten (an Anglicized version of Battenberg) from his mother's family.

The couple married on 20 November 1947 in Westminster Abbey in a ceremony attended by representatives of various royal families – but not Philip's three surviving sisters, who had married German aristocrats with Nazi connections and so stayed away. On the morning of the wedding, Philip was made Duke of Edinburgh, Earl of Merioneth and Baron Greenwich of Greenwich in the County of London. The previous day the King had bestowed on him the style of His Royal Highness.

The King's public speaking may have been getting better and better, but his health was worsening. He was still only forty-nine when the war ended, but in poor physical shape: the strain he had been under during the conflict was an important factor. Another was his chain-smoking: in July 1941, *Time* magazine reported that, in order to share the hardship of his people, he had cut down from twenty to twenty-five cigarettes a day to a mere fifteen. After the war, he started smoking more again.

Despite his poor health, the King set off in February 1947 on a ten-week tour of South Africa. The schedule was a gruelling one and the King tired easily; a warm reception from the Afrikaners, especially from those old enough to remember the Boer War, was not guaranteed. There was also an added psychological strain: Britain was again in the grip of a bitter winter, and the King suffered pangs of guilt at not sharing his subjects' suffering; at one point, he even suggested cutting short his trip. Attlee strongly advised against it, warning this would only add to the sense of crisis.

The King, Queen and their two daughters travelled more than 10,000 miles, much of it aboard a white royal train. Princess Elizabeth's twenty-first birthday fell during the trip and she marked it with a broadcast to the Empire in which she vowed to dedicate her life to 'our great imperial Commonwealth to which we all belong'. The royal party was greeted with large crowds wherever they went, although the Nationalists boycotted official gatherings and there was a lack of enthusiasm among many Afrikaners. The King found the heat and all the travel something of a trial, and lost an alarming amount of weight. Smuts, the Prime Minister, was facing a general election the following year, and had hoped to make political capital out of the royal visit. Instead it was the Nationalists who won, ushering in more than four decades of apartheid. The King got a foretaste of what was to come when he was told by his hosts that when giving medals to black South African servicemen, he should not speak to them or shake them by the hand. He objected but was told he must do as the government said.

Logue, who followed the King's progress through Africa from afar and listened to those of his speeches that were broadcast on the radio, was among the first to congratulate him on his return to Britain. 'It has been a great joy to me, to keep in touch with your travels during the last 100 days, and a wonderful pleasure to hear your speeches,' he wrote on 12 May. 'I come in for a large and, in many cases, undeserved glory, as everyone I come in contact with is enthusiastic about the trip and particularly the speeches. Almost every day someone says to me "Hasn't the King developed into a great speaker and what a beautiful voice he has"!!'

The King was beginning to suffer cramp in his legs, complaining in a letter to Logue of 'feeling tired and strained'. By October 1948, the cramps had become painful and permanent: his left foot was numb all day and the pain kept him awake all night; later, the problem seemed to shift to the right. The King was examined the following month by Professor James Learmouth, one of Britain's greatest authorities on vascular complaints, who diagnosed early arteriosclerosis; at one stage it was feared his right leg might have to be amputated because of fear of gangrene.

Logue wrote a few weeks later to express his concerns: 'As one who had the honour to be closely connected with you during those dreadful war years and had a glimpse of the enormous amount of work you did, and saw the strain that was constantly made on your vitality, it is very evident that you have driven yourself too hard and at last have had to call a halt,' he wrote. 'I know that rest, medical skill and your own wonderful spirit will restore you to health, and this will be the prayer of your devoted subjects, among whom is one that feels this matter very deeply.'

The King appeared to have recovered by December, but the doctors ordered continued rest, and a trip to Australia and New Zealand planned for early the next year had to be abandoned. The King nevertheless seemed upbeat in a letter he sent Logue on 10 December. 'Personally I am very surprised that something of the sort hadn't happened before as I was feeling tired & strained after South Africa,' he wrote:

> You will remember my laryngitis at the Guildhall. However, I am very glad it was forced out before going to Australia & New Zealand. What a disappointment that is to everyone there I'm afraid but our visit is only put off for a while. I am getting better with treatment & rest in bed & the doctors do have a smile on their faces, which I feel is all to the good. I hope you are well & are still helping those who cannot speak.

Logue was also having a bad year – and confined for some of the time to his new flat, which was on the eighth floor. As he wrote back to the King in his annual birthday letter a few days later, he was in such poor health that in August he collapsed. He had since recovered and was even working again, though was only 'allowed four patients a day'. He was heartened, though, by the apparent good news about the King's condition. 'I have followed the wonderful struggle you have made and rejoice the Almighty has brought you back to health,' Logue wrote.

Christmas was approaching – and with it the annual message. 'I have got a new type of broadcast this year from a more per-sonal angle which I hope will go well,' the King wrote back on 20

December. In a sign of the progress he had made over the years, he no longer looked to Logue to help him prepare for his broadcast, let alone to sit beside him as he had done for so many years, but he still urged him to telephone afterwards to give his opinion on his performance.

The King spoke from Sandringham; the personal angle he mentioned involved talking about 'three vivid personal experiences' that 1948 had brought: his silver wedding anniversary that April; the birth of Charles, his first grandchild, in November; and the bout of poor health at the end of the year that had forced postponement of his planned trip to Australia and New Zealand.

'As for the third, even this, like every other cloud, can have a silver lining, and it has had one striking result which it shares with the other two,' the King said. 'For the impression made equally by all three experiences is the grateful recollection of the volume of good will and affection that they brought from all over the world to me and mine.' They had also, he continued, left him with a fuller understanding of his role as monarch, which was 'no abstract symbol of constitutional theory' but rather 'one pole of a very real human relationship'.

The King's health continued to be so poor that he did not return to London until the end of February, when he resumed a limited programme of audiences and held an investiture. The following month brought more bad news, however. After a full examination, it became clear his recovery had not been as complete as the doctors had thought. Learmouth advised a right lumbar sympathectomy, a surgical procedure intended to free the flow of blood to his leg. The operation, carried out at the King's insistence in an impromptu operating theatre in Buckingham Palace rather than a hospital, went well. The King was under no illusions, however, that he would be completely restored to health. His doctors ordered him to rest much more, reduce his official engagements and cut down drastically on the smoking that had aggravated his condition. A second attack of thrombosis could be lethal, he was warned.

Logue wrote to the King on 28 March: 'It has been with a very anxious mind that I have watched the bulletin issued by your Doctor – and seen the gallant struggle you have made, but my mind has been greatly relieved by the utterance of The Princess Elizabeth at the headquarter of the WVS [Women's Voluntary Service] when she said: "My Father is getting on very well indeed", he wrote. 'It is only natural that I should be perturbed after having had the great honour of being associated with your Majesty over so many years.'

'My dear Logue,' the King wrote back two days later:

'Thank you so much for your letter, I am at last much better & hope in time to become a new man with a new lease of life.

'The rest & treatment have done me a world of good & once the effects of the operation have settled down I should feel quite different.'

The King's health did indeed appear to continue to improve through 1949, but the doctors nevertheless ordered as much rest as possible. That Christmas brought another message to the nation, the Commonwealth and the Empire. 'Once more I am in the throes of preparing my broadcast,' he wrote to Logue, thanking him for his annual birthday greetings, which were still accompanied, as they had been every year for almost three decades, by a gift of two or three books that Logue thought he would like. 'How difficult it is to find anything new to say in these days. Words of encouragement to do better in the New Year is the only thing to go on. I am longing to get it over. It still ruins my Christmas.'

Despite the King's usual reluctance, the broadcast went well. Afterwards, Michael Adeane, who in 1945 had become his assistant private secretary, wrote to Logue to congratulate him on all the work he had done with the King for previous years' broadcasts. 'I happened to be here & therefore listened from the next room but I have never heard a speech go smoother and better. Moreover,' Adeane wrote, 'I have never known the speaker more calm or more confident about the whole thing beforehand. One did not get the impression that he was in the least worried or anxious, & I don't believe he was. I know I would have been.' Adeane began his letter 'Dear Lionel', adding that he felt they knew each other sufficiently well for him to 'get away' with such an informal form of address – a contrast with other officials at the Palace and indeed, the King, himself, who would always refer to Logue by his surname.

Logue wrote back (beginning his letter 'Dear Michael') to say he was delighted that Adeane had liked the broadcast. 'I spoke to H.M. on the telephone at 5 o'clock & he was very pleased with the performance,' he said. 'I agree with you that it was the best ever, he worked up to 80 words to the minute which is excellent, his voice was well pitched, & very well controlled, & the whole effort was marked with smooth force. He is indeed reaping a reward for all his hard work & so many people have rung me up about the Broadcast.'

CHAPTER FOURTEEN

The Last Words

To the millions who gathered around their radios on Christmas Day 1951, the voice was both familiar and yet worryingly different. Delivering his message, the King sounded husky and hoarse, as if he were suffering from a particularly heavy cold. At times, his voice dropped to almost a whisper. He also seemed to be speaking slightly faster than usual. Yet few of those listening could have failed to have been moved by what their monarch had to say.

After beginning by describing Christmas as a time when everyone should count their blessings, the King struck a deeply personal note. 'I myself have every cause for deep thankfulness, for not only – by the grace of God and through the faithful skill of my doctors, surgeons and nurses – have I come through my illness, but I have learned once again that it is in bad times that we value most highly the support and sympathy of our friends,' he declared. 'From my peoples in these islands and in the British Commonwealth and Empire as well as from many other countries this support and sympathy has reached me and I thank you now from my heart. I trust that you yourselves realise how greatly your prayers and good wishes have helped and are helping me in my recovery.'

The King's five doctors telephoned their congratulations, but the newspapers both in Britain and beyond were shocked by what they had heard. Although it was a relief to hear the King speak for the first time since undergoing a major operation that September, the wavering tone of his voice made clear how poorly he was. 'Millions of people all over the world, listening to the King's Christmas Day broadcast, noticed with concern the huskiness in his voice,' the *Daily Mirror* reported two days later. 'The question at many Christmas firesides was: Is the King just suffering from a chill, or is the huskiness a sequel to the lung operation he had three months ago?'

For the first time since the King had delivered his first Christmas message in 1937, he had not spoken his words live but they had instead been pre-recorded. The explanation lay in a further deterioration in his health. After the various medical crises he suffered in the late 1940s, he had been ordered by his doctors to rest and relax as much as possible and to cut down his public appearances. A further strain came from the worsening economic and political situation: Attlee's Labour party, elected by a landslide in 1945, had seen its majority eroded to a handful in 1950 and was struggling to remain in power. A general election in October 1951 brought a change of government, with Winston Churchill, now aged seventy-six, returning to Downing Street.

The King had been well enough to open the Festival of Britain in May 1951, riding with the Queen in an open carriage through the streets of London, escorted by the household cavalry. 'This is no time for despondency,' he announced from the steps of St Paul's Cathedral. 'I see this festival as a symbol of Britain's abiding courage and vitality.' But many of those who saw him close up during the service remarked on how ill he looked – and that evening he took to his bed with influenza.

The King was slow to recover and also suffered from a persistent cough; he was initially diagnosed with a catarrhal inflammation of the left lung and treated with penicillin. The symptoms persisted, however, and that September he was found to have a malignant growth. Clement Price Thomas, a surgeon who specialized in such problems, told the King the lung should be removed as soon as possible – although, as was the practice of the day, he did not reveal to his patient that he was suffering from cancer.

The operation, carried out eight days later, went well. It had been feared that the King might lose certain nerves in the larynx, which would have made him unable to speak in more than a whisper. The fear proved unfounded. By October, he was writing to his mother expressing relief that he had not suffered complications, but he remained a sick man. During the State Opening of Parliament that November, his speech from the throne – exceptionally – was read for him by Lord Simonds, the Lord Chancellor. There were suggestions that he should not make his Christmas broadcast either. According to a newspaper report in the *Daily Express*,[190] it was proposed his place at the microphone be taken by his wife or by Princess Elizabeth. The King refused, even though it would undoubtedly have spared him considerable discomfort. 'My daughter may have her opportunity next Christmas,' he reportedly said. 'I want to speak to my people myself.' The King's determination to deliver his message in person – much he had always dreaded doing so – showed the extent to which, during the course of his reign, those few minutes on the afternoon of 25 December had been turned into one of the most important events in the national calendar.

The doctors warned, however, that a live broadcast could prove too much of a strain. Thus a compromise was found: the King recorded the message in sections, sentence by sentence, repeating some over and over again, until he was happy. Although the final product was barely six minutes long, the whole process took the best part of two days. The result was also far from perfect: imperfect editing led to what seemed to listeners an uncharacteristically fast delivery. For the King, though, it was far better than any of the alternatives. 'The nation will hear my message, although it might have been better,' he told the sound engineer and a senior official from the BBC, who were the only two people allowed to listen back with him to the final version before it was broadcast. 'Thank you for your patience.'

The letter that the King sent Logue in response to his customary birthday greetings reflected the poor spirits in which he found himself in the days before the recording. It was to be the last letter that he wrote him, and his remarks seemed all the more poignant because Logue, too, was in poor health.

'I am so sorry to hear that you have not been well again,' the King wrote:

As for myself, I have spent a wretched year culminating in that very severe operation, from which I seem to be making a remarkable recovery. The latter fact is in many ways entirely down to you. Before this operation, Price Thomas the surgeon asked to see me breathe. When he saw the diaphragm move up and down naturally he asked me whether I had always breathed in that way. I said no, I had been taught to breathe like that in 1926 & had gone on doing so. Another feather in your cap you see!!

Logue intended to reply after listening to the Christmas broadcast but was taken back into hospital on 28 December before he could do so. It was not until 19 January when he was finally discharged and back in his flat in Princes Court that he responded.

It is a wonderful thought to me that in 1924 when I left Australia, I could not get the medical profession to believe in Diaphragmatic Breathing, they imagined it was a fad. Then I had the wonderful fortune to have the Greatest in the Land as a patient & you & your letter have proved that I was right. We all listened with the greatest interest to your Majestic broadcast & I think it was very noble of you to do it & that is the general opinion & considering what you had been through, I think it came through wonderfully well.

The King had stayed on at Sandringham into the New Year with the Queen. The note of hope and confidence in his Christmas speech appeared to be justified. He was well enough to begin shooting again, and when his doctors examined him on 29 January, they pronounced themselves satisfied with his recovery. The next day the royal family went to the Theatre Royal Drury Lane to see Rodgers and Hammerstein's *South Pacific*. The outing had something of an air of celebration about it, partly because of the improvement in the King's health and partly because the following day, Princess Elizabeth and the Duke of Edinburgh were due to set off for East Africa. The improvement was illusory, however: a week later he died.

The King's death opened the way for discussion of something that had been rarely spoken of during his lifetime: the terrible toll that his stammer had taken on him and the importance of Logue's role in helping him to overcome it. Appropriately, it was John Gordon, the journalist who knew best the relationship between the two men, who led the way with an article entitled 'The King: a Story That Has Never Been Told', which dominated the front page of the *Sunday Express* on 10 February. In it, Gordon recounted at some length the story of 'the man who came to London unknown . . .

and gave the King the power to speak', beginning with their first meeting in Harley Street almost three decades earlier. The King's relationship with Logue, Gordon concluded, was 'more vital to a true understanding of his character than anything else in his reign'. A briefer and less prominent piece that appeared the same day in the *Sunday Pictorial*, penned by an unnamed 'special correspondent', explained to that newspaper's readers the role of Logue, who, it said, 'alone knows all the secrets of the King's dramatic and courageous struggle to conquer his stammer'. Both articles were widely quoted and reproduced in newspapers in Australia, which were keen to celebrate the important role played by their native son.

Logue, still the soul of discretion, was not directly quoted by either paper, although it was difficult to imagine that his old friend Gordon would have written his story without consulting him. Logue nevertheless shared his feelings with Alan Elliott, his patient from Northern Ireland, who was now fifteen. 'It has been a rather terrible time for me, but I rejoice that my King passed out so sweetly, & has left all his pain,' he wrote in a letter the day before the funeral. 'He was a very wonderful patient.'

Logue expanded on his thoughts in a letter he sent to the King's widow on 26 February, almost three weeks after her husband's death. He referred to the 'wonderful letter' that the King had sent him in December and expressed his regrets that his own illness had delayed his reply, which he feared the King had not seen.

'Since 1926 he honoured me, by allowing me to help him with his speech, & no man ever worked as hard as he did, & achieved such a grand result,' Logue wrote. 'During all those years you were a tower of strength to him & he has often told me how much he has owed to you, and the excellent result could never have been achieved if it had not been for your help. I have never forgotten your gracious help to me after my own beloved girl passed on.'

In her reply two days later, the Queen Mother was fulsome in her praise of Logue. 'I think that I know perhaps better than anyone just how much you helped the King, not only with his speech, but through that his whole life & outlook on life,' she wrote:

I shall always be deeply grateful to you for all you did for him. He was such a splendid person and I don't believe that he ever thought of himself at all. I did so hope that he might have been allowed a few years of comparative peace after the many anguished years he has had to battle through so bravely. But it was not to be. I do hope that you will soon be better.

That May, her daughter, now Queen Elizabeth II, mindful of how close Logue had been to her father, sent him a small gold snuff box that had belonged to the King, together with the following message:

I am sending you this little box which always stood on the King's table, & which he was rather fond of, as I am sure you would like a little personal souvenir of someone who was so grateful to you for all you did for him. The box was on his writing table, & I know that he would wish you to have it.

I do hope that you are feeling better, I miss the King more & more.

Yours v sincerely,

Elizabeth R.

Logue was delighted with the letter, which he showed off proudly a few months later at an annual dinner for alumni of Prince Alfred College, the school he had attended in Adelaide, which was held at the Oxford and Cambridge Club in Pall Mall. An insight into Logue's state of mind is provided by one of his own letters, dated 30 May

1952, which was found years later in a bookshop in New Zealand. It was addressed to 'my good friend' – a person whom Logue doesn't name but describes as a 'blast from the past', who has contacted him out of the blue. 'I had to sit down & concentrate, to call up your features – but I think I have got them now,' Logue began.

How nice of you to write to me. I have so very many letters these days & the way my old friends have rallied round is very heartening, in fact I didn't know I had so many.

These days, I do more consulting work than any other. If I didn't work I would go mad. It is very nice to be hailed as the greatest in the world at your job, but it is hard at my age (72) to live up to it.

My 3 sons have been a great credit to me. Laurie the eldest has an engineering shop in Nottingham, Val is a brilliant neurosurgeon, & the 'baby' (28) is a Barrister so I am very grateful, that they have done so well. My beloved King killed himself by working too hard, but – thank God – we have a much loved girl as Queen, to take his place & her husband will be a great help. I lost my beloved wife 6 years ago, & since then life has been very difficult.

That December, the Queen delivered her first Christmas message, from Sandringham. 'Each Christmas, at this time, my beloved father broadcast a message to his people in all parts of the world,' she said. 'As he used to do, I am speaking to you from my own home, where I am spending Christmas with my family.' Broadcasting in clear, firm tones – and without a trace of the impediment that had so clouded her father's life – the Queen paid tribute to those still serving in the armed forces abroad and thanked her subjects for the 'loyalty and affection' they had shown her since her accession to the throne ten months earlier. 'My father and my grandfather before him, worked hard all their lives to unite our peoples ever more closely, and to maintain its [the Commonwealth's] ideals which were so near to their hearts,' she said. 'I shall strive to carry on their work.'

Logue did not record what he thought of the speech – or indeed whether he even listened to it. Either way, his services were no longer required, and his health was failing. He spent Christmas in his flat surrounded by his three sons and their families: Valentine and his wife, Anne, with their two-year old daughter, Victoria; Laurie and Jo with their daughter, Alexandra, fourteen, and son Robert, ten, and Antony with Elizabeth, whom he was to marry the following November.

Shortly after New Year, Logue was taken ill for what was to be the last time. He remained bedridden for more than three months, and a live-in nurse was employed to look after him. Such was his dedication to his work, however, that he still attempted to see patients. Among them was Richard Oerton, who, then in his mid-teens, travelled with his mother from Devon for a consultation. 'The door of his flat was opened by a nurse who said he was too ill to keep the appointment,' Oerton recalled.[191]

Then there was a scurrying and Lionel Logue himself appeared in pyjamas and dressing gown, trying to push in front of the nurse.

'Oh,' he said, 'I want to see him. And his mother.' But the nurse hustled him away.

My mother, reasonably enough perhaps, though she seemed not to take in the pathos of what had just happened, complained that our appointment should have been cancelled before we set off from Devon. I myself was moved and saddened to have caught this glimpse of him. It proved to be the last.

Logue's condition continued to worsen, and he eventually fell into a coma. He died on 12 April 1953, less than two months after his seventy-third birthday. Among his effects were two invitations to the Queen's coronation, to be held that June – the second presumably sent because he had been too sick to respond to the first. Oerton thought back to the last abortive session with Logue when he turned on the radio and heard a bulletin that began: 'The death has been announced of Mr Lionel Logue.'

The obituaries that appeared in Britain, Australia and America were brief given the closeness of his relationship with the King – a reflection of the discretion with which he had always carried out his work. 'Mr Lionel Logue, C.V.O, who died yesterday at the age of 73, was one of the leading specialists in the treatment of speech defects and was mainly responsible for helping King George VI to overcome the impediment in his speech,' wrote *The Times*,[192] which sandwiched him in between the former President of Poland and the head of an American engineering company. 'He was on close personal terms with the King for a long time.' As for his techniques, the obituary writer merely noted: 'An important part of Logue's method was his instruction in how to breathe properly and so produce speech without strain.'

A few days later, readers added their comments: 'May I be allowed, through the courtesy of your columns, to pay a humble tribute to the great work of Mr Lionel Logue,' wrote a Mr J.C. Wimbusch.[193] 'As a patient of his in 1926, I can testify to the fact that his patience was magnificent and his sympathy almost superhuman. It was at his house in Bolton Gardens that I was introduced to the late King, then Duke of York. There must be thousands of people who, like myself, are living to bless the name of Lionel Logue.'

Logue's funeral was held on 17 April at Holy Trinity Church, Brompton, in South Kensington. He was cremated. The last person to enter the church, after the family, was a tall man of military bearing, bowler hat under his arm, who marched down to a front pew and was the first to leave at the end of the ceremony – the representative of the Queen. The Queen Mother and Australian High Commissioner also sent envoys. Afterwards the mourners went to Valentine's house. Logue's will, details of which were published in *The Times* that October, revealed his estate was valued at a fairly modest £8,605 – the equivalent of about £180,000 today. Logue's work with the King had brought him prominence and honours – although strangely, given the closeness of their relationship, not a knighthood. But it had not made him a wealthy man.

Epilogue

More than half a century on, it is difficult to identify the precise techniques that Lionel Logue used to treat the King. Although Logue left behind not only a diary, but also his letters and a myriad of newspaper cuttings and other mementos – upon which we have drawn extensively for this book – his patient records have disappeared. The sole exception is the record card he filled out after his first consultation with the then Duke of York in October 1926. Nor did Logue write up his cases in academic journals or publish papers detailing his techniques. This is not surprising, perhaps, given his lack of formal medical education – or indeed of any academic training in the course of a career that took him from drama and elocution to the newly emerging field of speech therapy.

The King did not leave any record of his dozens of sessions with Logue either – or at least not one that has been publicly accessible. His wartime diary, although running to several volumes, provides no insight into their relationship. He did, however, acknowledge the success of the breathing exercises Logue taught him; in his last letter in December 1951 (quoted in Chapter Fourteen), he described how Clement Price Thomas, the surgeon who removed his cancerous left lung, had praised his diaphragmatic breathing. Important, too, was the considerable effort Logue put into going through the texts of the King's speeches, removing words and phrases he feared would trip him up. In a sense this was not so much curing his problem as finding a way of living with it – yet by eliminating the largest of such stumbling blocks, Logue helped to build up the King's confidence, ensuring that the speech as a whole proved less daunting.

It is nevertheless possible to piece together a picture of what went on in Logue's consulting room from the testimony of other former patients, many of whom wrote to share their experiences after the publication of our book, *The King's Speech*, and the release of the film of the same name in 2010. Necessarily, most of the surviving patients were children at the time they had their consultations, almost all of them boys. All agreed on the importance Logue placed on breathing technique – a point made succinctly in a postcard dated 6 April 1951 that Alan Elliott, his teenaged patient from Northern Ireland, sent to his grandmother:

Dear Granny

I'm having a grand time in London. Mr Logue (the speech man) says my breathing has been wrong from the start.
    Love,
    Alan

Logue, himself, was more forthcoming in a letter he wrote to his young patient the same day:

My Dear Boy,

Of course you can write to me, any time you like, & I will always answer.
    So glad to receive such a cheerful letter, & to know that you

are getting to grips with your speech defect. It is bound to be harder, reading in school, you have an audience. In the same way you will find it easier to speak to certain people.

I would take a breath (not too big) between each word, & when you come & see me again we will probably alter all your exercises. It will depend on how you have progressed. Make sure when you do your exercises that you do not hold yourself stiffly. When reading, never go at more than 100 words to the minute. If you speak too quickly you will lose control of your speech, hence the defect.

Speech never stays on the same level, so do not worry if you are not so good at times, you soon pick up again.

Please remember me to your parents.

With every good wish,

Lionel Logue

An insight into Logue's technique was provided by Duncan Smith, who was taken as a seven- or eight-year-old to see him in 1951 or 1952. Although he had only a couple of sessions, Smith, who went on to work as a management consultant in a number of countries, said they contributed hugely to the 'almost cure' of his stammer – which in later life troubled him only when he was very stressed or tired. Retired and living in Virginia when he contacted us, Smith could still vividly recall the breathing and relaxation exercises that he had been taught:

'The breathing exercises consisted of: (1) exhale, then breath in slowly through my nose to the full capacity of my lungs, pause, then breath out slowly through my mouth until my lungs are completely empty, pause; (2) repeat this three times; (3) repeat, except this time only exhale half the air, pause, and then exhale the rest of the air and pause; (4) repeat this three times; (5) repeat, except only exhale one third of the air, pause, exhale another third, pause, exhale the final third, pause; (6) repeat this three times; (7) repeat, except this time only exhale one quarter of the air, pause, exhale another quarter, pause, exhale another quarter, pause, exhale the final quarter, pause; (8) repeat this three times.'

The emphasis was on doing all this slowly, making sure the lungs were completely filled after inhaling and completely empty again after exhaling. Logue told him that this exercise should be conducted in a relaxed pose – standing, legs apart, hands on hips. Smith was also taught to consciously relax his whole body, focused on each part in turn, starting from the feet and moving upwards.

Just as important were Logue's attempts to tackle the underlying reasons for the impediment through conversation – 'not about the psychological cause of my stammer, but more about how to gain the confidence I needed to reach my full potential, how to identify and prioritize the important things and not get agitated about the unimportant things', Smith recalled.

'I can distinctly remember the calm and friendly encouragement I received from him in our conversations: stay calm and relaxed, your views are really worth something, there is nothing that you cannot aspire to, keep your options open and opportunity will come your way, be interested in and empathetic with other people, etc.

'This actually was a significant confidence builder for me and I now believe it helped to put me on the path of exploring options, taking risks, not being afraid of consequences (the "worst case" was generally tolerable, and rarely happened anyway). Plus if I stammer then people just have to accept that and I should not be crippled with embarrassment. I did not get a complete cure of my stammer from LL, but I believe he gave me an important roadmap for building my confidence and gradually experiencing the disappearance (almost) of my stammer.'

Stephen Druce, who visited Logue as a ten- and eleven-year-old in the mid-1930s once a fortnight from his prep school in Wimbledon, also still had a vivid memory of their sessions and of 'the breathing exercises, and above all the elocution tricks and methods used on all the letters and sounds. He was charming, considerate, and clearly knew how to secure the confidence of a small boy. But a hard task master.

'The important elocution side of the method (if it should be called that) became a route into normal speech and gradually became assimilated into normality by the time I was fourteen/fifteen or so. The secret was to know exactly how to formulate each start point of difficult words and sound combinations to overcome any blockages.'

Logue's friendly manner – and sense of humour – also made an impression on one of his few female patients: Mary Graham née Ewart, who was born in 1925, was taken by her mother every Tuesday to his Harley Street practice, starting during the 1930s and continuing after the war. 'I was delighted to "escape" school for an afternoon,' she recalled. 'I was enthralled by his kindness, charm & friendliness. Having lost my father in 1937, he became a father figure. I made him a sleeveless navy blue sweater.'

'He was also very witty,' she continued. 'I loved the story of him and Myrtle attending the Cenotaph service when her knicker elastic broke. Myrtle nudged Lionel, and, looking down, he saw the knickers round her ankles. She stepped out of them and put them in his pocket.'

Logue's methods did not always bring success, however. Richard Oerton – one of Logue's last patients – saw him on and off for five years, but continued to struggle with his speech; the headmaster of his preparatory boarding school in Chichester claimed the sessions were actually making his stammer worse. 'When my father reported this to Logue, he spoke briefly about the pettiness of some schoolmasters and said that it was bound to be worse during a period of transition,' Oerton said.

They nevertheless pressed on. Logue, he said, 'offered a few techniques, such as starting a word softly and slowly, but I think his main concern was to give me the experience of fluency: he got me to read aloud, sometimes from newspapers (he favoured editorials in the *Daily Express*), and sometimes from exercise cards which he had prepared. I recall, for example, being made to intone, "This, that, these, those", "Lip, lap, lop", and similar sets of words, many times. And there was one exercise which sometimes reduced me, to Logue's delight, to helpless laughter: "Benjamin Bramble Blimber borrowed the baker's birchen broom to brush the blinding cobwebs from his brain".'

Despite all this, the stammer refused to go away. 'It may well be that Lionel Logue helped other people more than he did me, and it may also be that I could have been more committed than I was,' Oerton added.

'But I doubt whether his methods achieved anything very wonderful. To breathing and verbal exercises, I think he added some "techniques" to alleviate or control stammering and they may have helped people. Probably his "good fatherliness" helped them more. But clearly – as his relationship with the King showed – he could not produce the simple ease of speaking which most people have. Nor, to this day, can anyone else, so far as I know.'

Logue's methods worked better with David Radcliffe, who, like Oerton, was a patient in the early 1950s, while he was in his second or third year at Oundle School in Northamptonshire. Both he and his elder brother, Tony, struggled with their speech, but while Tony was able to stutter out words, David developed 'an acutely embarrassing total stoppage'. 'I would just clam up, and stand there looking like an idiot, and while I would be trying to get myself under control, people with misguided kindness would harass me with helpful suggestions,' he recalled. 'At times I felt like saying "Would you please shut up, and give me time to deal with this" (and for some reason I never felt that these words would be difficult to get out), but I never had the courage to try doing that.'

Radcliffe went on to Cambridge University and a career in academia; when he contacted us he was Professor Emeritus at the University of Western Ontario. He remembered Logue as a 'very dignified and smartly dressed man, in black jacket and pinstripe trousers.'

'Logue's treatment, as I recollect, was of course first of all to diagnose exactly what kind of stammer I had,' he recounted.

'This was a weird experience for me, because I found that I was quite able to talk quite freely about my problem without stammering. I felt like a fraud. I wondered whether he was going to take me seriously. For me it was a new experience, but of course for Logue it must have been a well-known phenomenon.

'Although few people would recognize it in me now, I think once a stammerer, always a stammerer. But certainly it was Lionel Logue who helped me to cope with my disability, and turn things around for the rest of my schooldays and university. And I think there was something, too, in the example of King George, who after all was King through all my childhood, and very much a hero of the war years, which framed much of my childhood. If he could do it, so could I.'

Notes

This book draws extensively on the Logue Archive, which is made up of diary entries by Lionel and Myrtle Logue, letters Lionel received from the King and drafts of those he sent him, together with a variety of documents, mementos and other items collected by the Logue family. Material taken from the archive – including verbatim accounts of conversations between the principal actors – is quoted without attribution.

1 Theo Aronson, *The Royal Family at War*, London: John Murray, 1993, p. 13.
2 Letter to authors.
3 Aronson, *op. cit.*, p. 94.
4 Robert Wood, *A World in Your Ear*, London: Macmillan, 1979, p. 130.
5 Aronson, *op. cit.*, p. 24.
6 *Ibid.*, p. 25.
7 Felicity Goodall, 'Life during the blackout', *Guardian*, 1 Nov 2009.
8 *Ibid.*
9 Lord Killearn, *The Killearn Diaries, 1934–1946: the Diplomatic and Personal Record of Lord Killearn (Sir Miles Lampson), High Commissioner and Ambassador, Egypt*, London: Sidgwick & Jackson, p. 107.

10 *The Times*, 2 September 1939.

11 *The Times*, 5 September 1939.

12 Denis Judd, *King George VI*, London: Michael Joseph, 1982, p. 39

13 *Ibid.*, 1982, p. 176.

14 Sarah Bradford, *George VI*, London: Weidenfeld & Nicolson, 1989, p. 403.

15 *Ibid.*, p. 403.

16 William Shawcross, *Queen Elizabeth the Queen Mother: The Official Biography*, London: Macmillan, 2009, p. 498.

17 Bernard Gray, 'The King was with His Troops', *Daily Mirror*, 5 December 1939.

18 *Ibid.*

19 Aronson, *op. cit.*, p. 15.

20 John W. Wheeler-Bennett, *King George VI, His Life and Reign*, London: Macmillan, 1958, p. 429.

21 Wood, *op. cit.*, p. 116.

22 'How 30 men with cutlasses and grappling irons seized Altmark', *Sunday Express*, 18 February 1940.

23 Wheeler-Bennett, *op. cit.*, p. 436.

24 Shawcross, *op. cit.*, p. 503.

25 Wheeler-Bennett, *op. cit.*, p. 433.

26 A.J.P. Taylor, (ed.), W.P. Crozier, *Off the Record: Political Interviews, 1933–43*, London: Hutchinson, 1973.

27 Henry Channon, ed. Robert Rhodes James, *'Chips': The Diaries of Sir Henry Channon*, London: Weidenfeld & Nicolson, 1967, p. 229.

28 *Ibid.*, p. 230.

29 Wheeler-Bennett, *op. cit.*, p. 437.

30 *Daily Mirror*, 27 October 1939.

31 *Daily Mirror*, 15 March, 1940.

32 Judd, *op. cit.*, p. 166.

33 Wheeler-Bennett, *op. cit.*, p. 420.

34 *Ibid.*, p. 436.

35 Bradford, *op. cit.*, p. 40.

36 Meryle Secrest, *Kenneth Clark, A Biography*, London: Weidenfeld & Nicolson, 1984, p. 118.

37 Ed. Nigel Nicolson, Sir Harold Nicolson, *The War Years 1939–45, Volume II of Diaries and Letters*, London: Collins, 1966, entry for 10 December 1936.

38 Ed. Nigel Nicolson, Sir Harold Nicolson, *The Later Years 1945–62, Volume III of Diaries and Letters*, London: Collins, 1968, entry for 21 March 1949.

39 Philip Ziegler, *King Edward VIII: The Official Biography*, London: Collins, 1990, p. 404.

40 *Ibid.*, p. 404.

41 *Ibid.*, p. 404.

42 R.J. Minney, *The Private Papers of Hore-Belisha*, London: Collins, 1960, p. 237–8.

43 Martin Gilbert, *The Churchill War Papers: At the Admiralty, September 1939–May 1940*, London: Heinemann, 1993, p. 369.

44 Frazier Hunt, '"Come on Hitler!" Dares Ironside', *Daily Express*, 5 April 1940.

45 Wheeler-Bennett, *op. cit.*, p. 439–40.

46 Martin Gilbert, *Churchill: A Life*, 1991, London: Heinemann, p. 642.

47 George VI's War Diary, Volume II, entry for 11 May 1940.

48 Shawcross, *op. cit.*, p. 537.

49 Andrew Roberts, *Eminent Churchillians*, London: Weidenfeld & Nicolson, 1994, p. 45.

50 Sir John Colville, *The Fringes of Power: Downing Street Diaries 1939–55*, London: Hodder & Stoughton, 1985, entry for 7 August 1940.

51 Philip Ziegler, *London at War*, London: Sinclair-Stevenson, 1995, p. 81.

52 Wood, *op. cit.*, p. 103.

53 Wheeler-Bennett, *op. cit.*, p. 449.

54 'The King Masters Speech Defect', *Sunday Express*, 26 May 1940.

55 Davidson papers, box 275, quoted in Andrew Roberts, *op. cit.*, p. 41.

56 Headlam diary, entry for 24 May 1940, p. 111, quoted in Andrew Roberts, *op. cit.*, p. 41.

57 Wheeler-Bennett, *op. cit.*, p. 454.

58 George VI's War Diary, Volume II, entry for 26–28 May 1940, quoted in Deborah Cadbury, *Princes at War: The British Royal Family's Private Battle in the Second World War*, London: Bloomsbury, 2015, p. 149.

59 Ed. Nigel Nicolson, Sir Harold Nicolson, *The War Years 1939–45, Volume II of Diaries and Letters*, London: Collins, 1966, p. 186.

60 Wheeler-Bennett, *op. cit.*, p. 457.

61 Wood, *op. cit.*, p. 147.

62 Elizabeth Longford, *The Queen Mother*, London: Weidenfeld & Nicolson, 1981, p. 80.

63 'The King's Shelter', *Sunday Express*, 15 September 1940.

64 Wheeler-Bennett, *op. cit.*, p. 464.

65 Ed. Nigel Nicolson, Sir Harold Nicolson, *The War Years 1939–45, Volume II of Diaries and Letters*, London: Collins, 1966, p. 188.

66 Shawcross, *op. cit.*, p. 514.

67 *Ibid.*, p. 513.

68 Brian Green, *Dulwich: The Home Front, 1939–1945*, pamphlet published by the Dulwich Society, 1995.

69 http://www.dulwichsociety.com/journal-archive/74-winter-2011/681dads-army

70 'Home Guards on Parade', *The Times*, 12 August 1940.

71 Betty Wilson, 'Australia has a social centre in London', *Sydney Morning Herald*, 24 October 1940.

72 Noble Frankland, *Prince Henry, Duke of Gloucester*, London: Weidenfeld & Nicolson, 1980, p. 185.

73 Aronson, *op. cit.*, p. 34.

74 Ziegler, *King Edward VIII*, p. 422.

75 Sir John Colville, *op. cit.*, entry for 3 July 1940.

76 Bradford, *op. cit.*, p. 577.

77 Ziegler, *King Edward VIII*, p. 427.

78 Shawcross, *op. cit.*, p. 520.

79 Martin Gilbert, *Finest Hour: Winston S. Churchill, 1939–41*, London: Minerva, 1989, p. 700.

80 Ziegler, *King Edward VIII*, p. 428.

81 Wheeler-Bennett, *op. cit.*, p. 465.

82 Peter Stansky, *The First Day of the Blitz*, New Haven and London: Yale University Press, 2007, p. 30.

83 Ed. Nigel Nicolson, Sir Harold Nicolson, *The War Years 1939–45, Volume II of Diaries and Letters*, London: Collins, 1966, p. 111.

84 Ziegler, *London at War*, p. 113.

85 Stansky, *op. cit.*, p. 1.

86 *Ibid.*, p. 69.

87 *Ibid.*, p. 28.

88 Ziegler, *London at War*, p. 115.

89 Bradford, *op. cit.*, p. 430.

90 Norman Hartnell, *Silver and Gold*, London: Evans Brothers, 1955, p. 102.

91 Longford, *op. cit.*, 1981, p. 86.

92 Shawcross, *op. cit.*, p. 522.

93 Wheeler-Bennett, *op. cit.*, p. 468.

94 *Ibid.*, p. 469.

95 Shawcross, *op. cit.*, p. 524.

96 'The East Enders' Angel', *Evening Standard*, 2 April 2002.

97 Shawcross, *op. cit.*, p. 523.

98 'In an Air Raid', *Adelaide Chronicle*, 16 January 1941.

99 Ed. Nigel Nicolson, Sir Harold Nicolson, *The War Years 1939–45, Volume II of Diaries and Letters*, London: Collins, 1966, p. 114.

100 Philip Ziegler, *Crown and People*, London: Collins, 1978, p. 72.

101 Wheeler-Bennett, *op. cit.*, p. 469.

102 *Ibid.*, p. 469.

103 Jeffery Richards and D. Sheridan, *Mass-Observation at the Movies*, London: Routledge & Kegan Paul, 1987, p. 213.

104 *Ibid.*, p. 402.

105 Ziegler, *Crown and People*, p. 78.

106 Dorothy Laird, *Queen Elizabeth the Queen Mother and Her Support to the Throne During Four Reigns*, London: Hodder and Stoughton, 1966, p. 293.

107 'In an Air Raid', *Adelaide Chronicle*, 16 January 1941.

108 Shawcross, *op. cit.*, p. 165.

109 Elizabeth Grice, 'Nicholas Mosley: "The King's Speech therapist gave me hope, too"', *Daily Telegraph*, 3 February 2011.

110 William Sansom, *Westminster in War*, London: Faber & Faber, 1947, p. 92.

111 Shawcross, *op. cit.*, p. 541.

112 Wheeler-Bennett, *op. cit.*, p. 533.

113 *Ibid.*, p. 535.

114 *Ibid.*, p. 537.

115 *Daily Express*, 9 May 1942.

116 Wheeler-Bennett, *op. cit.*, p. 548.

117 *Ibid.*, p. 549.

118 *Ibid.*, p. 543.

119 *Ibid.*, p. 553.

120 Martin Gilbert, *Road to Victory: Winston S. Churchill 1941–1945*, London, Heinemann, 1966, p. 251.

121 Amanda Cable, 'We saw the Nazi pilot wave at us – then he bombed our school: Survivors remember the day the Luftwaffe massacred 38 pupils at a London school', *Daily Mail*, 4 September 2009.

122 'Shot down by RAF', *The Times*, 21 January 1943.

123 'Propaganda Bombing', *The Times*, 21 January 1943.

124 Wheeler-Bennett, *op. cit.*, p. 564.

125 *Ibid.*, p. 564.

126 *Ibid.*, p. 567.

127 *Ibid.*, p. 568.

128 Bradford, *op. cit.*, p. 431.

129 Hugo Vickers, *Vivien Leigh: A Biography*, London: Penguin, 1988, p. 156.

130 Michael Carver, *Out of Step: Memoirs of a Field Marshal*, London: Hutchinson, 1989, p. 166.

131 Wheeler-Bennett, *op. cit.*, p. 578.

132 Harold Macmillan, *War Diaries: The Mediterranean, 1943–45*, London: Macmillan, 1984, p. 120.

133 Ed. Duff Hart-Davis, King's Counsellor, *Abdication and War: the Diaries of Sir Alan Lascelles*, London: Weidenfeld & Nicolson, p. 139.

134 Hart-Davis, *op. cit.*, p. 140.

135 'Court Circular', *The Times*, 17 July 1943.

136 Lionel Logue papers, November 30, 1943.

137 Lionel Logue papers, December 29, 1943.

138 George VI's War Diary, Volume VIII, entry for 21 December 1943.

139 Marion Crawford, *The Little Princesses*, London: Odhams, 1950, p. 59.

140 *Ibid.*, p. 85.

141 *Ibid.*, p. 86.

142 Hart-Davis, *op. cit.*, p. 189.

143 Wheeler-Bennett, *op. cit.*, p. 589.

144 *Ibid.*, p. 589.

145 Don Whitehead, 'So Easy, So Simple', *Sunday Express*, 23 January 1944.

146 'Beached: German losses staggering', *Daily Express*, 19 February 1944.

147 Basil Gingell, 'Hitler's order: Take it', *Sunday Express*, 20 February 1944.

148 'Scots Guard in the Beach-Head: Valour against odds', *The Times*, 29 March 1944.

149 'The Victory of Rome', *New York Times*, 6 June1944.

150 Wheeler-Bennett, *op. cit.*, p. 599.

151 Bradford, *op. cit.*, p. 474.

152 Wheeler-Bennett, *op. cit.*, p. 600.

153 Hart-Davis, *op. cit.*, p. 224.

154 *Ibid.*, p. 225.

155 *Ibid.*, p. 227.

156 Aronson, *op. cit.*, p. 158.

157 *Ibid.*, p. 158.

158 King's diary, 6 June 1944.

159 Wheeler-Bennett, *op. cit.*, p. 608.

160 *Ibid.*, p. 608.

161 Wheeler-Bennett, *op. cit.*, p. 608.

162 Hart-Davis, *op. cit.*, p. 234.

163 Wheeler-Bennett, *op. cit.*, p. 609.

164 *Ibid.*, p. 610.

165 Arthur L. Woolf, 'The Battle of South London', http://www.camberwell-boroughcouncil.co.uk/battle-south-london.

166 Aronson, *op. cit.*, p. 170.

167 John Bettinson, letter to authors.

168 Wheeler-Bennett, *op. cit.*, p. 612.

169 Bradford, *op. cit.*, p. 480.

170 Nigel Hamilton, *Monty, The Making of a General, 1887–1942*, London: Hamish Hamilton, 1981, p. 116.

171 Patrick Howarth, *George VI*, London: Hutchinson, 1987, p. 168.

172 Shawcross, *op. cit.*, p. 590.

173 Wheeler-Bennett, *op. cit.*, p. 625.

174 *Ibid.*, p. 624.

175 Hart-Davis, *op. cit.*, p. 321.

176 Ed. Nigel Nicolson, Sir Harold Nicolson, *The War Years 1939–45, Volume II of Diaries and Letters*, London: Collins, 1966, p. 462.

177 Wheeler-Bennett, *op. cit.*, p. 627.

178 Aronson, *op. cit.*, p. 212.

179 Judd, *op. cit.*, p. 217.

180 Wheeler-Bennett, *op. cit.*, p. 635.

181 *Ibid.*, p. 636.

182 *Ibid.*, p. 636.

183 Channon, *op. cit.*, p. 501.

184 Judd, *op. cit.*, p. 219.

185 John Lehmann, *I Am My Brother*, London: Longmans, 1960, pp. 296–7.

186 'Potato Rationing', *Spectator*, 14 November, 1947.

187 Christopher Wilson, 'The night a bogus medium conned the Queen into trying to contact her beloved father', *Daily Mail*, 24 Oct, 2014.

188 William F. Neech, *Death Is Her Life*, London: Psychic Book Club, 1957, quoted in *Paranormal Review*, 12 December 2010.

189 Interview with authors, June 2010.

190 *Daily Express*, 7 February 1952.

191 R.T. Oerton, 'Remembering Lionel Logue', *Speaking Out*, spring 2011, pp. 8–9.

192 *The Times*, 13 April 1953.

193 *The Times*, 17 April 1953.

Index

Dornier bombers, 105, 121
Dover Castle, Kent, 82
Druce, Stephen, 265
Drury Lane theatre, Covent Garden, 95, 254
Dulwich, London, 18, 95–6, 120, 206–7, 209, 226
Dulwich & Sydenham Golf Club, 95, 120–22
Dunkirk evacuation (1940), 82–7, 92
Dutch East Indies, 144
Dynamo Room, Dover Castle tunnels, 82
dysentery, 190, 208, 230

East India Company, 18
Eaton Square, Belgravia, 71
Eden, Anthony, 71, 86, 94, 211
Edgware Road, London, 6
Edinburgh, Duke of, *see* Philip, Duke of Edinburgh
Edinburgh, Scotland, 226
Edward VII, King of the United Kingdom, 88
Edward VIII, King of the United Kingdom, xi, 2, 14, 29, 45–6, 57, 62–7, 72, 98–101, 149, 172, 229
Edward, Duke of Kent, 2
Egan, Simon, ix
Egypt, 145, 152–4, 155, 165
Ehle, Jennifer, viii
Eindhoven, Netherlands, 213
Eisenhower, Dwight David, 154–5, 169, 197, 199, 200, 201, 202, 213
Elbe river, 152
elections, *see* general elections
Elephant and Castle, London, 136
Elizabeth, Queen consort of the United Kingdom, Queen Mother

1923 marries George, 64
1927 tour of Australia and New Zealand, 12, 150
1938 Munich Agreement, 16
1939 tour of North America, 59–60; outbreak of war, 9, 17; Edward's visit, 65; Scotland visit, 39; Armistice Day speech, 41–2; George's Christmas speech, 45, 47, 48; princesses sent to Royal Lodge, 56–7, 89
1940 George's Empire Day speech, 76, 80; moves to Windsor Castle, 89; learns to use revolver, 91; Blitz, 107–14, 117; Christmas, 124, 126
1941 Wales visit, 141
1942 Baedeker Raids, 144; Christmas, 157–8, 159
1943 George's North African tour, 169; resignation of Hardinge, 172, 173
1944 D Day, 198, 201, 203; V-1 attacks, 206, 207; Christmas, 216
1945 VE Day, 221, 224–6; death of Myrtle Logue, 231; State Opening of Parliament, 233–4
1948 silver wedding anniversary, 247
1951 George's Christmas broadcast, 252
1952 watches *South Pacific* at Drury Lane, 254; funeral of George, 1; letter from Logue, 255–6
1953 Logue's funeral, 260
Elizabeth II, Queen of the United Kingdom
1936 abdication of Edward VIII, 97
1939 outbreak of war, 9; moves to Royal Lodge, 56–7, 89
1940 moves to Windsor Castle, 89;